# Enterprise Project Management

## Using Microsoft® Office Project Server 2007

## Best Practices for Implementing an EPM Solution

### Hagit Landman, PMP

Copyright © 2008 by Hagit Landman

ISBN-13: 978-1-932159-97-4

Printed and bound in the U.S.A. Printed on acid-free paper
10  9  8  7  6  5  4  3  2  1

**Library of Congress Cataloging-in-Publication Data**

Landman, Hagit, 1965-
   Enterprise project management using Microsoft Office Project Server 2007 :
best practices for implementing an EPM solution / by Hagit Landman.
        p. cm.
   Includes index.
   ISBN 978-1-932159-97-4 (pbk. : alk. paper)
   1. Microsoft Project. 2. Project management—Computer programs. I.
Title.
   HD69.P75L356 2008
   658.4′04028553—dc22                                      2008011786

Microsoft is a registered trademark of Microsoft Corporation in the United States and/or other countries.

PMBOK is a registered mark of Project Management Institute, Inc. PMI does not endorse or otherwise sponsor this publication.

Phone: (954) 727-9333
Fax: (561) 892-0700
Web: www.jrosspub.com

# Dedication

To my loving family, Naftali and Elad,
who were patient with me during the writing of this book

In memory of my parents,
Rachel and Alexander Zygler

Special thanks to Aaron Graves
for his significant and instrumental advice, guidance, and support,
without which this book would not have been possible

# Table of Contents

# Preface

Enterprise Project Management (EPM) or organization project management is a methodology that combines standardized project management processes and supporting tools to meet an organization's project management goals.

Tools that provide a business solution for EPM are available from Microsoft®. The solution is comprised of Microsoft® Office Project Professional, Microsoft® Office Project Server, and the Microsoft® Windows SharePoint technology.

The Project Management Institute (PMI) offers a set of proven project management processes described in the Project Management Body of Knowledge (PMBOK®). These processes are widely applied and are recognized as good project management practices.

Implementing an EPM solution that combines project management methodology and supporting tools to enable all project stakeholders in your organization to perform the processes defined effectively is not a simple task. It includes:

- Defining the organization's project goals and objectives
- Defining the project management methodology and processes aligned with the above goals
- Establishing tools that support the above processes
- Training all the stakeholders in the methodology developed and its implementation with the use of the supporting tools

◆ Ongoing support from the project management office (PMO) to ensure that all the stakeholders adhere to the methodology and that they have all they need to perform their work efficiently

## Purpose and Scope

This book provides you with the principles and guidelines you will need to define, implement, and deploy an EPM solution in your organization. It is based on the author's experience and best practices and includes numerous examples that demonstrate how to configure the EPM system to support your implementation. It does not explain how to implement a PMO.

This book describes each stage of the EPM implementation methodology and explains how to carry out the tasks that must be performed to achieve the objectives of each stage. These stages are:

◆ **Establishing technology environments**—Establish a technological foundation for development, testing, training, and deployment of the EPM solution.
◆ **Defining requirements and goals**—Gather and categorize the requirements and goals for the EPM implementation.
◆ **Establishing project management processes and supporting tools**—Define the project management processes aligned with your organization's and stakeholders' goals and establish the procedures and tools required to support those processes.
◆ **Testing the solution with a pilot team/project**—The solution is tested by the pilot team/project for a period of several months in preparation for organization-wide deployment.
◆ **Deploying the solution to organization units**—The solution is fine-tuned based on the feedback received from the pilot team and is then deployed according to the deployment plan.

## Audience

This book is designed for personnel in charge of defining and deploying EPM solutions. Typically, such personnel are part of an organization's PMO and are experienced in performing business analysis, defining the solution, and managing the implementation and deployment of the solution.

# About the Author

**Hagit Landman** is a program and project management consultant and subject matter expert with more than 17 years of experience in multidisciplinary projects. She is a certified Project Management Professional (PMP®) with an MBA and bachelor of science degree in industrial engineering and management.

Ms. Landman specializes in program and project management methodology and implementation and has defined and implemented Enterprise Project Management solutions in several large IT companies. She has extensive experience in the development and implementation of program management office methodologies and best practices in large organizations in Israel, as well as in various international companies, based on the Project Management Body of Knowledge (PMBOK®) and on the Office of Government Commerce's PRINCE 2®, a process-based method for effective project management used extensively throughout Europe in the private sector and the standard to be used for all government information system projects. She has also managed large-scale development and production programs.

Ms. Landman is an active member of the Project Management Institute. She has participated in writing items for both the Program Management Professional (PgMP)SM and the Certificate Associate in Project Management (CAPM®) certification exams administered by the Project Management Institute. As a recognized subject matter expert fluent in both English and Hebrew, she has participated in the translation of the Project Management Professional (PMP®) certification exam into Hebrew.

Ms. Landman can be contacted at www.hlandman.com or by e-mail at hagit@hlandman.com.

*Free value-added materials available from*
*the Download Resource Center at www.jrosspub.com*

At J. Ross Publishing we are committed to providing today's professional with practical, hands-on tools that enhance the learning experience and give readers an opportunity to apply what they have learned. That is why we offer free ancillary materials available for download on this book and all participating Web Added Value™ publications. These online resources may include interactive versions of material that appears in the book or supplemental templates, worksheets, models, plans, case studies, proposals, spreadsheets and assessment tools, among other things. Whenever you see the WAV™ symbol in any of our publications, it means bonus materials accompany the book and are available from the Web Added Value Download Resource Center at www.jrosspub.com.

Downloads available for *Enterprise Project Management Using Microsoft® Office Project Server 2007: Best Practices for Implementing an EPM Solution* consist of a project plan template, project closure checklist, and matrices for stakeholders, requirements, supplier evaluations, and communication.

# Introduction: Enterprise Project Management Implementation Principles and Workflow

Enterprise Project Management (EPM) is a solution that integrates processes, people, organization strategy, and technology to provide real value to you and all the stakeholders in your organization, as illustrated in Figure 1.

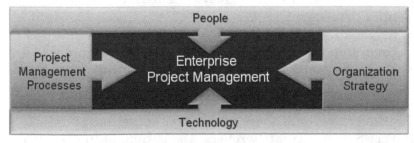

**Figure 1. EPM: Integration of People, Processes, Strategy, and Technology**

Essential prerequisites of any EPM implementation are executive management buy-in, a clear understanding of the business cases to be supported, and the impact the initiative will have on the organization.

The EPM initiative involves organizational and cultural changes, which require the backing of organizational management. Backing can be provided by either or both of the following:

◆ **Champion**—An executive within the organization who lobbies for the EPM initiative

◆ **Sponsor**—An executive within the organization who provides financing for the EPM initiative

When implementing an EPM solution in your organization, keep in mind the following general guidelines:

◆ Deploy the solution in one department or business unit at a time.

◆ Use the standard features and functions of Microsoft® Office Project Server as much as possible in the first stage of the implementation; leave code development, such as integration with the line-of-business machines, for the later stages.

◆ Clearly define the primary business challenges the EPM solution will address.

◆ Understand the impact the EPM solution will have on your organization.

◆ Obtain full support of executive and mid-level management for the deployment.

◆ Use a Microsoft® Project deployment partner to assist you in the solution implementation.

In order to maintain the EPM solution and ensure that projects are managed according to project management methodology that is aligned with the organization's strategy and goals, the project management officer must:

◆ Continuously verify that information stored on Microsoft® Office Project Server accurately reflects the current status of each project

◆ Provide support to all stakeholders to help them perform their project management duties effectively

Figure 2 depicts the stages of an EPM solution implementation.

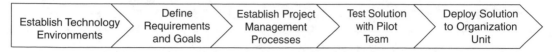

**Figure 2. Stages of an EPM Solution Implementation**

Figure 3 depicts the tasks to be performed in each of the EPM implementation stages.

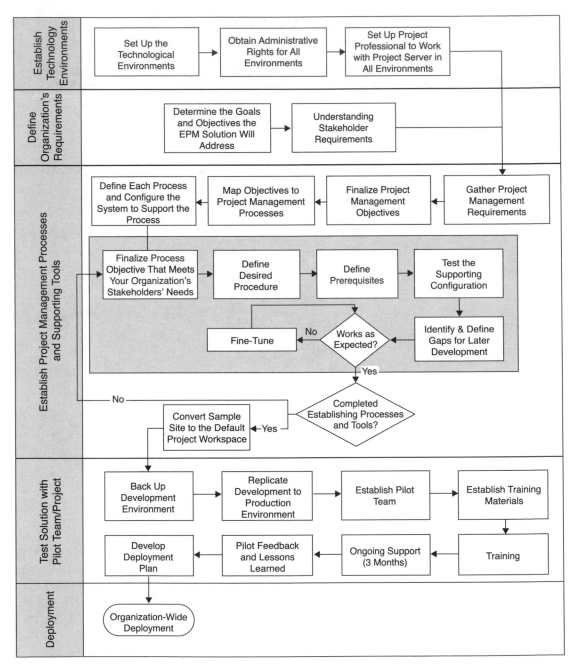

**Figure 3. EPM Implementation and Deployment Methodology and Workflow**

# Part I.
# Enterprise Project
# Management Foundation,
# Goals, and Requirements

# Establishing
# Technology Environments

Before you begin to define the project management processes and configure the system to support these processes, you need to understand the Microsoft® Enterprise Project Management (EPM) system components and establish technology environments to serve as a foundation for subsequent stages. The technology environments stage includes the following tasks (see Figure 1.1):

1. Setting up the development, training, and production environments

2. Obtaining administrative rights for all of the above environments

3. Setting up Microsoft Office Project Professional to work with Microsoft Office Project Server in all of the above environments

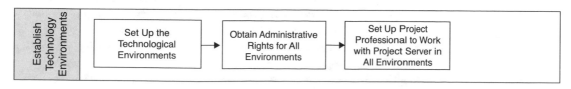

**Figure 1.1. Main Tasks of the Technology Environments Stage**

## Overview of the Microsoft EPM System

The Microsoft EPM 2007 solution is an integrated system that is comprised of the products listed in Table 1.1.

### Table 1.1. EPM Components

| Components | Description |
| --- | --- |
| **Server Side** | |
| Microsoft® Windows 2003 Server with Service Pack 1 or higher | The server that hosts the Microsoft Project Server and Microsoft SharePoint needs to be based on the Windows 2003 Server Operating System. |
| Microsoft® SQL Server 2000 with Service Pack 3 or higher, or Microsoft® SQL Server 2005 | The database management system for Project Server 2007 and Windows SharePoint Services 2007. |
| Microsoft® SQL Server 2000 Analysis Services | Provides Online Analytical Processing (OLAP) services, which is required to use the Portfolio Analyzer feature of Project Server 2007. |
| Microsoft® Windows SharePoint Services 2007 | Provides web-based project workspaces for each project published in Project Server, to manage project information such as documents, issues, risks, and other project information lists. |
| Microsoft® Office Project Server 2007 | The server-side application that provides a collaborative project management environment to support communication between project stakeholders; it also provides a centralized data store for project information. It is used to drive the process of managing projects, facilitating team interaction, and providing personalized access to project information. Microsoft Project Server is essentially a web server with a database engine serving web pages which are accessed by anyone who has an interest in a project using their web browser. |

**Table 1.1. EPM Components (continued)**

| Components | Description |
| --- | --- |
| **Client Side** | |
| Microsoft® Office Project Professional 2007 | A desktop client that allows project managers to create and edit project plans. Project plans are saved to the Project Server 2007 databases. |
| Microsoft® Office Project Web Access 2007 | User access to Project Server 2007 is through Project Web Access 2007, which is a browser-based client that allows team members, resource managers, and executives to enter and view timesheet information and view portfolio reports. |
| Microsoft® Office 2003 or 2007 | Used to create supporting project information materials such as the project charter, product specification, and more. |

The EPM system can be installed on a single host or on multiple hosts, depending on the size of your organization. Figure 1.2 is an example of a single-host topology.

 It is assumed that your IT group has already installed the EPM system in your organization. If not, have your IT group refer to the Microsoft® documentation to size the topology and hardware requirements that will best serve your organization and install the EPM components.

## Setting Up the Technological Environments

Once the Microsoft EPM system is installed, it is recommended that your IT group prepare three EPM environments:

◆ **Development**—The development environment is a replica of the production environment. This is where you configure the solution to

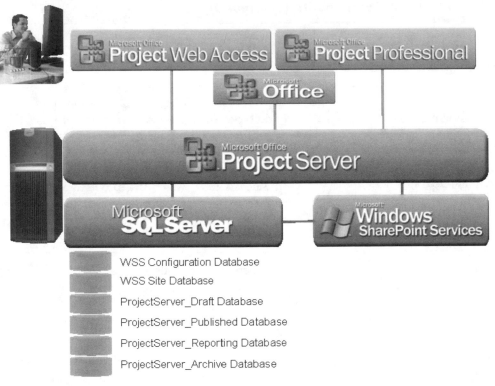

WSS Configuration Database

WSS Site Database

ProjectServer_Draft Database

ProjectServer_Published Database

ProjectServer_Reporting Database

ProjectServer_Archive Database

**Figure 1.2. Single-Host Topology**

meet the project management needs of your organization, test it, modify it, and test it again until you are ready to release the solution or modification to the production environment.

◆ **Production**—The production environment is where the users in your organization perform their project management duties.

◆ **Training**—The training environment is where you train project managers, project executives, and project team members in how to use the EPM solution that will enable them to perform their duties more efficiently.

For small organizations, the three environments can be set up on a single host, using a different IIS port for each environment.

 IIS stands for Internet Information Services. IIS must be configured on Windows 2003 Server prior to the Project Server installation.

For example:

◆ **Production environment** is on port 80 of your IIS server:

| Site URL | Description |
| --- | --- |
| http://<servername>:80 | The Windows SharePoint Services top-level site in the production environment |
| http://<servername>/ProjectServer:80 | Project Web Access in the production environment |

◆ **Training environment** is on port 81 of your IIS server:

| Site URL | Description |
| --- | --- |
| http://<servername>:81 | The Windows SharePoint Services top-level site in the training environment |
| http://<servername>:81/ProjectServer | Project Web Access in the training environment |

◆ **Development environment** is on port 82 of your IIS server:

| Site URL | Description |
| --- | --- |
| http://<servername>:82 | The Windows SharePoint Services top-level site in the development environment |
| http://<servername>:82/ProjectServer | Project Web Access in the development environment |

These environments can also be on the same port with different environment names, such as:

◆ http://<servername>:ProjectServer
◆ http://<servername>:ProjectDev
◆ http://<servername>:ProjectTraining

For larger organizations, the three environments can be set up on different hosts. For example:

◆ **Production environment** is on <servername1>:

| Site URL | Description |
|---|---|
| http://<servername1> | The Windows SharePoint Services top-level site in the production environment |
| http://<servername1>/ProjectServer | Project Web Access in the production environment |

◆ **Training environment** is on <servername2>:

| Site URL | Description |
|---|---|
| http://<servername2> | The Windows SharePoint Services top-level site in the training environment |
| http://<servername2>/ProjectServer | Project Web Access in the training environment |

◆ **Development environment** is on <servername3>:

| Site URL | Description |
|---|---|
| http://<servername3> | The Windows SharePoint Services top-level site in the development environment |
| http://<servername3>/ProjectServer | Project Web Access in the development environment |

## Obtaining Administrative Rights

After setting up all the required environments, your IT group must assign administrative rights to all of these environments, so that you can configure the server to meet your business project management needs.

 Having administrative rights is different than being an administrator on the server. You need to be an administrator only on the sites and not on the server(s).

The following procedure is performed by the IT group to assign administrative rights to the Windows SharePoint Services site collection and the Project Server environment.

**To assign administrative rights to the Windows SharePoint Services site collection:**

1. Open Internet Explorer and enter the top-level site collection URL of the development environment (for example, http://<servername>:82). The **Windows SharePoint Services** site opens.

2. Select **Site Actions > Site Settings**:

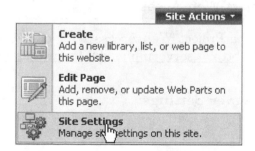

The **Site Settings** page opens.

3. Under **Users and Permissions**, click **Site collection administrators**:

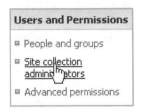

The list of **Site Collection Administrators** is displayed.

4. In the **Site Collection Administrators** field, enter the user name of each person who will be responsible for setting up and configuring the EPM solution ("Aaron Graves" and "Hagit Landman" in the sample screen shot below):

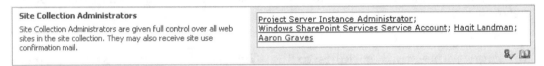

5. Click **OK**. The above users are now authorized to configure and administer Windows SharePoint sites.

6. Repeat steps 1 through 5 for the production and training environments, entering the appropriate URL in step 1.

## To assign administrative rights to Project Web Access:

1. Open Internet Explorer and enter the Project Web Access URL of the development environment (for example, http://<servername>:82/ProjectServer). The **Project Web Access** site opens.

2. On the side navigation bar, click **Server Settings**:

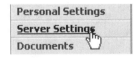

The **Server Settings** page opens.

3. In the **Security** section, click **Manage Users**:

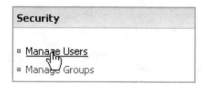

The **Manage Users** page opens.

4. Click **New User**:

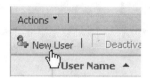

The **New User** page opens.

5. Enter the **Display Name** and **E-mail address** of the user ("Aaron Graves" in the sample screen shot below):

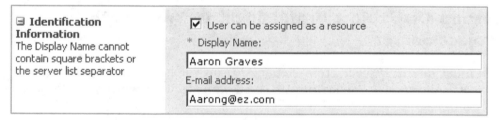

6. Enter the user's Windows logon credentials, using the <domain name\ username> format:

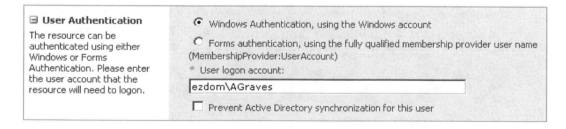

7. In the **Available Groups** pane of the **Security Groups** section, select **Administrators** and click **Add**:

8. Click **Save**. The user can now define and configure the Project Server environment.

9. Repeat steps 3 through 8 for each site collection administrator.

10. Repeat steps 1 through 9 for the production and training environments, entering the appropriate URL in step 1.

## Setting Up Project Professional to Work with Project Server

You must install Project Professional 2007 on your computer and then notify the Project Professional application that you want to work with your Project Server environments.

**To set up the Project Professional connection to the Project Server environments:**

1. Open Project Professional 2007 and click **Tools > Enterprise Options > Microsoft Office Project Server Accounts...**:

The **Project Server Accounts** dialog opens.

2. In the **When starting** section, select **Manually control connection state**:

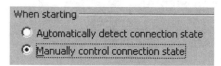

3. Click **Add**. The **Account Properties** dialog opens:

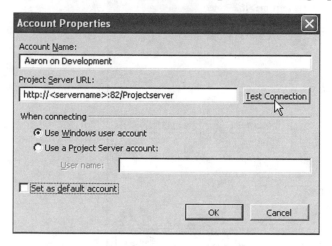

4. To establish connection to the development environment:
   a. In the **Account Name** field, enter your name and an identifier for the development environment.
   b. In the **Project Server URL** field, enter the URL address of the development environment.

5. Click **Test URL** to verify successful connection.

6. In the **When connecting** section, select **Use Windows user account**.

7. Click **OK**.

8. Repeat steps 3 through 7 for the production and training environments, entering the appropriate URL and identifier in step 4:

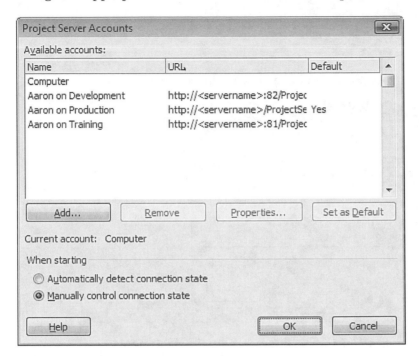

9. Click **OK**, and exit Project Professional.

## To verify that Project Professional is working correctly with Project Web Access:

1. Open Project Professional. The **Login** dialog opens:

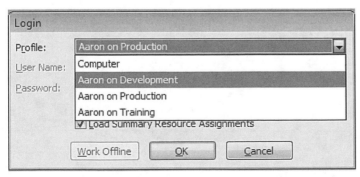

2. From the **Profile** drop-down list, select your login to the development environment and click **OK**. The Project Professional application launches.

3. Verify that the application is connected to the server; the **Status** bar must show **Connected**:

 Figure 1.17

If the connection is not established, contact the IT administrator.

4. Enter tasks of different durations in the new project plan.

---

 **NOTE** Every time you open Project Professional (not from the EPM system), it opens a new project (usually project 1).

---

5. Select **File > Save**. The **Save to Project Server** dialog opens:

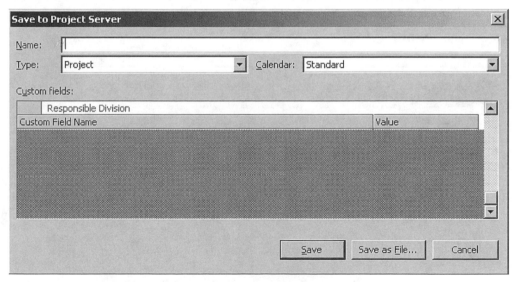

6. Enter a name for your test project and click **Save**.

7. Check that the project is synchronized with the server; the **Status** bar should change from **0 percent complete...** to **Save job completed successfully**:

If the **Save** operation fails, contact the IT administrator.

8. Select **File > Publish**. The **Publish Project: Test Plan Connection** dialog opens:

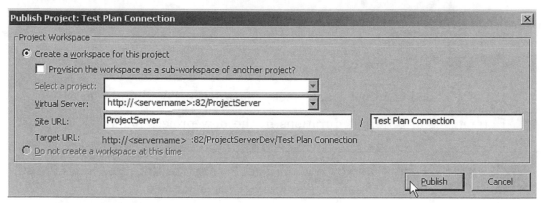

9. Enter the location where you want the project workspace to be created for the project you are saving (for example, "Test Plan Connection" in the development environment, as in the sample screen shot above).

10. Click **Publish**.

---

 Subsequent sections discuss the use of the project workspace and explain when to publish a plan.

---

11. Verify that the **Status** bar shows **Save job completed successfully**. If the **Publish** operation fails, contact the IT administrator.

12. Open Internet Explorer and enter the development environment URL (for example, http://ps2007demo/dev/default.aspx). The **Project Web Access** page opens:

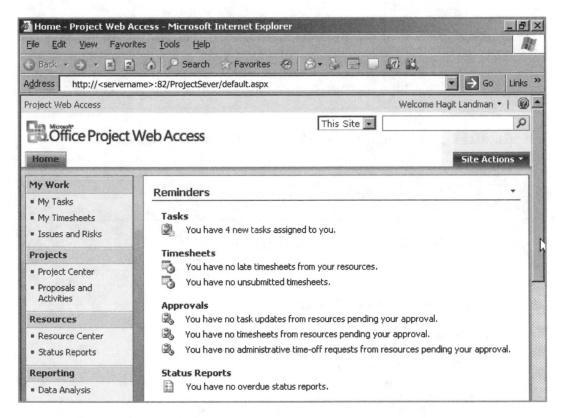

13. Click **Project Center** and verify that you can see the published project on the **Project Center** web page:

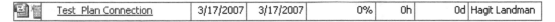

| | | Test_Plan Connection | 3/17/2007 | 3/17/2007 | 0% | 0h | 0d | Hagit Landman |
|---|---|---|---|---|---|---|---|---|

**NOTE** If this is the first time the workstation is used to access Project Center, you may need to click **Install the Active X controllers** as indicated on the web page.

 If you do not see the plan, verify that you clicked the **Save and Publish** button, not **Save**. If you still cannot see the plan, advise your IT administrator. Otherwise, users will not be able to view their project information via Project Web Access.

14. Click the project plan name. The plan's Gantt chart opens:

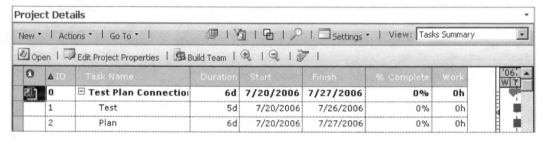

15. Select **Go To > Project Workspace**:

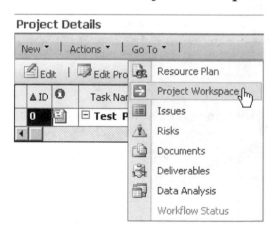

The project workspace of the test plan opens in a separate window:

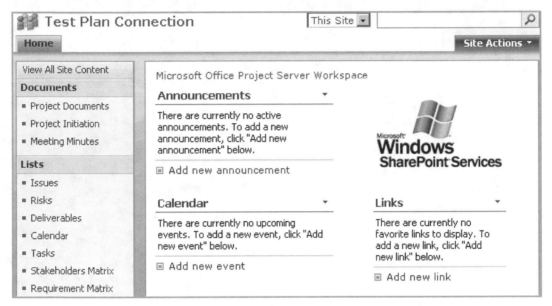

 If you do not see the project workspace, advise your IT administrator. Otherwise, neither you nor the project stakeholders can manage project information such as requirement documents, risks, issues, etc.

You have established the technology foundation. Now you can begin to define the organization requirements and goals for your EPM solution.

# Organizational Goals, Objectives, and Requirements

To implement Enterprise Project Management (EPM) successfully, you need to know the goals and objectives that the EPM solution will address (see Figure 2.1). You also need to have a clear understanding of the project management requirements of all the stakeholders in your organization. This knowledge will enable you to define the project management logical and physical processes needed to meet those requirements.

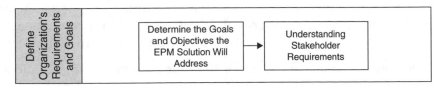

**Figure 2.1. Define the Organization's Requirements and Goals**

## Defining Organizational Goals and Objectives

**To determine the goals and objectives the EPM solution will address:**

1. Discuss with the champion of the EPM initiative, and with each of the other executives, what they perceive to be the goals and objectives of the EPM solution.

2. Consolidate the goals and objectives in a single document (table), clarifying as needed and highlighting gaps and inconsistencies.

3. Present the table to the champion and the executives involved to resolve issues and achieve consensus.

Table 2.1 is an example of a document that describes business project management goals and objectives.

## Understanding Stakeholder Requirements

To configure and deploy the EPM solution so that it provides benefits to all stakeholders:

1. Classify your stakeholders based on the organizational breakdown structure. For example:
   - ◆ **Executives**—Top management level that needs overall project management information
   - ◆ **Resource managers**—Users who need information regarding their resources
   - ◆ **Project managers**—Users in charge of managing the projects
   - ◆ **Other**

2. Record the names of the users who fall under each stakeholder classification using a Microsoft Word file or Excel worksheet. A sample stakeholder classification table is provided in Table 2.2.

3. Select one or two people from each of the stakeholder types and set up a meeting to gather their requirements. Use an Excel spreadsheet to capture and organize the requirements. The spreadsheet

### Table 2.1. Organization's Project Management Goals and Objectives

| Goals | Objectives |
|---|---|
| Have business insight | ◆ Monitor key performance indicators of projects across the portfolio and drill into the details as needed.<br>◆ Evaluate and model schedule, resource, and cost data over time and across projects to identify trends and address problem areas. |
| Optimize work management | ◆ Effectively assign people to projects, and track and manage resources across the organization with skill-based resource assignment tools.<br>◆ Ensure that the organization has the right people and the capacity to take on future projects.<br>◆ Improve project management processes by establishing standards and best practices across the organization.<br>◆ Establish processes and rules for reporting and approving time spent on projects to ensure data accuracy and validity. |
| Improve collaboration | ◆ Enhance project information sharing and coordination across project teams and stakeholders.<br>◆ Improve project notification and communication to enable a more efficient and effective workforce.<br>◆ Centrally store, link, and share documents and information, such as issues and risks related to project plans. |

must list the implementation stages, or project process groups as depicted in the PMBOK®, and define the requirements for each of these stages/groups, as well as those stakeholders who mentioned the same or similar requirements.

Sample spreadsheets for the initiation, planning, execution, monitoring and control, and closing phases appear in Tables 2.3 to 2.7.

## Table 2.2. Stakeholder Classification Table

| Stakeholder Type | Name | Title | Phone and E-mail | Comments |
|---|---|---|---|---|
| Executives | John Kul | Director | 052-555-1213 JohnK@company.com | |
| | Mark Calton | V.P. Development | 052-555-1214 MarkC@company.com | |
| | Chris Webner | V.P. Operations | 052-555-1221 ChrisW@company.com | |
| | Ben Hertzman | V.P. Engineering | 052-555-1241 BenH@company.com | |
| Division Managers | Nave Benisti | Technology Division Manager | 052-555-1244 NaveB@company.com | |
| | Sari Malenali | Network Infrastructure Division Manager | 052-555-1237 SariM@company.com | |
| Program Managers | Emanual Lev | Product Pluto Program Manager | 052-555-1216 EmanualL@company.com | |
| | Dominique Martinelli | Product Jupiter Program Manager | 052-555-1253 DominiqueM@company.com | |
| Project Managers | Brad Masters | Project Manager | 052-555-1295 BradM@company.com | |
| | Rachel Brol | Project Manager | 052-555-1214 RachelB@company.com | |
| | Merav London | Project Manager | 052-555-1229 MeravL@company.com | |
| Team Leaders | Lucy Schultz | Pluto Development Manager | 052-555-1238 LucyS@company.com | |
| | Bernard Bolder | Jupiter Development Manager | 052-555-1227 BernardB@company.com | |
| Team Members | Ruth Bark | Web Developer | 052-555-1321 RuthB@company.com | |
| | Alex Metali | Developer | 052-555-1247 AlexM@company.com | |
| | Samuel Malone | Developer | 052-555-1251 SamuelM@company.com | |

## Table 2.3. Requirements for the Initiation Phase

| Requirement | Stakeholder | | | | | | | | | |
|---|---|---|---|---|---|---|---|---|---|---|
| | Executive/ Steering Committee | Division Manager | Program Manager | Project Manager | Resource Manager | Team Leader | Team Member | PMO | Project Client | Project End User |
| Define high-level project schedule | | | x | x | | | | x | x | |
| Create central location to manage all potential project information | | | | x | | | | x | | |
| Gather project's relevant documentation | | | x | x | | | | x | | |
| Analyze stakeholders | | | x | x | | | | x | | |
| Gather and manage project's requirements and needs (business and technology) | | | x | x | | | | x | | |
| Develop project charter | x | x | x | x | | | | x | | |
| ◆ Define proposed solution | | x | x | | | | | | | |
| ◆ Define preliminary budget and return on investment | | x | x | | | | | | | |
| ◆ Define high-level project risks | | x | x | x | | | | x | | |
| Develop preliminary project scope statement | | x | x | x | | | | x | x | |
| Finalize high-level milestone plan | | | x | x | | | | | | |
| Review and approve proposed projects based on strategic alignment | x | x | x | x | | | | x | x | |

## Table 2.4. Requirements for the Planning Phase

| Requirement | Executive/ Steering Committee | Division Manager | Program Manager | Project Manager | Resource Manager | Team Leader | Team Member | PMO | Project Client | Project End User |
|---|---|---|---|---|---|---|---|---|---|---|
| **Integration Management** | | | | | | | | | | |
| Develop the project management plan | | | x | x | x | x | | x | x | |
| **Scope Management** | | | | | | | | | | |
| Plan and define the project scope | x | x | x | x | x | x | | x | x | x |
| Define deliverable acceptance | | | x | x | | | | x | x | |
| Create the work breakdown structure | | | x | x | | | | x | | |
| Define the change request management process | | | x | x | | | | x | x | |
| **Time Management** | | | | | | | | | | |
| Define the project-level work plan | | | | x | x | x | | x | | |
| Identify delivery activities | | | x | x | | | | x | x | |
| Define the team-level work plan | | | | x | | x | x | x | | |
| Determine project schedule based on actual resource capacity and availability | | | x | x | x | x | | x | | |
| Perform the critical path analysis | | | x | x | | | | x | | |
| Approve the schedule | | x | x | x | x | x | | x | x | |
| Baseline the project schedule | | | x | x | | | | x | | |
| **Cost Management** | | | | | | | | | | |
| Plan cost definitions | | | x | x | | | | x | | |
| Define the project costs | | | x | x | | | | x | | |
| View the project costs | | | x | x | | | | x | | |
| Define the project budget | | | x | x | | | | x | | |
| Approve and baseline the project budget | x | x | x | x | | | | x | | |
| **Quality Management** | | | | | | | | | | |
| Define the quality management plan | | | x | x | | | | | | |

## Table 2.4. Requirements for the Planning Phase (continued)

| Requirement | Executive/ Steering Committee | Division Manager | Program Manager | Project Manager | Resource Manager | Team Leader | Team Member | PMO | Project Client | Project End User |
|---|---|---|---|---|---|---|---|---|---|---|
| **Human Resource Management** | | | | | | | | | | |
| Create the project organizational breakdown structure | | x | x | x | x | | | | | |
| Define roles and responsibilities | | | x | x | x | | | x | | |
| Plan human resources | | | | | | | | | | |
| View the project assignments by resource team | | | x | x | x | x | x | x | | |
| Define the staffing management plan | | | x | x | x | | | x | | |
| **Communication Management** | | | | | | | | | | |
| Define the project communication plan | | | x | x | | | | x | x | |
| Define the project communication plan document | | | x | x | | | | x | | |
| Define the project glossary | | | | | | | | x | | |
| Define the governance procedures | | x | x | x | | | | x | x | |
| Define the documentation deliverable management procedure | | | x | x | | | | x | x | |
| **Risk Management** | | | | | | | | | | |
| Identify the project risks | | | x | x | | x | | x | | |
| Perform the qualitative risk analysis | | | x | x | | | | x | | |
| Perform the quantitative risk analysis | | | x | x | | | | x | | |
| Define the risk mitigation plans | | | x | x | | | | x | | |
| View the project risks | x | x | x | x | x | x | x | x | x | |
| **Procurement Management** | | | | | | | | | | |
| Define the procurement management plan | | | x | x | | | | x | | |
| Define the supplier evaluation criteria | | | x | x | x | | | x | | |

## Table 2.5. Requirements for the Execution Phase

| Requirement | Stakeholder | | | | | | | | | |
|---|---|---|---|---|---|---|---|---|---|---|
| | Executive/ Steering Committee | Division Manager | Program Manager | Project Manager | Resource Manager | Team Leader | Team Member | PMO | Project Client | Project End User |
| **Integration Management** | | | | | | | | | | |
| Hold the project execution kickoff meeting | x | x | x | x | x | x | x | x | x | |
| **Scope Management** | | | | | | | | | | |
| Manage change requests | | | x | x | | | | x | x | |
| Report change request status | | | x | x | | | | x | | |
| Create, manage, and deliver the program/ project document deliverables | | | x | x | | x | x | x | | |
| Create, manage, and deliver the program/ project deliverables | | | x | x | | x | x | x | | |
| **Time Management** | | | | | | | | | | |
| View and manage assignments that were supposed to be completed in the previous reporting period | | | x | x | | x | x | | | |
| Approve/disapprove reported tasks | | | x | x | | | | | | |
| Define the method of progress reporting | | | x | x | | | | x | | |
| Review impact on the project schedule | | | x | x | | x | | x | | |
| Report schedule progress | | | x | x | | | | x | | |
| **Cost Management** | | | | | | | | | | |
| Collect the project costs and expenses | | | x | x | | | | x | | |
| **Quality Management** | | | | | | | | | | |
| Perform quality audits and report quality progress | | | | | | x | | | | |
| **Human Resource Management** | | | | | | | | | | |
| Perform orientation and coaching for new team members | | | | | | x | x | | | |
| Communicate new and/or changed assignments | | | x | x | x | x | x | x | | |
| Develop the project team | | | x | x | x | x | x | x | | |
| Manage human resources | | | x | x | x | x | x | | | |
| Perform team-building activities | | | x | x | x | x | x | x | | |

## Table 2.5. Requirements for the Execution Phase (continued)

| Requirement | Stakeholder | | | | | | | | | |
|---|---|---|---|---|---|---|---|---|---|---|
| | Executive/ Steering Committee | Division Manager | Program Manager | Project Manager | Resource Manager | Team Leader | Team Member | PMO | Project Client | Project End User |
| **Communication Management** | | | | | | | | | | |
| Manage the communication management plan and distribute information | | | x | x | | | | x | | |
| Manage the project event calendar | | | x | x | | | | x | | |
| Manage action items | | | | | | | | x | | |
| **Risk Management** | | | | | | | | | | |
| Log new risks | | | x | x | | x | | x | | |
| Assess risks | | | x | x | | x | | x | | |
| Manage risks | | | x | x | | x | | x | | |
| Manage the risk mitigation plans | | | x | x | | x | | x | | |
| Escalate risks | | | x | x | | x | x | | | |
| Report risk status | | | x | x | | x | x | | | |
| **Issues Management** | | | | | | | | | | |
| Upgrade risks to issues | | | x | x | | x | | x | | |
| Open new issues | | | x | x | | x | | x | | |
| View the issues log | | | x | x | | x | | x | | |
| **Procurement Management** | | | | | | | | | | |
| Receive sellers' responses | | | x | x | | | | x | | |
| Select sellers | | | x | x | | | | x | | |
| Issue purchase orders | | | | | | | | x | | |
| Manage sellers | | | x | x | | | | x | | |

## Table 2.6. Requirements for the Monitoring and Control Phase

| Requirement | Stakeholder | | | | | | | | | |
|---|---|---|---|---|---|---|---|---|---|---|
| | Executive/ Steering Committee | Division Manager | Program Manager | Project Manager | Resource Manager | Team Leader | Team Member | PMO | Project Client | Project End User |
| **Scope Management** | | | | | | | | | | |
| Administer contracts | | | x | x | | | | x | | |
| Monitor change requests | | | x | x | | | | x | x | |
| **Time Management** | | | | | | | | | | |
| Collect reports | | | | | | | | x | | |
| View actual finish dates vs. planned finish dates for primary tasks and milestones | | | x | x | | | | x | | |
| View achieved milestones vs. planned milestones | | | x | x | | | | x | x | |
| View actual schedule progress vs. planned schedule progress | x | | x | x | | x | | x | | |
| Identify tasks that cause slippage | | | x | x | | | | x | | |
| Identify interdependencies | | | x | x | | x | | x | | |
| Perform critical path analysis | | | x | x | | | | x | | |
| **Cost Management** | | | | | | | | | | |
| Collect the cost reports | | | x | x | | x | | x | | |
| View actual costs vs. scheduled costs | | | x | x | | x | | x | | |
| Control costs and budget | | | x | x | | x | | x | | |
| **Quality Management** | | | | | | | | | | |
| Perform quality control | | | x | x | | x | | | | |
| **Human Resource Management** | | | | | | | | | | |
| View actual resource assignment load vs. planned resource assignment load | | | x | x | x | | | x | | |
| **Communication Management** | | | | | | | | | | |
| Manage performance and status reports | x | x | x | x | | | | x | x | |
| Manage stakeholders | | | x | x | | | | x | | |
| **Risk Management** | | | | | | | | | | |
| Monitor and control risks | | | x | x | | x | | | | |
| **Procurement Management** | | | | | | | | | | |
| Contract administration | | x | x | x | | | | | x | |

## Table 2.7. Requirements for the Closing Phase

| Requirement | Executive/ Steering Committee | Division Manager | Program Manager | Project Manager | Resource Manager | Team Leader | Team Member | PMO | Project Client | Project End User |
|---|---|---|---|---|---|---|---|---|---|---|
| **Integration Management** | | | | | | | | | | |
| Sponsor closure letter | | | x | | | | | | | |
| Create and manage the project closure checklist | | | x | x | | | | x | | |
| Hold the lessons learned meeting and save the results to the database | x | x | x | x | x | x | x | x | x | x |
| Issue the end of program/project/phase report | | | x | | | | | x | | |
| **Scope Management** | | | | | | | | | | |
| Verify that all the deliverables have been delivered | | | x | | | | | | x | |
| Close the contract | | | x | | | | | x | | |
| **Time Management** | | | | | | | | | | |
| Close the project plan | | | x | x | | | | x | | |
| **Cost Management** | | | | | | | | | | |
| Close all work packages and budget codes | | | | | | | | x | | |
| **Human Resource Management** | | | | | | | | | | |
| Assign resources to other projects | | | x | x | x | x | x | | | |
| **Communication Management** | | | | | | | | | | |
| Save all relevant information in the database for future use | | | | | | | | x | | |
| Close all open action items | | | x | x | | | | x | | |
| **Risk Management** | | | | | | | | | | |
| Close risks | | | x | x | | | | x | | |
| **Procurement Management** | | | | | | | | | | |
| Close contracts with subcontractors | | | x | | | | | x | | |

This book has free materials available for download from the Web Added Value™ Resource Center at www.jrosspub.com.

# Part II.
# Project Management Processes and Enterprise Project Management Solution Deployment

# Establishing Project Management Processes and Supporting Tools

## Overview

Having defined the organization's project management goals and objectives, as well as gathered all of the stakeholder requirements, you can begin to define the project management processes and supporting tools.

Figure 3.1 is an adaptation of the project management life cycle suggested in the PMBOK® that you can use as a general guideline for establishing the project management processes.

Processes are built of tasks. For each task, you need to define the following:

1. **Objectives**—What the objectives of the task are

2. **Procedure**—How the user must use the Enterprise Project Management solution to achieve the objective for each procedure

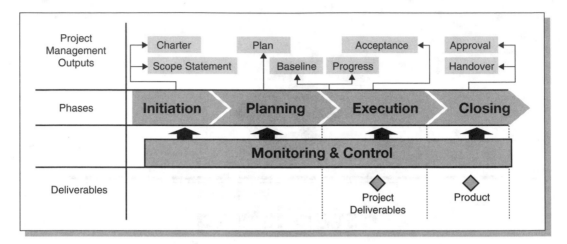

**Figure 3.1. Project Management Life Cycle**

3. **Prerequisites**—What data items and software settings are required to perform the task and support the procedure

## Definitions

**Management**—Roles and responsibilities established to manage a project according to its scope and in line with contract terms and conditions.

**Organization**—Organizational units and structures, groupings, and coordinating mechanisms (such as a steering committee) established within an organization and in partnership with external bodies, for the delivery of a project.

**Policies**—Frameworks and boundaries established for making decisions to manage and deliver a project.

**Program**\*—A group of related projects managed in a coordinated way to obtain benefits and control not available by managing them individually. Programs may include elements of related work outside the scope of the discrete projects in the program.

---

\* Project Management Institute *A Guide to the Project Management Body of Knowledge (PMBOK® Guide)—Third Edition,* Project Management Institute, Inc., 2004. Copyright and all rights reserved. Material from this publication has been reproduced with the permission of PMI.

**Program management office (PMO)**\*—The centralized management of a particular program or programs such that the corporate benefit is realized by the sharing of resources, methodologies, tools, and techniques and related high-level project management focus.

**Project**\*—A temporary endeavor undertaken to create a unique product, service, or result.

**Project charter**\*—A document issued by the project initiator or sponsor which legalizes the existence of a project and provides the project manager with the authority to use the organization's resources in the project activities.

**Project initiator**—The person responsible for the initiation process. Preferably, this person is the assigned project manager.

**Project management office (PMO)**\*—An organizational body or entity assigned various responsibilities related to the centralized and coordinated management of those projects under its domain. The responsibilities of a PMO can range from providing project management support functions to actually being responsible for the direct management of a project.

**Project management plan**\*—A formal, approved document that defines how a project is executed, monitored, and controlled. It may be summary or detailed and may be composed of one or more subsidiary management plans and other planning documents.

**Project process groups**\*—The five process groups required for any project that have clear dependencies and that are required to be performed in the same sequence on each project, independent of the application area or the specifics of the applied project life cycle. The process groups are initiating, planning, executing, monitoring and controlling, and closing.

**Requirement**\*—A condition or capability that must be met or possessed by a system, product, service, result, or component to satisfy a contract, standard, specification, or other formally imposed documents. Requirements include the quantified and documented needs, wants, and expectations of the sponsor, customer, and other stakeholders.

---

\* Project Management Institute *A Guide to the Project Management Body of Knowledge (PMBOK® Guide)—Third Edition,* Project Management Institute, Inc., 2004. Copyright and all rights reserved. Material from this publication has been reproduced with the permission of PMI.

**Stakeholder***—Persons and organizations, such as customers, sponsors, performing organization, and the public, that are actively involved in a project or whose interests may by positively or negatively affected by execution or completion of a project. They may also exert influence over a project and its deliverables.

**Work breakdown structure (WBS)***—A deliverable-oriented hierarchical decomposition of the work to be executed by the project team to accomplish the project objectives and create the required deliverables. It organizes and defines the total scope of the project. Each descending level represents an increasingly detailed definition of the project work. The WBS is decomposed into work packages. The deliverable orientation of the hierarchy includes both internal and external deliverables.

## Acronyms

| | |
|---|---|
| EPM | Enterprise Project Management |
| IIS | Internet Information Services |
| KPI | Key performance indicator |
| OBS | Organizational breakdown structure |
| PMBOK® | Project Management Body of Knowledge |
| PMI | Project Management Institute |
| PMO | Project management office |
| Project Professional | Microsoft® Office Project Professional |
| ROI | Return on investment |
| SOW | Statement of work |
| WBS | Work breakdown structure |

---

\* Project Management Institute *A Guide to the Project Management Body of Knowledge (PMBOK® Guide)—Third Edition,* Project Management Institute, Inc., 2004. Copyright and all rights reserved. Material from this publication has been reproduced with the permission of PMI.

# Initiation Process

Initiation is the first of the project/program management processes. In the course of this process, the project/program boundaries are defined and examined:

◆ Where the project starts and where it stops

◆ What information is needed to make the right decision in terms of going ahead with or not going ahead with the project

## Overview

The initiation process is performed to define and approve the scope of a new project and to determine if the project is worth doing.

The main outputs of the initiation process are:

◆ Stakeholder analysis

◆ Project charter (the "contract" between the project/program manager and the organization)

◆ Preliminary scope statement

 For better buy-in by the project manager, it is advisable that he or she be involved in the project from the very beginning. After all, the project manager has to deliver the result. This way, he or she will understand all the project constraints and will deal with them better later on.

Initiation is a very important process, and it must not be skipped.

## Workflow

To provide a solution that meets the requirements that are defined for the initiation process, the features/functions listed in Table 4.1 must be implemented.

**Table 4.1. Initiation Feature/Function Processes**

| Requirement | Solution Feature/ Function Guidelines | Relevant Procedure |
|---|---|---|
| Define high-level project schedule | Use Project Web Access Proposal Project Plan | ◆ "To create a new proposed project plan"<br>◆ "To enter phases, main tasks, and milestones |
| Create central location to manage all potential project information | Use Windows SharePoint Services to manage all project-related information | "To create a project workspace" |
| Gather project's relevant documentation | Use Windows SharePoint Services document library list | "To enter initial project information in the project workspace" |

## Table 4.1. Initiation Feature/Function Processes (continued)

| Requirement | Solution Feature/ Function Guidelines | Relevant Procedure |
|---|---|---|
| Analyze stakeholders | Use Windows SharePoint Services list to gather and manage requirements (stakeholders analysis) | "To fill out the stake-holders matrix" |
| Gather and manage project's requirement and needs (business and technology) | Use Windows SharePoint Services list to gather and manage requirements | "To fill out the require-ments matrix" |
| Develop project charter<br>◆ Define proposed solution<br>◆ Define preliminary budget and return on investment<br>◆ Define high-level project risks | Use Microsoft Word document to develop project charter | "Creating the project charter" |
| Develop preliminary project scope statement | Use Microsoft Word document to develop preliminary project scope statement | "To create a preliminary scope statement" |
| Finalize high-level mile-stone plan | Use Project Web Access Proposal Project Plan | "To finalize the high-level milestone project plan" |
| Review and approve proposed projects based on strategic alignment | Use Windows SharePoint Services document library metadata to manage workflow | "To approve the project for planning" |

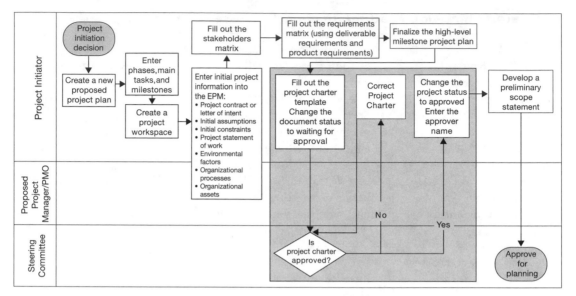

**Figure 4.1. Initiation Process Workflow**

Figure 4.1 depicts the initiation process workflow based on the solution feature/ function guidelines.

## Creating the Proposed Project Plan

The project plan created in the course of the initiation process serves as a basis for the project schedule.

### Objective

The objective of the project plan is to set a rough estimate of the project duration and main milestones. These milestones enable the project manager to define what type of resources will be required for each major milestone and when.

## Procedures

First, the project initiator creates a proposal to house the activities of the proposed project.

### To create a new proposed project plan:

1.  Open Internet Explorer and enter the URL of Project Web Access (for example, http://<Servername>/ProjectServer). The **Project Web Access** site opens:

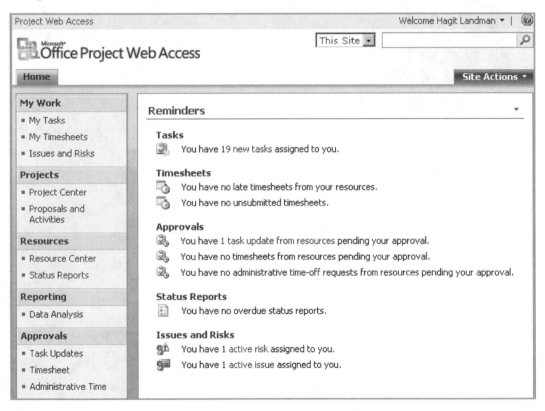

2. In the quick launch menu, click **Proposals and Activities**:

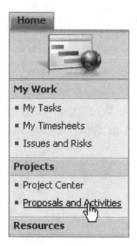

The **Proposals and Activities** page opens.

3. Select **New > Proposal**:

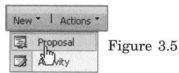　Figure 3.5

The **New Proposal** or **Plan** page opens:

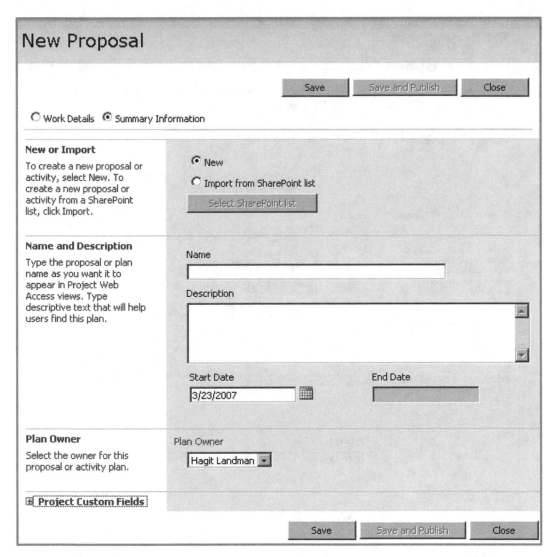

4. Select the **Summary Information** option button and then the **New** option
   button in the **New or Import** section.

5. In the **Name** field, type the proposed project name (for example, "Upgrading CRM System").

6. In the **Description** field, type a brief description of the proposed project.

7. In the **Start Date** field, enter the proposed start date of the project.

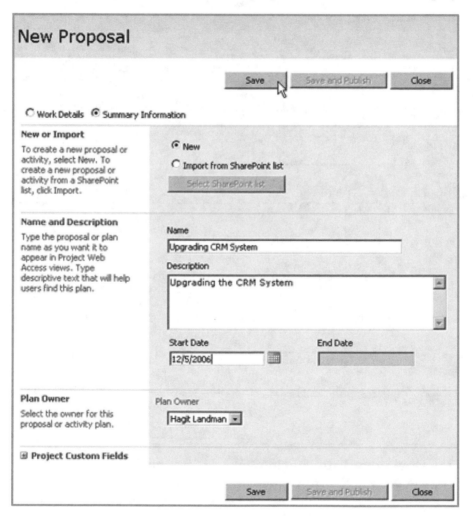

8. Click **Save**.

## To enter phases, main tasks, and milestones:

1.  Select the **Work Details** option button. The **Actions** grid is displayed:

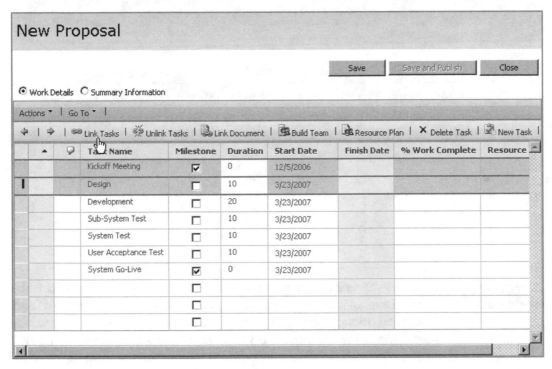

2.  Enter the main tasks and milestones required to achieve the proposed project objectives.

3.  To link between activities:
    a.  Select an activity in the grid. (You must select the entire grid line to link an activity; this is done by pressing on the box at the far left of the activity line.)
    b.  Select the activity that you want to link to by pressing the control key and clicking to the left of the activity. (In the example above, the activities are **Kickoff Meeting** and **Design**.)
    c.  On the toolbar, click **Link Tasks**.
    d.  The chain sign ⊕ will appear next to the tasks to show that they are linked activities.
    e.  Repeat steps a to c for all activities you want to link.

4. Click **Save**. The proposed project plan is created:

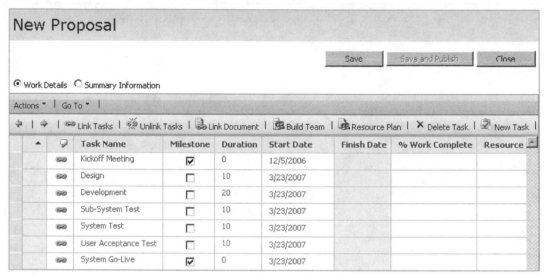

 There is an important difference between **Save** vs. **Save and Publish**. **Save** places the proposed plan only on the **Proposed and Activity Plan** page. **Save and Publish** also creates a project workspace for the proposed project where all documents, issues, risks, and other project information items are managed.

## Prerequisites

This task is built into the application, in the server. No adaptations or configurations are needed. There are no prerequisites for it.

## Creating the Project Workspace

Project Server uses the Windows SharePoint Services component to create a project workspace for every published project plan or proposed project plan. The project workspace enables you to create, store, and share project-related information such as documents, requirements, contracts, contacts, news, events, and other information and to efficiently collaborate with other stakeholders.

## Objective

The objective of this task is to establish a central repository of project-related information to assist the project initiator in gathering and managing project-related information such as the statement of work, requirements, project charter, etc.

## Procedure

### To create a project workspace:

1. Go to **Proposals and Activities**, and select the proposal that you have created. In the example below, it is **Upgrading CRM System**:

| | Name ▲ | Published | Checked Out By | State | Start Date | Finish Date | Resource Plan |
|---|---|---|---|---|---|---|---|
| | Change the CR SW | Yes | | Proposed | 2/26/2007 | 2/26/2007 | |
| | Upgrading CRM System | Yes | Hagit Landman | Proposed | 12/5/2006 | 2/26/2007 | |
| | Upgrading the SW | No | | Proposed | 2/26/2007 | 2/26/2007 | |

**Proposals and Activities**

Use this page to create a project proposal or track activity, open an existing proposal or activity, or delete an obsolete proposal or activity.

New ▾ | Actions ▾ |

Open Read-Only | ✕ Delete | Convert | Check In | Build Team | Resource Plan |

The proposal page opens.

2. In the proposed project plan that you have created, click **Save and Publish**:

This enables Project Server to create a project workspace for the proposed project selected.

3. Project Server will now create the workspace. The **Checking Queue Status** screen will open while Project Server is creating the workspace:

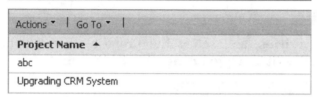

Publishing project. Waiting for the queue...

4. Click **Close**.

5. Now the project will appear in the list of **Project Workspaces** on the **Project Web Access** home page:

Project Workspaces

| Actions ▾  │  Go To ▾  │ |
| --- |
| **Project Name** ▲ |
| abc |
| Upgrading CRM System |

## Prerequisites

This task is built into the application. There is no need for any adaptations. There are no prerequisites for it.

# Entering the Initial Project Information

## Objectives

Collecting and entering the initial project information in the project workspace ensures that you can find all the relevant project documentation in one place. This documentation serves as a basis for the project charter and the preliminary scope statement.

The relevant project documentation might include the following:

- ◆ Project contract or letter of intent
- ◆ Initial assumptions
- ◆ Initial constraints
- ◆ Project statement of work (SOW)
- ◆ Environmental factors
- ◆ Organizational processes
- ◆ Organizational assets
- ◆ Product description
- ◆ Organizational policies and procedures
- ◆ Other relevant documentation
- ◆ Historical information such as
  - ◇ Lessons learned
  - ◇ Risks
  - ◇ Work breakdown structure
  - ◇ Estimates
  - ◇ Project plans

## Procedure

### To enter initial project information in the project workspace:

1. Open the project workspace. On the **Project Web Access** home page, click the proposed project name in the **Project Workspaces** section:

Project Workspaces

| Actions ▾     Go To ▾ | | View: All Workspaces |
|---|---|---|
| **Project Name** ▲ | **Date Created** | **Owner** |
| Upgrading CRM System | 3/23/2007 | Hagit Landman |
| Upgrading test | 3/1/2007 | Hagit Landman |

The project workspace opens:

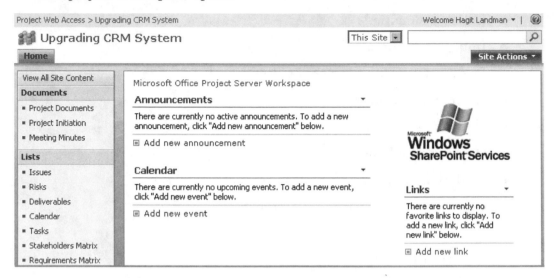

2. To load documentation to the project initiation library, under **Documents**:
   a. Select **Documents > Project Initiation**:

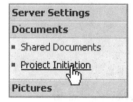

The **Project Initiation** page opens:

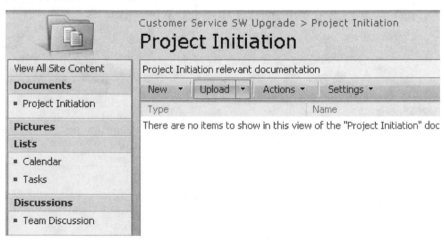

b.  Under **Upload**, select **Upload Document** or **Upload Multiple Documents**:

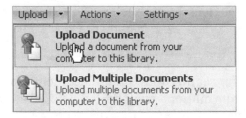

c.  Browse to the document(s) you want to upload, and select the relevant document(s):

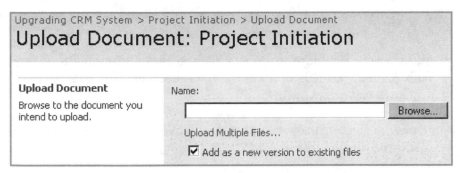

d.  Click **Open**, then **OK**. The document metadata fields appear.
e.  Enter the relevant metadata:

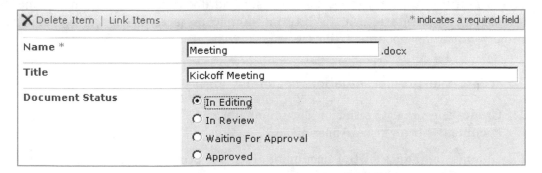

f.  When you finish entering the metadata, click **OK**.
g.  Repeat the above procedure for all the documents you want to upload.

## Prerequisite

Project workspace is based on Windows SharePoint Services and is automatically created when a project plan or proposed plan is published. The native project workspace does not include the required lists and documents described in the above procedure.

Instead of making the end user create the required lists and documents for every project and then manage the project information, use the following method:

1. Use a sample project workspace as an interim solution to create the required lists and documents.

2. When all the required lists are built, save the sample project workspace as a site template.

3. Add the site template to Project Web Access and indicate to Project Web Access that this template is to be used as the basis for all new project workspaces.

Now every new project or proposed plan published on the server will include the required lists and documents.

The above procedures are described in Chapter 9 on converting your sample site to be the default project workspace and are performed only when you have completed defining the project workspace lists and documents. In the meantime, to support the procedure, use the interim sample project workspace to create the project initiation document library.

## To create the project initiation document library:

1. Create the project initiation document library. For the procedure to create a document library, see Appendix A.3.

2. Change metadata of the document. For the procedure to change document metadata, see Appendix A.4.

# Performing the Preliminary Stakeholder Analysis

## Objectives

One of the key success factors in a project is the fulfillment of the stakeholders' requirements. The role, position, communication needs, and influence on the project life cycle must be identified for each stakeholder at the beginning of a project.

Stakeholders are tracked using a log table that maps the project stakeholders and their position in the organization, influence on the project, requirements, and the response to these requirements.

In the course of a project, the log table is reviewed regularly to ensure that the requirements are met.

This table can also serve as a tool to verify that no out-of-scope deliverables are included in the requirements matrix.

## Procedure

The project initiator uses the project workspace of the project selected to manage the stakeholder information.

### To fill out the stakeholders matrix:

1. Open Project Web Access.

2. Select the project workspace:

**Project Workspaces**

| Actions ▾ | Go To ▾ | | | View: | All Workspaces ▾ |
| --- | --- | --- | --- | --- | --- |
| **Project Name** ▲ | | **Date Created** | **Owner** | | |
| abc | | 3/19/2007 | Hagit Landman | | |
| Upgrading CRM System | | 3/23/2007 | Hagit Landman | | |

The project workspace selected opens:

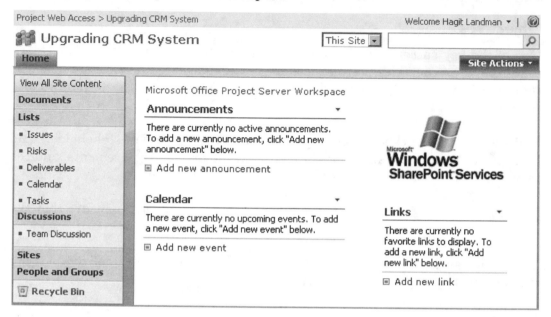

3. In the **Lists** section of the quick launch menu, click **Stakeholders Matrix**:

The **Stakeholders Matrix** page opens:

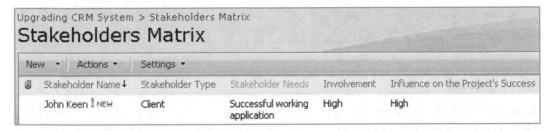

4. On the toolbar, click **New**. A new (blank) **Stakeholders Matrix** item opens:

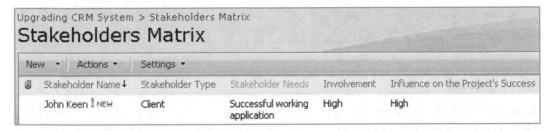

5. Fill out the stakeholder's information.

6. Click **OK**.

7. Repeat steps 4 to 6 for each stakeholder.

### Prerequisite

As a prerequisite for this task, you must create a table of the project stakeholders (the stakeholders matrix). Table 4.2 is a sample stakeholders matrix that contains the minimum information to be captured and managed.

### To create the stakeholders matrix:

1. Open Project Web Access (development environment).

2. Follow the procedure in Appendix A.7 for creating a new list. Use the fields and field types included in the sample stakeholders matrix in Table 4.2.

## Filling Out the Requirements Matrix

### Objectives

The requirements matrix is a tool used to collect all the requirements in a project from all the sources, such as the contract, letter of intent, meetings with the client, etc. Gathering all the requirements in one place ensures that nothing is missed and enables you to monitor the requirements.

The requirements can be administrative (for example, meeting arrangements), technical, managerial, etc.

The requirements matrix also maps the requirements to the personnel who handle these requirements, to their origin, and to the stakeholders who initiated these requirements.

The requirements matrix serves as the basis for the preliminary scope statement and for the scope statement in the planning process.

## Table 4.2. Stakeholders Matrix

| Field Name | Description | Field Type |
| --- | --- | --- |
| Stakeholder Name | Name of the stakeholder | Text field |
| Stakeholder Type | Classifies the user's stakeholder type; possible values:<br>◆ Executive ◆ End User<br>◆ Project Sponsor ◆ Client<br>◆ Project Manager ◆ Vendor/Supplier<br>◆ Program Manager ◆ Team Leader<br>◆ Resource Manager ◆ Team Member | Choice (value list) |
| Stakeholder Needs | Brief description of the stakeholder's needs | Multiple-line text field |
| Involvement | Describes the stakeholder's involvement in the project | Multiple-line text field |
| Influence on the Project's Success | Describes the degree of influence the stakeholder has on project success; possible values:<br>◆ Very High ◆ Low<br>◆ High ◆ Very Low<br>◆ Medium | Choice (value list) |
| Benefits from the Project | Describes the stakeholder's benefits from the project | Multiple-line text field |
| Belong to Organization? | Defines if the stakeholder is within the organization; possible values: yes/no | Yes/no (check box) |
| If No, Company Name | Stakeholder's company name | Text field |
| Title and Role in Organization | Stakeholder's official title | Multiple-line text field |

## Procedure

The project initiator uses the selected project's workspace to manage the requirements information.

### To fill out the requirements matrix:

1. Open Project Web Access.

2. Select the project workspace:

The project workspace selected opens.

3. In the side menu, click **Requirements Matrix**:

The **Requirement Matrix** page opens.

4. Click **New**. The requirement fields are displayed:

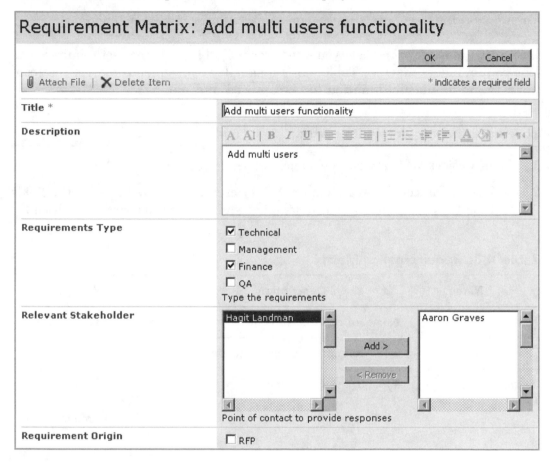

5. Fill in the requirement fields.

6. Click **OK**.

7. Repeat steps 4 to 6 for each requirement identified.

## Prerequisite

To support this task, use the interim project workspace as a template.

As a prerequisite for this task, you must create a table of the project requirements (the requirements matrix). Table 4.3 is a sample requirements matrix that contains the minimum information to be captured and managed.

### To create the requirements matrix:

1. Open Project Web Access (development environment).

2. Follow the procedure in Appendix A.7 for creating a new list. Use the fields and field types included in the sample requirements matrix in Table 4.3.

### Table 4.3. Requirements Matrix

| Field Name | Description | Field Type |
|---|---|---|
| Title | Name of the requirement | Single line of text |
| Description | Brief description of the requirement | Multiple lines of text |
| Requirements Type | Type of the requirement | Choice (check boxes):<br>◆ Technical<br>◆ Management<br>◆ Finance<br>◆ QA<br>◆ Other |
| Relevant Stakeholder | Name of the relevant stakeholder who is connected directly to the requirement | Lookup to the "Stakeholder Name" in the stakeholders matrix |
| Requirement Origin | Origin of the requirement: RFP, SOW, etc. | Choice (check boxes):<br>◆ RFP<br>◆ RFI<br>◆ SOW<br>◆ Change Request |

## Table 4.3. Requirements Matrix (continued)

| Field Name* | Description | Field Type |
|---|---|---|
| Requirement Reference | Reference to the origin of the requirement | Multiple lines of text |
| Responsible Department | Name of the department that will be responsible for handling the requirement | Choice (check boxes):<br>◆ R&D<br>◆ Engineering<br>◆ Integration<br>◆ Training<br>◆ Testing<br>◆ Management<br>◆ Finance<br>◆ HR<br>◆ Contracts<br>◆ Other |
| Requirement Compliance | Level of the solution compliance with the requirement | Choice (drop-down list):<br>◆ Fully complies<br>◆ Partially complies<br>◆ Does not comply |
| Solution Response and Reference | The solution that will fulfill the requirement | Multiple lines of text |
| HLE | High-level effort estimate | Choice (drop-down list):<br>◆ High ◆ Med ◆ Low |
| In-house Effort Estimate | An estimate of the number of work hours the requirement will take to develop using existing manpower | Number |
| Average In-house MP Cost per Hour | Average rate of in-house work hour | Currency |
| Total In-house MP Cost | In-house effort estimate × the average rate | Currency, calculated |

* MP = manpower.

**Table 4.3. Requirements Matrix (continued)**

| Field Name* | Description | Field Type |
|---|---|---|
| External Effort Estimate | Estimate of the number of out-sourced hours required | Number |
| Average External MP Cost per Hour | Average rate of external work hour | Currency |
| Total External MP Cost | External effort estimate × the average rate | Currency, calculated |
| Total Work Hours | Sum of in-house and external effort in hours | Number |
| Material Cost | Estimate of the material and purchasing costs | Currency |
| Total Estimated Cost | Total cost of fulfilling the require-ment (in-house + external + materials) | Currency, calculated |

* MP = manpower.

## Finalizing the High-Level Milestone Plan

### Objectives

◆ To define the program/project time frame more accurately prior to producing the project charter

◆ To identify the main milestones and main deliverables and their estimated schedules

◆ To help define high-level budget and resource allocation

### Procedure

The desired workflow is depicted in Figure 4.1.

## To finalize the high-level milestone project plan:

1. Open the proposed project plan from the **Proposals and Activities** quick launch menu:

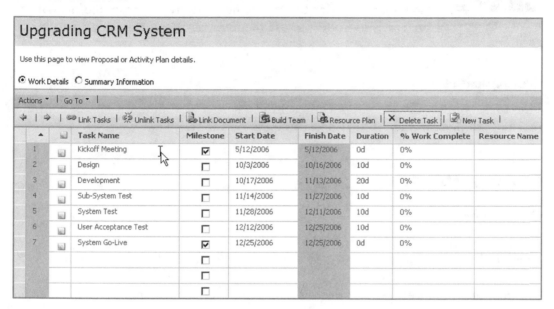

2. Update the project schedule:

| | | Task Name | Milestone | Start Date | Finish Date | Duration | % Work Complete | Resource Name |
|---|---|---|---|---|---|---|---|---|
| 1 | | Kickoff Meeting | ☑ | 5/12/2006 | 5/12/2006 | 0d | 0% | |
| 2 | | ⊟ **Phase 1** | ☐ | 10/4/2006 | 10/4/2006 | 1d? | 0% | |
| 3 | | Design | ☐ | 10/3/2006 | 10/16/2006 | 10d | 0% | |
| 4 | | Development | ☐ | 10/17/2006 | 11/13/2006 | 20d | 0% | |
| 5 | | Sub-System Test | ☐ | 11/14/2006 | 11/27/2006 | 10d | 0% | |
| 6 | | System Test | ☐ | 11/28/2006 | 12/11/2006 | 10d | 0% | |
| 7 | | User Acceptance Test | ☐ | 12/12/2006 | 12/25/2006 | 10d | 0% | |
| 8 | | System Go-Live | ☑ | 12/25/2006 | 12/25/2006 | 0d | 0% | |
| 9 | | ⊟ **Phase 2** | ☐ | 10/4/2006 | 12/26/2006 | 60d? | 0% | |
| 10 | | Development | ☐ | 12/26/2006 | 12/26/2006 | 20 | 0% | |
| 11 | | Sub-System Test | ☐ | 10/4/2006 | 10/4/2006 | 10 | 0% | |
| 12 | | System Test | ☑ | 10/4/2006 | 10/4/2006 | 8 | 0% | |
| 13 | | User Acceptance Test | ☐ | 10/5/2006 | 10/5/2006 | 5 | 0% | |
| 14 | | Phase 2 Go-Live | ☑ | 10/5/2006 | 10/5/2006 | 0d | 0% | |

Save | Save and Publish | Cancel

3. Click **Save and Publish** to update the plan on the server.

 Technically, at this time, the plan does not have to be detailed. However, in order to define the time frame, resource allocation, etc., it is in your interest to enter as many details as possible.

## Prerequisites

This task is built into the application, in the server. No adaptations or configurations are needed. There are no prerequisites for it.

# Creating the Project Charter

## Objectives

The project charter is the document that formally authorizes a project; it is the "contract" for a project. It provides a clear statement of the project scope.

The charter must define the project in a robust manner, so that it does not need to be changed if the project is modified during its life cycle.

Some of the major objectives of the project charter are to:

- ◆ Officially assign a project manager
- ◆ Establish the boundaries of the project
- ◆ Define the end deliverables
- ◆ Define the project time frame and major milestones
- ◆ State the business case
- ◆ Identify major risks
- ◆ Present the results of the project's preliminary stakeholder analysis
- ◆ Set the key performance indicators

The project charter must be written by the project/program initiator and approved by the project steering committee.

## Procedures

The desired workflow is depicted in Figure 4.1.

### To fill out the project charter template:

1. On the **Project Web Access** home page (development environment), select the project workspace.

2. From the quick launch menu, select **Documents > Project Initiation**. The **Project Initiation** page opens:

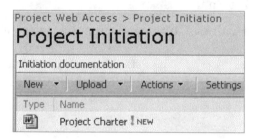

3. From the scroll-down menu of the **Project Charter** document, select **Check Out**:

The following message is displayed:

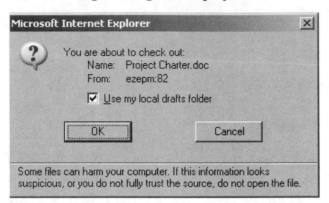

4. Click **OK**. When a document is checked out, a small (green) arrow appears in the Microsoft Word icon next to its name: .

5. From the scroll-down menu of the **Project Charter** document, select **Edit in Microsoft Office Word**:

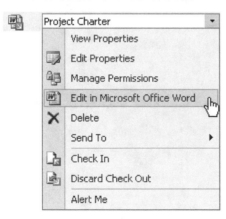

The **Project Charter** document opens:

## Project Charter

### <u>\<Project Name\></u>

1. Project's Description (What is the project):
2. Project Manager:
3. Leading Business Unit:
4. Objectives:
5. Major Stakeholders:

| Stakeholder | Name | Division/Department | Influence |
|---|---|---|---|
| Project Initiator | John Smith | | |
| Program Manager | | | |
| Project Manager | | | |
| Project Client | | | |
| Project Sponsor | | | |

6. Fill in the project charter information.

7. Save and close the document. The following dialog opens:

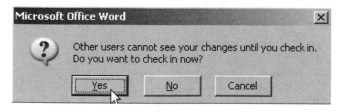

8. Click **Yes**. The **Check In** dialog opens:

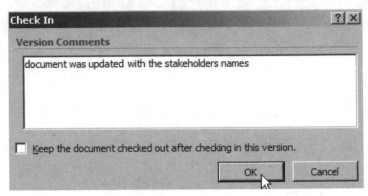

9. Enter the **Version Comments** and click **OK**. The updated document is saved in the project workspace.

10. Refresh the screen by pressing **[F5]** on the keyboard. The **Initiation documentation** page opens:

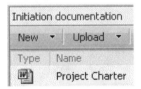

## To change the document status to waiting for approval:

1. From the scroll-down menu of the **Project Charter** document, select **Edit Properties**:

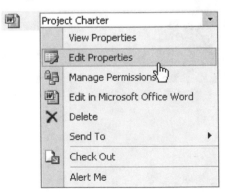

The document's properties are displayed:

2. If the document is ready for approval, from the **Document Status** group of option buttons, select **Waiting For Approval**.

3. Click **OK**. The system sends the members of the project's steering committee e-mail messages asking for approval of the document. The e-mail messages include a link to the document.

### To revise the project charter:

1. The steering committee representatives who have been chosen to review the document check the document out to review it and change the **Document Status** to **In Review**.

2. The steering committee representatives enter revisions using the track changes option.

3. The steering committee representatives check the document in and change the **Document Status** to **Waiting For Approval**.

4. If the document is approved, the steering committee representatives change the document status to **Approved** (see the procedure below).

5. If the document is not approved because it requires changes, the steering committee representatives change the status to **In Editing**.

### To update the project charter:

If changes are required in the project charter document, the project initiator updates the document and resubmits it for approval.

## To change the project charter status to approved:

1. From the **Document** menu, select **Project Initiation**.

2. From the scroll-down menu of the **Project Charter** document, select **Edit Properties**:

3. Change the document status to **Approved**:

4. Click **OK**.

## Prerequisite

### To upload the project charter template:

1. Create a template for the project charter.

2. Upload the document to the project initiation document library.

To upload the sample project charter document as a template, use the procedure in Appendix A.6 for uploading a document to a document library.

# Creating the Preliminary Scope Statement

## Objectives

The preliminary scope statement is used to define what is in scope and what is out of scope of a project.

It is very important to define what is in and out of the scope to avoid tension and conflicts in the future, in order to budget and estimate the time frame of the project correctly.

Some of the requirements that appear in the scope statement may not appear in the contract and/or SOW because they might be added as a result of meetings with the client or from other documents. As soon as the final scope statement is completed, the client and the provider will have to agree on and approve the scope.

## Procedure

### To create a preliminary scope statement:

1. On the **Project Web Access** home page (development environment), select the project workspace.

2. From the quick launch menu, select **Documents > Project Initiation**.

3. Check out the preliminary scope statement template using steps 2 to 5 described in the section above on "To fill out the project charter template", but check out the preliminary scope statement template.

4. Fill out the preliminary scope statement using the requirements matrix, SOW, and other supporting documentation.

5. Change the **Document Status** to **Waiting For Approval**.

6. Make sure that the steering committee members receive the request for approval.

## Prerequisite

**To upload the preliminary scope statement:**

1. Create a template for the preliminary scope statement.

2. Upload the document to the project initiation document library.

To upload the sample preliminary scope statement document as a template, use the procedure in Appendix A.6 for uploading a document to a document library.

# Approving the Project for Planning

## Objectives

The documentation produced in the course of the initiation process serves as a basis for decisions made by the steering committee. Based on the information in the project charter and the preliminary scope statement, the committee makes a "go" or "no-go" decision regarding the project.

## Procedure

**To approve the project for planning:**

1. Request a meeting for approval to continue to the next process, planning.

2. Select **Documents > Project Initiation > Approve for Planning**:

3. Use the approve for planning document as a template to prepare for the approve for planning meeting.

4. During or after the meeting, select **Documents > Meeting Minutes > Minutes of Meeting Template**.

5. Fill out the template.

6. Distribute the minutes of the meeting to everyone on the distribution list.

7. From the quick launch menu, select **Lists > Project Approvals**:

The **Project Approvals** page opens:

8. From the **New** menu, select **New Item**. The item fields are displayed:

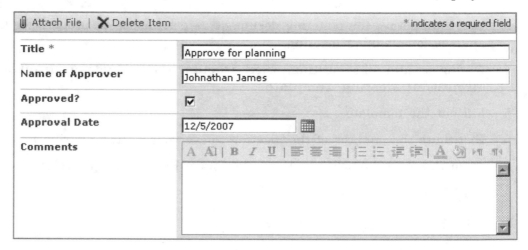

9. Enter the name of the approver and check the **Approved?** box.

10. Click **OK**.

## Prerequisites

### To use the approve for planning presentation template:

1. Create the approve for planning presentation template.

2. Upload the sample approve for planning presentation template using the procedure in Appendix A.6 for uploading a document to a document library.

## To create the meeting minutes library:

Create the meeting minutes document library under the **Documents** section of the quick launch menu. Use the procedure in Appendix A.3 for creating a document library.

## To upload the minutes of meeting template:

1. Create the minutes of meeting presentation template.

2. Upload the sample minutes of meeting presentation template using the procedure in Appendix A.6 for uploading a document to a document library.

## To create the project approval list:

Follow the procedure in Appendix A.7 for creating a new list to build the project approval list with the fields and field types included in Table 4.4.

## Table 4.4. Project Approval List

| Field Name | Description | Field Type |
| --- | --- | --- |
| Title | Approval type | Single line of text |
| Name of Approver | Name of the person who approves the item | Single line of text |
| Approved? | Indicates if the item is approved | Yes/no (check box) |
| Approval Date | Date of the approval | Date and time |

## To create the approve for planning item:

1. On the **Project Approvals** page, click **New**:

The **Project Approvals** page opens:

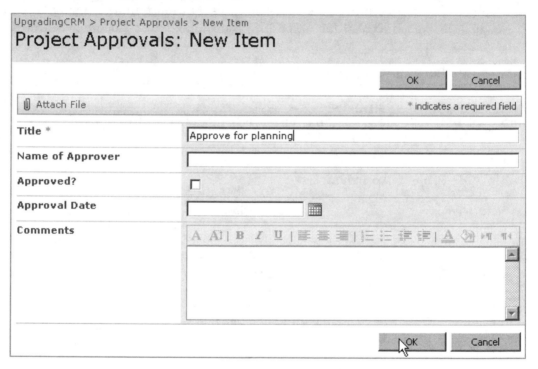

2. In the **Title** field, type "Approve for planning".

3. Click **OK**.

# Planning Process

The planning process is one of the most critical parts of a project. It is vital for the success of a project. Effective planning helps you predict the outcome of a project in terms of time scale, cost, risk, and quality. It can help ensure that the project objectives are met.

## Overview

Within the planning process, the people, resources, finances, suppliers, and tasks must be correctly scheduled, so that project management will be able to monitor and control project delivery effectively. The main output of this process is the project management plan.

The project management plan is critical for the success of a project. It contains the following:

- ◆ Scope management plan
- ◆ Time management plan
- ◆ Cost management plan
- ◆ Quality management plan
- ◆ Human resource management plan

♦ Communication management plan

♦ Risk management plan

♦ Procurement management plan

## Workflow

To provide a solution that meets the requirements that are defined for the planning process, the features/functions listed in Table 5.1 must be implemented.

### Table 5.1. Planning Feature/Function Processes

| Requirement | Solution Feature/ Function Guidelines | Relevant Procedure |
|---|---|---|
| **Integration Management** | | |
| Develop the project management plan | Use the Windows SharePoint Services document library list | "To upload the required documents to the project management plan library" |
| **Scope Management** | | |
| Plan and define the project scope | Use the SharePoint list to gather and manage requirements | "To prepare the detailed project scope statement" |
| Define deliverable acceptance | Use a Microsoft Word document to develop the scope management plan | "To define the process for format verification and acceptance of the completed project deliverables" |
| Create the work breakdown structure | Use Project Professional and Visio to create the work breakdown structure | "To create the program/ project WBS" |
| Define the change request management process | Use the SharePoint list to gather and manage process requirements | ♦ "To fill out the change requests log" <br> ♦ "To view the change requests log" |

## Table 5.1. Planning Feature/Function Processes (continued)

| Requirement | Solution Feature/ Function Guidelines | Relevant Procedure |
|---|---|---|
| **Time Management** | | |
| Define the project-level work plan | Use Project Professional to define the detailed project plan | "To build the project-level work plan" |
| Identify delivery activities | Use Project Professional to define the delivery activities | "To identify activities that represent deliverables" |
| Define the team-level work plan | Use Project Professional to define the detailed project plan | "To build the team-level work plan" |
| Determine project schedule based on actual resource capacity and availability | Use Project Professional to assign resources | ◆ "To assign team members to activities in the work plan" <br> ◆ "To allocate resources to resource types" |
| Perform the critical path analysis | Use Project Professional to analyze the critical path | "To analyze the critical path" |
| Approve the schedule | Use the SharePoint list to save the project approvals | "To approve the schedule" |
| Baseline the project schedule | Use Project Professional to baseline the project work plans | "To baseline the schedule" |
| **Cost Management** | | |
| Plan cost definitions | Use Microsoft Word document to define cost and budget rules | ◆ "To define budget and cost rules" <br> ◆ "To defined earned value rules" <br> ◆ "To define reporting formats in Project Professional" |

## Table 5.1. Planning Feature/Function Processes (continued)

| Requirement | Solution Feature/ Function Guidelines | Relevant Procedure |
|---|---|---|
| Define the project costs | Use Project Professional to plan and estimate costs | "To plan costs using Project Professional" |
| View the project costs | Use Project Professional to view the project's costs | ◆ "To plan costs using Project Professional"<br>◆ "To define reporting formats in Project Professional" |
| Define the project budget | Use Project Professional to define the project budget | "To plan costs using Project Professional" |
| Approve and baseline the project budget | Use Project Professional to baseline the project budget | "To baseline the schedule" |
| **Quality Management** | | |
| Define the quality management plan | Use Microsoft Word document to create the quality management plan | ◆ "To gather quality standards to be used in the program/project"<br>◆ "To create the quality management plan" |
| **Human Resource Management** | | |
| Create the project organizational breakdown structure | Use Visio to create organization charts | "To define program/project organization charts" |
| Define roles and responsibilities | Use Microsoft Word document to develop the roles and responsibilities document | "To define roles and responsibilities" |
| Plan human resources | Use Microsoft Word document to develop the human resource management plan | "To create the human resource management plan" |

## Table 5.1. Planning Feature/Function Processes (continued)

| Requirement | Solution Feature/ Function Guidelines | Relevant Procedure |
|---|---|---|
| View the project assignments by resource team | Use Project Professional to assign resources | ◆ "To build the program/ project team from the enterprise resource pool"<br>◆ "To assign team members to activities in the work plan" |
| Define the staffing management plan | Use Project Professional to manage resources | "To define the staffing management plan" |
| **Communication Management** | | |
| Define the project communication plan | Use the SharePoint list to create the communication matrix | "To fill out the communication matrix" |
| Define the project communication plan document | Use Microsoft Word to create the communication management plan | ◆ "To define area reports and the views for each reporting level"<br>◆ "To define the escalation procedure" |
| Define the project glossary | Use Microsoft Word to create the glossary document | "To prepare the project glossary" |
| Define the govern-ance procedures | Use Microsoft Word docu-ment to create the governance procedures | ◆ "To define area reports and the views for each reporting level"<br>◆ "To define the escalation procedure" |
| Define the document-ation deliverable management procedure | | ◆ "To define program/ project deliverables"<br>◆ "To define the documen-tation deliverable management procedure"<br>◆ "To update the deliver-ables log" |

**Table 5.1. Planning Feature/Function Processes (continued)**

| Requirement | Solution Feature/<br>Function Guidelines | Relevant Procedure |
|---|---|---|
| **Risk Management** | | |
| Define the risk management plan | Use Microsoft Word document to define the risk management plan | ◆ "To host the risk planning meeting"<br>◆ "To define the risk methodology"<br>◆ "To define risk budgeting"<br>◆ "To define risk timing"<br>◆ "To define risk categories"<br>◆ "To define the risk escalation procedure" |
| Identify the project risks | Use the Windows SharePoint Services risks list to create the risks log | "To update the risks log" |
| Perform the qualitative risk analysis | Use the Windows SharePoint Services risks list to create the risks log | "To update the risks log" |
| Perform the quantitative risk analysis | Use the Windows SharePoint Services risks list to create the risks log | "To update the risks log" |
| Define the risk mitigation plans | Use the Windows SharePoint Services risks list to create the risks log | "To update the risks log" |
| View the project risks | Use the Windows SharePoint Services risks list to view the project risks | "To view the risks log" |

**Table 5.1. Planning Feature/Function Processes (continued)**

| Requirement | Solution Feature/ Function Guidelines | Relevant Procedure |
|---|---|---|
| **Procurement Management** | | |
| Define the procurement management plan | Use Microsoft Word document to define the procurement management plan | "To create the procurement management plan" |
| Define the supplier evaluation criteria | Use the Windows SharePoint Services list to create the supplier evaluation criteria | "To fill out the supplier evaluation criteria list" |

Figure 5.1 depicts the recommended workflow for the planning process based on the solution feature/function guidelines.

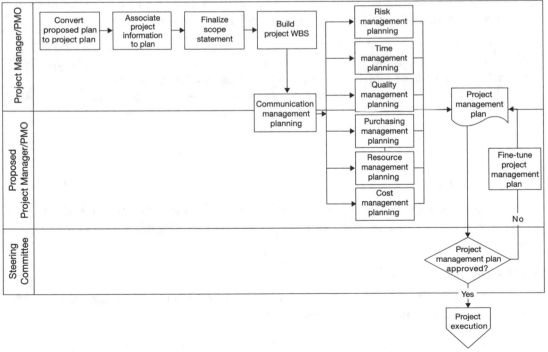

**Figure 5.1. Planning Process Workflow**

# Converting the Proposed Project to the Project Plan

## Objectives

◆ To convert the proposed project plan to a project plan in Project Professional

◆ To move the plan to the project center

◆ To start working on it as a plan and not as a proposal

## Procedure

The assigned project manager carries out this procedure.

### To convert the proposed project plan to the project plan:

1. Open Project Web Access (development environment).

2. In the quick launch menu, click **Proposals and Activities**. The **Proposals and Activities** page opens.

3. Select the row of the proposed plan to convert to a project plan by clicking anywhere in the row (except on the project hyperlink):

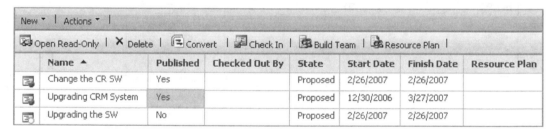

4. Click **Convert**.

5. In the message dialog that is displayed, click **Yes**. The proposed plan is converted to a project plan that is accessible via Project Professional.

## Prerequisites

This task is built into the application. No adaptations or configurations are needed. There are no prerequisites for it.

# Associating Project Information with the Project Plan

To associate project information with the project plan, you need to:

◆ Define custom project information (enterprise fields and values)

◆ Apply the appropriate values within the project plan

---

**RECOMMENDATION**

Apply appropriate project information metadata to each project so that you can filter the projects in different ways to answer questions such as:

◆ Which projects are carried out under a particular budget code?

◆ What active projects are worked on for which client?

◆ What projects are worked on to enable the organization to enter a new market with a new product?

◆ Which projects are the responsibility of a particular division?

◆ Which projects are high priority?

---

## Objective

◆ To apply metadata to projects in order to filter the projects in different ways

## Procedure

This procedure is carried out by the assigned project manager.

### To apply project information to the project plan:

1. Open Project Professional and log in to the server (development environment).

2. From the **File** menu, select **Open**.

3. Double-click **Retrieve the list of all projects from Project Server**.

4. Select the project plan you have converted and click **Open**. The converted project plan opens:

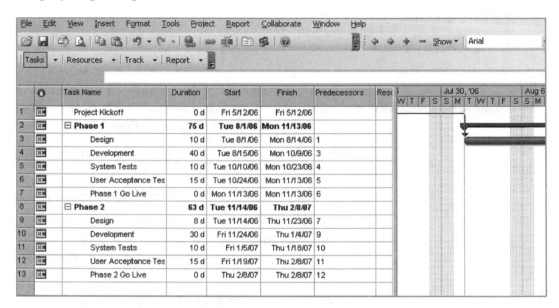

5. From the **Project** menu, select **Project information**.

6. Enter the following required project information:
   ◆ From the **Proj Type** drop-down list, select the project type (for example, Enhancement, Add-On Module, Service Pack, Product Fixes).
   ◆ From the **Project Status** drop-down list, select the project status (for example, Proposed, Approved, Rejected, On hold, Active).
   ◆ From the **Responsible Division** drop-down list, select the division/department/business unit responsible for carrying out the project.
   ◆ In the **Budget Code** field, type the budget code under which the project is to be funded.
   ◆ From the **Project Exposure** drop-down list, select the project exposure risk (exposure level) (for example, Very High, High, Medium, Low).
   ◆ If the project is for a client, in the **Client** field, type the client's name. For an internal project, type "Internal".
   ◆ From the **KPI** drop-down list, select the key performance indicator for the project (for example, Improve Customer Satisfaction, Improve Products and Service, Improve Operation Efficiency).

 It is recommend that you add the project summary task. To add the project summary task, select **Tools > Options > View**, and then check the **Show project summary task** box.

7. From the **File** menu, select **Publish**.

8. In the **Publish Project: Test Plan Connection** dialog, click **Publish**.

## Prerequisites

Before you can associate project information with your project plan, you must create the appropriate fields and lookup tables with the required values. Table 5.2 shows examples of project metadata (enterprise custom fields and values) used by the author when implementing an EPM solution for a client.

The procedure that follows the table shows how to define these fields and values so the project manager can associate the appropriate project metadata with the proposed project.

### Table 5.2. Examples of Project Metadata

| Field Name | Purpose | Field Type | Table Name or Formula |
|---|---|---|---|
| Project Type Table | Value list for the **Proj Type** field | Lookup table | The following are the project type values:<br>◆ Enhancement<br>◆ Add-on Module<br>◆ Service Pack<br>◆ Product Fixes<br>◆ Client Fixes<br>◆ New Product<br>◆ Client Implementation<br>◆ Client Customization |
| Proj Type | Select a project type for the project plan | Project | Lookup in the **Project Type Table** |

**Table 5.2. Examples of Project Metadata (continued)**

| Field Name | Purpose | Field Type | Table Name or Formula |
|---|---|---|---|
| State | Value list for the **Project Status** field | Lookup table | The following are the project state values:<br>◆ Proposed<br>◆ Approved<br>◆ Rejected<br>◆ On hold<br>◆ Active<br>◆ Completed |
| Project Status | Select the project status for the project plan | Project | Lookup in the **State** table |
| OBS | Organizational break-down structure value list for the **Responsible Division** field | Lookup table | The following are the business unit values:<br>◆ US<br>Sales<br>Marketing<br>Operations<br>R&D<br>QA<br>Documentation<br>◆ UK<br>Sales<br>Marketing<br>Operations<br>Development<br>◆ Australia<br>Sales<br>Marketing<br>Operations<br>Development |
| Responsible Division | Select the division/department/business unit responsible for carrying out the project | Project | Lookup in the **OBS** table |

**Table 5.2. Examples of Project Metadata (continued)**

| Field Name | Purpose | Field Type | Table Name or Formula |
|---|---|---|---|
| Budget Code | The budget code used to fund the project | Project | Free text |
| Exposure | Value list for the **Project Exposure** field | Lookup table | The following are the exposure risk values:<br>◆ Very High<br>◆ High<br>◆ Medium<br>◆ Low |
| Project Exposure | Select the risk of the project | Project | Lookup in the **Exposure** table |
| Client | Client name | Project | Free text |
| KPI Table | Value list for the **KPI** field | Lookup table | The following are the key performance indicator values:<br>◆ Improve Customer Satisfaction<br>◆ Improve Products and Services<br>◆ Improve Operation Efficiency<br>◆ New Product for New Market<br>◆ New Product for Increased Market Share |
| KPI | Select the key performance indicator (business driver) for the project plan | Project | Lookup in the **KPI Table** |

## Generic Procedure

The following generic procedure shows how to begin to define an enterprise custom field or a lookup table in Project Web Access. It is used at the start of each of the field-specific procedures.

### To begin to define an enterprise custom field or a lookup table:

1. Open Internet Explorer and enter the URL of Project Web Access in the development environment (for example, http://<servername>/ProjectServer). The **Project Web Access** site opens:

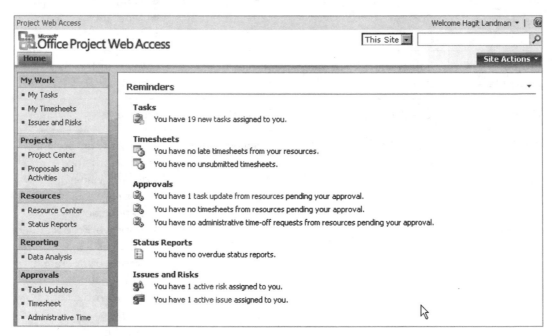

In the side menu bar, click **Server Settings**:

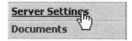

The **Server Settings** page opens.

2. Under the **Enterprise Data** options, click **Enterprise Custom Field Definition**:

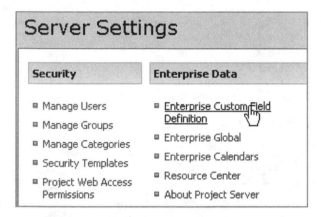

3. The **Custom Fields and Lookup Tables** page opens:

From here you can create a new custom field or a lookup table.

To allow the user to choose a value from a list, define a "lookup table" that contains the permissible values, and then create a custom field and associate the field with the lookup table.

## Field-Specific Procedures

The following procedures show how to create specific enterprise custom fields, including, if necessary, creation of the corresponding lookup tables.

### To define the Proj Type enterprise custom field:

1. Perform steps 1 to 3 of the generic procedure (see above).

2. On the **Custom Fields and Lookup Tables** web page, under the **Lookup Tables for Custom Fields** section, click **New Lookup Table**:

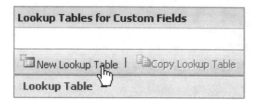

The **New Lookup Table** page opens:

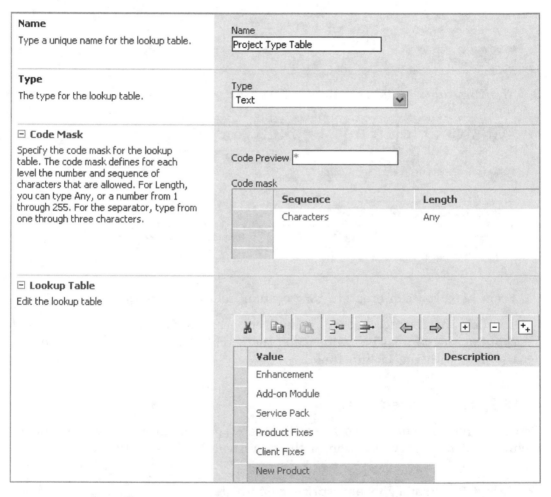

3.  In the **Name** field, type "Project Type Table".

4.  From the **Type** drop-down list, select **Text**.

5.  For **Code Mask**, use the default **Sequence** and **Length**.

6.  In the **Lookup Table** pane, enter the project type values from the table.

7.  Click **Save**.

8.  On the **Custom Fields and Lookup Tables** web page, under the **Enterprise Custom Fields** section, click **New Field**:

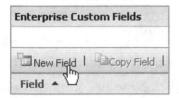

The **New Custom Field** page opens:

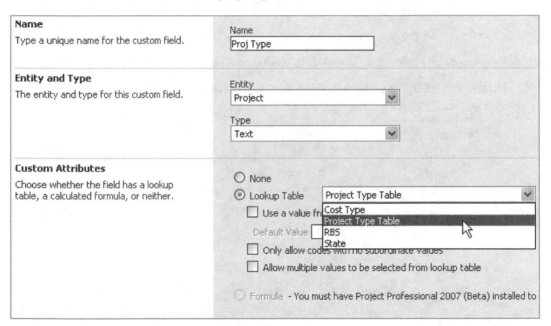

9.  In the **Name** field, type "Proj Type".

 **NOTE**   "Project Type" is a reserved term in Microsoft Project Professional.

10. From the **Entity** drop-down list, select **Project**.

11. From the **Type** drop-down list, select **Text**.

12. From the **Custom Attributes** options, check **Lookup Table**.

13. From the **Lookup Table** drop-down list, select **Project Type Table**.

14. Click **Save**. The **Proj Type** field is now available for use in Microsoft Project Professional.

### To define the project status enterprise custom field:

1. Perform steps 1 to 3 of the generic procedure (see above).

2. Under **Lookup Tables for Custom Fields**, click **New Lookup Table**. The **New Lookup Table** page opens.

3. In the **Name** field, type "State".

4. From the **Type** drop-down list, select **Text**.

5. For **Code Mask**, use the default **Sequence** and **Length**.

6. In the **Lookup Table** pane, enter the state values from the table:

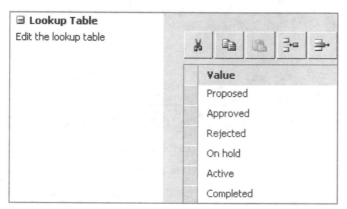

7. Click **Save**.

8. Under **Enterprise Custom Fields**, click **New Field**. The **New Custom Field** page opens.

9. In the **Name** field, type "Project Status".

10. From the **Entity** drop-down list, select **Project**.

11. From the **Type** drop-down list, select **Text**.

12. From the **Custom Attributes** options, check **Lookup Table**.

13. From the **Lookup Table** drop-down list, select **State**:

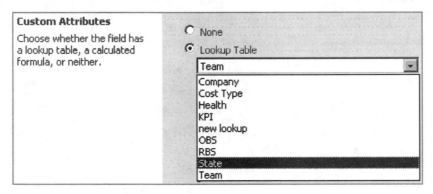

14. Click **Save**.

## To define the responsible division enterprise custom field:

1. Perform steps 1 to 3 of the generic procedure (see above).

2. Under **Lookup Tables for Custom Fields**, click **New Lookup Table**. The **New Lookup Table** page opens.

3. In the **Name** field, type "OBS".

4. From the **Type** drop-down list, select **Text**.

5. In the **Code Mask** section, enter another level of character sequence code mask with length "Any". This permits a tree value list of up to two levels.

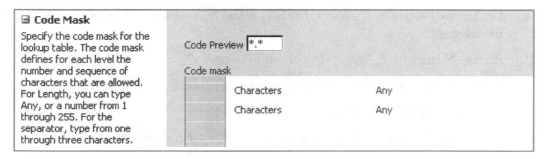

6. In the **Lookup Table** pane, enter the business unit values from the table.

7. Use the ⇐ ⇒ buttons to set the levels as follows:

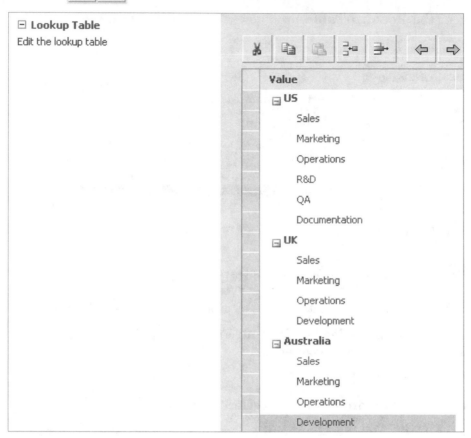

8. Click **Save**.

9. Under **Enterprise Custom Fields**, click **New Field**. The **New Custom Field** page opens.

10. In the **Name** field, type "Responsible Division".

11. From the **Entity** drop-down list, select **Project**.

12. From the **Type** drop-down list, select **Text**.

13. From the **Custom Attributes** options, check **Lookup Table**.

14. From the **Lookup Table** drop-down list, select **OBS**.

15. Click **Save**.

## To define the budget code enterprise custom field:

1. Perform steps 1 to 3 of the generic procedure (see above).

2. Under **Enterprise Custom Fields**, click **New Field**.

3. In the **Name** field, type "Budget Code".

4. From the **Entity** drop-down list, select **Project**.

5. From the **Type** drop-down list, select **Text**.

6. In the **Custom Attributes** section, check the **None** box.

7. In the **Values to Display** field, check the **Data** box.

8. In the **Required** field, check whether or not this field is required.

9. Click **Save**.

## To define the project exposure enterprise custom field:

1. Perform steps 1 to 3 of the generic procedure (see above).

2. Under **Lookup Tables for Custom Fields**, click **New Lookup Table**. The **New Lookup Table** page opens.

3. In the **Name** field, type "Exposure".

4. From the **Type** drop-down list, select **Text**.

5. For **Code Mask**, use the default **Sequence** and **Length**.

6. In the **Lookup Table** pane, enter the priority values from the table.

7. Click **Save**.

8. Under **Enterprise Custom Fields**, click **New Field**. The **New Custom Field** page opens.

9. In the **Name** field, type "Project Exposure".

10. From the **Entity** drop-down list, select **Project**.

11. From the **Type** drop-down list, select **Text**.

12. From the **Custom Attributes** options, check **Lookup Table**.

13. From the **Lookup Table** drop-down list, select **Exposure**.

14. Click **Save**.

## To define the client enterprise custom field:

1. Perform steps 1 to 3 of the generic procedure (see above).

2. Under **Enterprise Custom Fields**, click **New Field**.

3. In the **Name** field, type "Client".

4. From the **Entity** drop-down list, select **Project**.

5. From the **Type** drop-down list, select **Text**.

6. In the **Custom Attributes** section, check the **None** box.

7. In the **Values to Display** field, check the **Data** box.

8. In the **Required** field, check whether or not this field is required.

9. Click **Save**.

## To define the KPI enterprise custom field:

1. Perform steps 1 to 3 of the generic procedure (see above).

2. Under **Lookup Tables for Custom Fields**, click **New Lookup Table**. The **New Lookup Table** page opens.

3. In the **Name** field, type "KPI Table".

4. From the **Type** drop-down list, select **Text**.

5. For **Code Mask**, use the default **Sequence** and **Length**.

6. In the **Lookup Table** pane, enter the KPI values from the table.

7. Click **Save**.

8. Under **Enterprise Custom Fields**, click **New Field**. The **New Custom Field** page opens.

9. In the **Name** field, type "KPI".

10. From the **Entity** drop-down list, select **Project**.

11. From the **Type** drop-down list, select **Text**.

12. From the **Custom Attributes** options, check **Lookup Table**.

13. From the **Lookup Table** drop-down list, select **KPI Table**.

14. Click **Save**.

## To check configuration:

1. If Microsoft Project Professional is active, exit it.

2. Open Microsoft Project Professional and log in to the server.

3. From the **Project** menu, select **Project Information**:

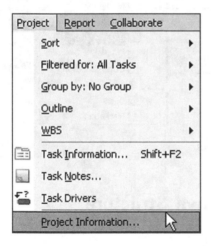

The **Project Information** dialog opens:

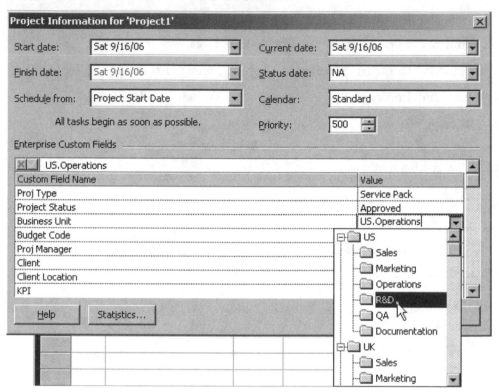

Now it is possible to define enterprise fields.

# Building the Project Work Breakdown Structure

## Objectives

◆ To define and organize the total scope of the project into a hierarchical tree structure

◆ To break down the project scope into deliverable-oriented units

## Procedure

**To finalize the WBS activity plan:**

1. Open Microsoft Project Professional and log in to the server.

2. From the **File** menu, select **Open**.

3. Double-click **Retrieve the list of all projects from Project Server**.

4. Select the relevant project plan and click **Open**.

5. Click **View > 1 WBS Planning**:

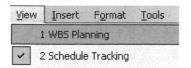

6. Organize tasks according to the desired WBS structure. For every task, set the values for the following:
   ◆ **Responsible Division**—The division responsible for the task.
   ◆ **Responsible Company**—The company or vendor responsible for performing the work for the task.
   ◆ **Assignment Owner**—The person responsible for reporting progress on the task assignments.
   ◆ **Resource Name**—The resource required to perform the task. To assign an enterprise resource, you first need to build your resource team using **Tools > Build Team from Enterprise...**:

- ◆ **Duration**—The estimated duration of the task.
- ◆ **Cost**—The estimated cost of the task.
- ◆ **Work**—The estimated effort required to perform the task.
- ◆ **Deliverable Name**—The name of the deliverable (relevant in a master project where there are interdependent projects).
- ◆ **Output Description**—A brief description of the outcome of the task.
- ◆ **Predecessor**—A task that must start or finish before another task can start or finish.
- ◆ **Steering Committee Flag**—Specifies if the task is shown in the steering committee reports.
- ◆ **Management Flag**—Specifies if the task is shown in the management reports.
- ◆ **Project Management Flag**—Specifies if the task is shown in the project manager reports.

7. Click **Save and Publish**.

## Prerequisites

The following are the steps required to support WBS planning:

- ◆ Create custom fields to support the WBS planning procedure.
- ◆ Create a view in Project Professional to display the fields that the project manager needs to complete.

Table 5.3 shows examples of WBS planning workflow metadata (enterprise custom fields and values) used by the author when implementing an EPM solution for a client.

The procedure after Table 5.3 shows how to define these fields and values.

### Table 5.3. WBS Planning Metadata

| Field Name | Purpose | Entity | Graphical Indicators | Field Type | Lookup Table |
|---|---|---|---|---|---|
| Responsible Division | Select the division/ department/business unit responsible for carrying out the project | Task | No | Text | OBS |

## Table 5.3. WBS Planning Metadata (continued)

| Field Name | Purpose | Entity | Graphical Indicators | Field Type | Lookup Table |
|---|---|---|---|---|---|
| Company | Value list for the **Responsible Company** field | Task | No | Lookup table | The following are the valid values:<br>◆ Microsoft<br>◆ EZPM<br>◆ SAP<br>◆ ACME<br>◆ Other |
| Responsible Company | Select the company responsible for executing the task | Task | No | Text | Company |
| Output Description | Free text used to briefly describe the output of the task | Task | No | Text | |
| Budget Code | The budget code given to the team members in order to collect costs | Task | No | Text | |
| Steering Committee Flag | A flag that marks whether the activity is reported to the steering committee | Task | Yes | Flag | |
| Management Flag | A flag that marks whether the activity is reported to the management level | Task | Yes | Flag | |
| PM Flag | A flag that marks whether the activity is reported to the project management level | Task | Yes | Flag | |

## To create custom fields to support WBS planning:

1. Create the fields according to the WBS planning metadata in Table 5.3.

2. To create enterprise custom fields and lookup tables, refer to the procedure "To begin to define an enterprise custom field or a lookup table" in the section on "Associating Project Information with the Project Plan" above.

3. Pay attention because some of the fields may have already been created in previous procedures, such as "Associating Project Information with the Project Plan".

## To create the WBS view in Project Professional:

1. Open Project Professional. The **Login** dialog opens:

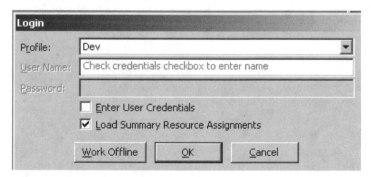

2. From the **Profile** drop-down list, select your login to the development environment and click **OK**. The Project Professional application launches.

3. From the **Tools** menu, select **Enterprise Options > Open Enterprise Global**:

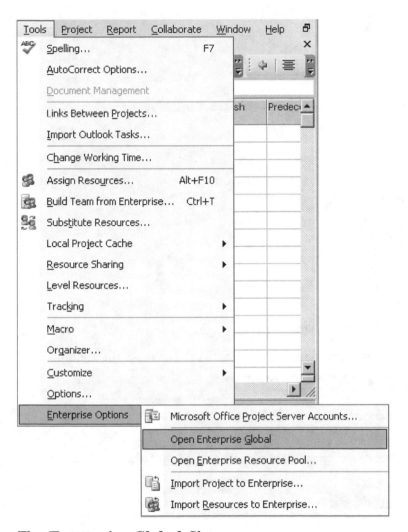

The **Enterprise Global** file opens:

4.  In this file, you define the views that apply to your project (for example, the "1 WBS Planning" view) and create a table named "WBS Planning" with the following fields (these are examples only):

◆ ID
◆ Indicators
◆ WBS
◆ Name
◆ Duration
◆ Start
◆ Finish
◆ Predecessors
◆ Work
◆ Cost
◆ Assignment Owner
◆ Resource Names
◆ Deliverable Name
◆ Output Description
◆ Steering Committee Flag
◆ Project Management Flag
◆ Management Flag

5. Select **View > Table > More Tables...** and then select **New**.

6. The **Table Definition** dialog opens. Fill in the relevant fields:

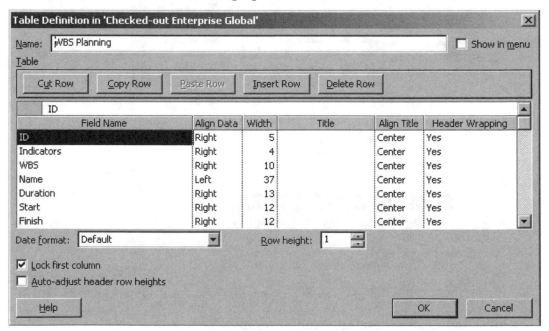

7. Click **OK**.

8. To create a view, select **View > More Views... > New**.

9. The **View Definition** dialog opens:

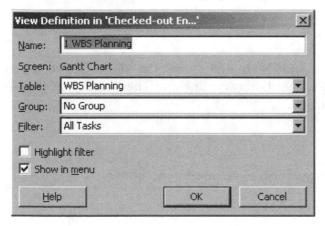

10. In the **Name** field, type "1 WBS Planning". The number "1" makes this view appear first in the list of views.

11. From the **Table** drop-down list, select **WBS Planning**.

12. From the **Group** drop-down list, select the grouping that you want to use (if you want to group the activities in the plan by, for example, team, division, etc.). In the example above, **No Group** has been selected.

13. From the **Filter** drop-down list, select the filter that you want to use in this view. (You can select which activities you want to show in this view, whether they are critical, filtered by date, and so on.) In the example above, the view will display all activities (**All Tasks**). Click **OK**.

14. Save the **Enterprise Global** file (**File > Save**) and exit Project Professional. Now whenever you open a project from the server, you can see and select this view.

## Integration Management: Project Management Plan

### Objectives

Integration management documents the processes in each management area and defines how these processes interface with each other. Management plans are stored in the project management plan document library.

## Procedure

**To upload the required documents to the project management plan document library:**

For the procedure, see Appendix A.6 on uploading a document to a document library.

Upload each management plan that is created during the planning process to the project management plan document library. Include the quality management plan, risk management plan, etc.

## Prerequisite

**To create the project management plan document library:**

For the procedure, see Appendix A.3 on creating a document library.

# Defining the Scope Management Plan

## Objectives

Scope management determines the scope of the program/project and manages changes made to that scope.

The scope management plan (see Figure 5.2), based on the requirements matrix, determines the program/project WBS.

Every change to the defined scope as it appears in the requirements matrix will be considered a change request and is handled according to the change request process defined in the scope management plan.

## Procedures

**To prepare the detailed project scope statement:**

Finalize all of the project requirements and log them in the requirements matrix.

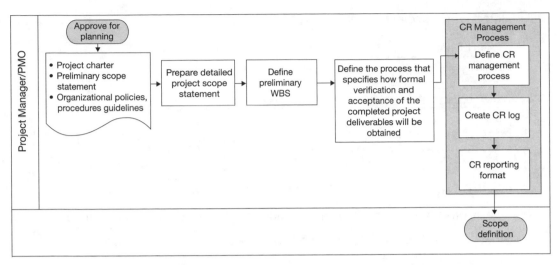

**Figure 5.2. Scope Management Plan Workflow**

## To define the process for format verification and acceptance of the completed project deliverables:

1. Define the process and record it in the scope management plan.

2. Upload the scope management plan to the project workspace under the project management plan document library.

## To create the program/project WBS:

1. Open Internet Explorer and enter the URL of Project Web Access (development environment). The **Project Web Access** site opens.

2. In the quick launch menu, click **Project Center**:

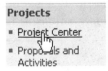

The **Project Center** page opens.

3. Select your project:

| Project Center | | |
|---|---|---|
| New ▾ | Actions ▾ | Go To ▾ | | |
| ☑ Edit | 📝 Edit Project Properties | 📇 Build Team | | |
| ❶ | Project Name | Start |
| 📱📋 | Upgrading CRM System | 12/5/2006 |
| 📱📋 | abc | 3/19/2007 |

4. Click **Edit**.

5. The project you have chosen will now open in Project Professional.

6. Select the WBS view (**1 WBS Planning** in the example below):

The **WBS** view opens:

| | ❶ | WBS | Task Name | Duration | Start | Finish |
|---|---|---|---|---|---|---|
| 1 | | P | Kickoff Meeting | 0 days | Tue 11/7/06 | Tue 11/7/06 |
| 2 | | 2 | Design | 10 days | Tue 11/7/06 | Mon 11/20/06 |
| 3 | | 3 | Development | 20 days | Tue 11/7/06 | Mon 12/4/06 |
| 4 | | 4 | Sub System Test | 10 days | Tue 11/7/06 | Mon 11/20/06 |
| 5 | | 5 | System Test | 10 days | Tue 11/7/06 | Mon 11/20/06 |
| 6 | | 6 | User Acceptance Test | 10 days | Tue 11/7/06 | Mon 11/20/06 |
| 7 | | 7 | System Go Live | 0 days | Tue 11/7/06 | Tue 11/7/06 |

 The page shows the document you created in the section on "Creating the Proposed Project Plan" and later published.

7. Add detailed activities to the plan, sometimes using each of the existing tasks as rollup tasks. For example:

| 1 | Kickoff Meeting | 0 days |
|---|---|---|
| 2 | ⊟ **Design** | **1 day?** |
| 2.1 | High Level Design | 1 day? |
| 2.2 | Detailed Design | 1 day? |
| 2.3 | Design Review | 1 day? |
| 3 | ⊟ **Development** | **1 day?** |
| 3.1 | ⊟ **Sub System A** | **1 day?** |
| 3.1.1 | Sub System A Development | 1 day? |
| 3.1.2 | Sub System A Unit Test | 1 day? |
| 3.2 | ⊟ **Sub System B** | **1 day?** |
| 3.2.1 | Sub System B Development | 1 day? |
| 3.2.2 | Sub System B Unit Test | 1 day? |
| 4 | ⊟ **Sub System Test** | **1 day?** |
| 4.1 | Sub System A Test | 1 day? |
| 4.2 | Sub System B Test | 1 day? |
| 5 | ⊟ **Integration** | **1 day?** |
| 5.1 | Sub System Integration | 1 day? |
| 6 | ⊟ **System Test** | **3 days?** |
| 6.1 | System Test Design | 1 day? |
| 6.2 | System Test | 1 day? |
| 7 | ⊟ **User Acceptance Test** | **1 day?** |
| 7.1 | User Acceptance Test Calendars | 1 day? |
| 7.2 | User Acceptance Tests | 1 day? |
| 7.3 | System Bug Fixes | 1 day? |
| 8 | System Go Live | 0 days |

8. Save the plan (**File > Save**).

9. From the **Report** menu, select **Visual Reports...**:

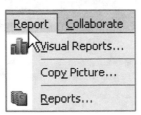

The **Visual Reports – Create Report** page opens:

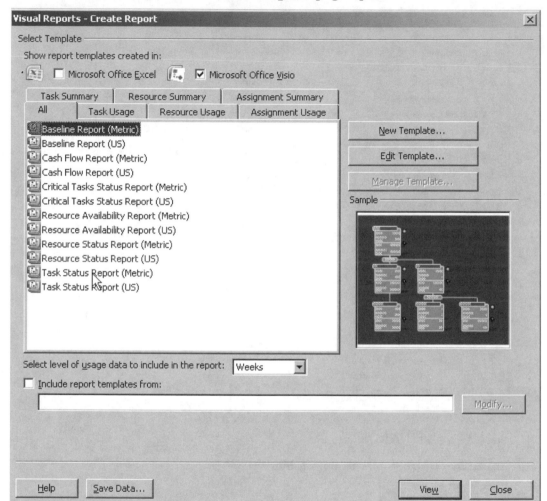

10. Check the **Microsoft Office Visio** box.

11. Select **Task Status Report**.

12. Click **View**.

13.  The system will display the following message:

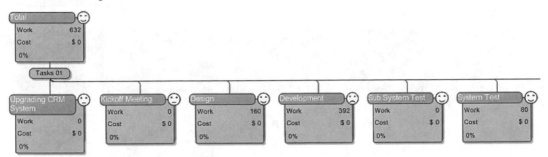

     Gathering reporting data...

     Microsoft Office Visio opens, displaying a diagrammatic view of the WBS at
     the rollup task level:

14.  To display the sub-tasks of an activity:
     ◆ Select the activity.
     ◆ From the context (right-click) menu, select **Tasks**:

The sub-tasks are displayed:

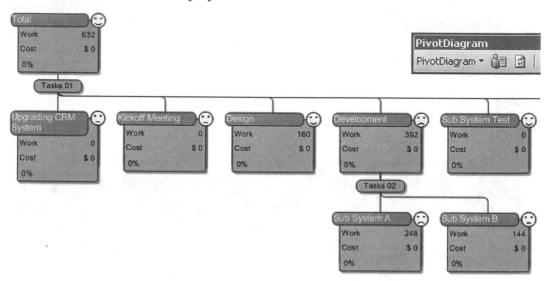

15. Repeat step 14 until you see all the required details:

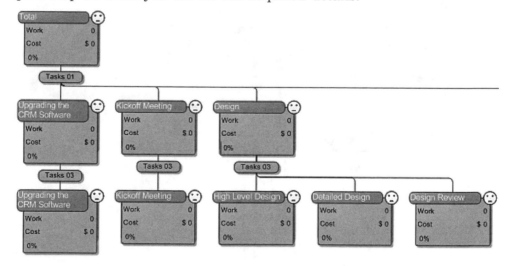

16. To expand all of the tasks to the same level, on the shortcut menu at the left, click **Tasks** and then select the level in the hierarchy that you want to show (in the example below, it is level 3):

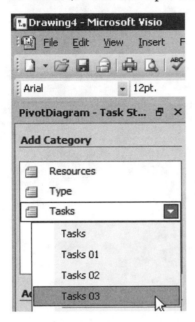

## To modify the data shown in the Visio diagram:

1. Select the tasks that you want to change. To avoid confusion in using the diagram, it is recommended that you use **Edit > Select All** and make the same changes across the entire diagram.

2. Right-click on any of the tasks selected and select **Data > Edit Data Graphic...**:

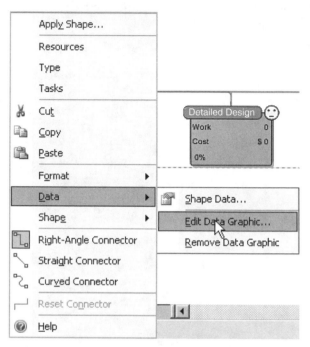

The **Edit Data Graphic** page opens:

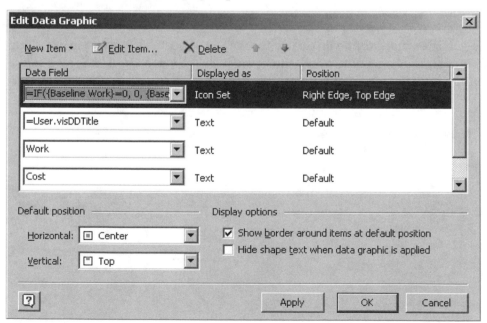

3. From the **Data Field** drop-down lists, select the data fields to be displayed. For example, you can display **WBS** instead of **Work** and **Duration** instead of **Cost**:

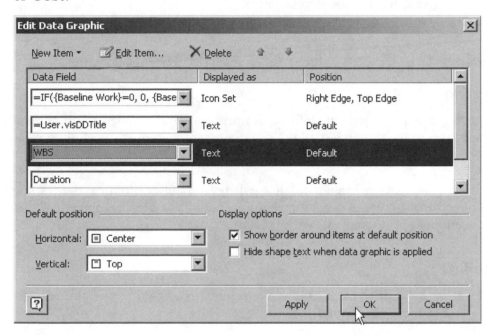

4. Click **OK**. The diagram changes to display the fields selected:

### Prerequisites

This function is already built into the system. No additional configuration is required to perform the above procedure.

## Defining the Change Request Management Process

### Objectives

Change request management defines the process for monitoring and controlling change requests for the project plan. The main control tool is the change requests log.

The change requests management log will be part of the requirements matrix, as it is necessary to capture all the requirements for a project regardless of their origin (contract, statement of work, meetings, etc.).

### Procedures

The information needed for each change request is shown in the change request logging fields table (see Table 5.4).

**To fill out the change requests log:**

1. Open Project Web Access.

2. Select the project workspace. The project workspace selected opens:

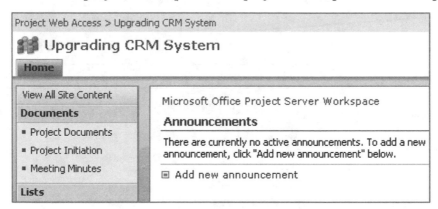

3. In the **Lists** section of the quick launch menu, click **Requirements Matrix**:

The **Requirements Matrix** page opens:

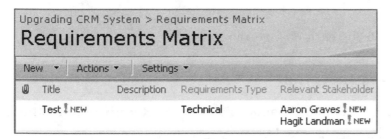

4. On the toolbar, click **New**. A new (blank) **Requirements Matrix** item opens:

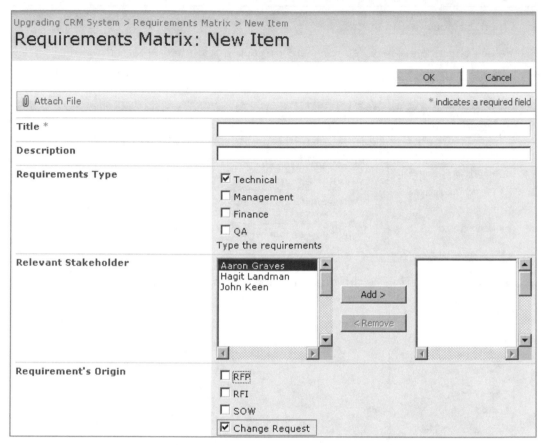

5. Fill out the change request information. In the **Requirement's Origin** section, check the **Change Request** box.

6. Click **OK**.

7. Repeat steps 4 to 6 for each change request.

## To view the change requests log:

1. In the **Lists** section of the quick launch menu, click **Requirements Matrix**.

2. In the **View** section, select **Change Requests Log**:

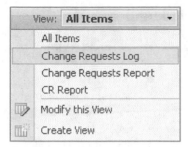

The **Change Requests Log** view is now displayed.

## Prerequisites

To support change request logging, add the change request fields (see Table 5.4) to the requirements matrix that was defined in the initiation process.

### Table 5.4. Change Request Logging Fields

| Field Name | Description | Field Type |
|---|---|---|
| CR ID | Uniquely identifies the change request | Single line of text |
| Current Status | Status of the change request | Choice (drop-down list): <br>◆ Pending <br>◆ On hold <br>◆ HLE received <br>◆ Waiting for IA/DLE <br>◆ Pending approval <br>◆ Approved <br>◆ Deferred <br>◆ Declined <br>◆ Implemented <br>◆ Closed |
| Current Status Date | Date the change request status was changed | Date |

**Table 5.4. Change Request Logging Fields (continued)**

| Field Name | Description | Field Type |
| --- | --- | --- |
| Raised By | Name of the stakeholder who initiated the change request | ◆ Lookup to the "Stakeholder Name (linked to item)" in the stakeholders matrix<br>◆ Allow multiple values |
| Date Raised | Date the change request was raised | Date |
| Priority | Priority of the change request set by the PMO based on customer input and an assessment of impact/urgency | Choice (drop-down menu):<br>◆ High<br>◆ Medium<br>◆ Low |
| Impact Assessment | Link to the impact assessment document (for impact on the project) | Link |
| Affected | Components affected by the change; this should include the projects and teams that will be affected | Choice (check boxes that allow multiple selections):<br>◆ Component "A"<br>◆ Component "B"<br>◆ Other |
| Solution Response and Reference | Description of the solution that will fulfill the change request | Multiple lines of text |
| Component "A" | Detailed cost estimate for the changes to Component "A" | Multiple lines of text |
| Component "B" | Detailed cost estimate for the changes to Component "B" | Multiple lines of text |
| CR Owner (Name) | Name of the stakeholder who owns the product description and who is responsible for assessing the impact of and accepting or rejecting the change request | ◆ Lookup to the "Stakeholder Name (linked to item)" in the stakeholders matrix<br>◆ Allow multiple values |

**Table 5.4. Change Request Logging Fields (continued)**

| Field Name | Description | Field Type |
|---|---|---|
| Reasons for Change | Reasons for the change, what scenarios the change request covers, and any workarounds currently being used | Multiple lines of text |
| Target Date | Date the change request owner has targeted for making the change (from the work plan) | Date |
| Comments | Free text that describes the various statuses, considerations, assumptions, etc. | Multiple lines of text |

### To create the change requests management log and view:

For the procedure to add the required fields to the requirements matrix, see Appendix A.20 on modifying an existing list.

For the procedure to create the change requests log view, see Appendix A.21 on creating a list view.

Create a view that includes fields for the information to be completed by the project manager.

## Defining the Time Management Plan

### Objectives

Time and schedule management includes the processes required to ensure the timely completion of a project.

The time management plan describes the process for controlling and reporting the project schedule.

The goal of the time management plan is to ensure that clear and unambiguous program management information is provided at the appropriate level and time. Achieving this goal ensures the following:

◆ The project delivery teams and management understand the status of the program through separate and integrated plans. This information forms the basis for decisions that are made to manage future activities and deliveries.

◆ All program teams (projects) interact with each other to ensure alignment of plans and clear understanding of interdependencies.

◆ The individual project plans are consolidated in the integrated program plan.

The time management plan includes the following tasks:

◆ Define the level of project schedule reporting

◆ Define the schedule activities

◆ Define the program/project deliverables

◆ Define dependencies between the activities and sub-projects

◆ Define the duration of the activities

◆ Estimate resources (this is also a part of the resource management plan)

◆ Analyze the schedule, taking into consideration all the above tasks, checking the critical path, resource leveling, etc.

The time management plan (see Figure 5.3) describes the management, tracking, and escalation procedures for the schedule.

## Procedures

### To build the project-level work plan:

1. Enter the URL of Project Web Access (development environment).

2. The **Project Web Access** site opens.

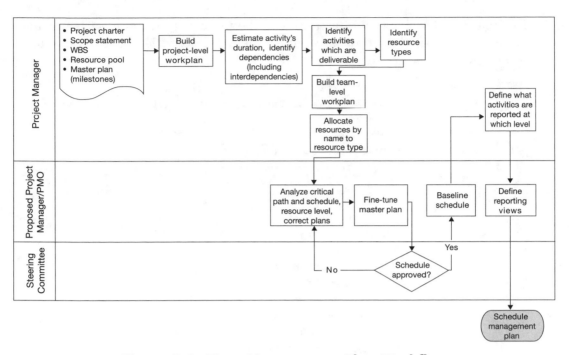

**Figure 5.3. Time Management Plan Workflow**

3.  On the side navigation bar, click **Project Center**:

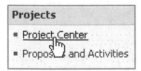

The **Project Center** page opens.

4.  Select the project and click **Edit**:

| Project Center | | |
|---|---|---|
| New ▾ | Actions ▾ | Go To ▾ | | |
| 📝 Edit | 📄 Edit Project Properties | 🔧 Build Team | | |
| ❶ | Project Name | Start |
| | Upgrading CRM System | 12/5/2006 |
| | abc | 3/19/2007 |

5. In Project Professional, add activities to the project, at the project level and/
   or team level. In the following example, detailed activities have been added
   to sub-systems A and B:

| | ❶ | WBS | Name | Duration |
|---|---|---|---|---|
| 9 | | **3** | ⊟ **Development** | **31 d** |
| 10 | | **3.1** | ⊟ **Sub System A** | **31 d** |
| 11 | | **3.1.1** | ⊟ **Sub System A Development** | **23 d** |
| 12 | 🖼 | 3.1.1.1 | Sub System A Infrastructure Ready | 0 d |
| 13 | | 3.1.1.2 | Sub System A S/W Development | 20 d |
| 14 | | 3.1.1.3 | Sub System A S/W Installation | 3 d |
| 15 | | 3.1.2 | Sub System A Unit Test | 8 d |
| 16 | | 3.1.3 | Sub System A Ready for Sub System Test | 0 d |
| 17 | | **3.2** | ⊟ **Sub System B** | **18 d** |
| 18 | | **3.2.1** | ⊟ **Sub System B Development** | **13 d** |
| 19 | | 3.2.1.1 | Sub System B Infrastructure Ready | 0 d |
| 20 | | 3.2.1.2 | Sub System B S/W Development | 10 d |
| 21 | | 3.2.1.3 | Sub System B S/W Installation | 3 d |
| 22 | | 3.2.2 | Sub System B Unit Test | 5 d |
| 23 | 🖼 | 3.2.3 | Sub System B Ready for Sub System Test | 0 d |
| 24 | | 4 | Sub System Test | 10 d |
| 25 | | **5** | ⊟ **System Test** | **51 d** |
| 26 | | 5.1 | System Test Design | 10 d |
| 27 | | 5.2 | Testing Environment Ready | 0 d |
| 28 | | 5.3 | System Test | 10 d |
| 29 | | **6** | ⊟ **User Acceptance Test** | **73 d** |
| 30 | | 6.1 | User Acceptance Test Calendars | 10 d |
| 31 | | 6.2 | User Acceptance Tests | 11 d |
| 32 | | 6.3 | System Bug Fixes | 10 d |
| 33 | | 6.4 | Go/No Go Decision | 1 d |
| 34 | 🖼 | 7 | System Go Live | 2 d |

6. For each activity in the project plan, add **Duration** and/or **Start** and **Finish** dates, and identify dependencies using the **Predecessor** field:

| | ❶ | WBS | Name | Duration | Start | Finish | redecessor | eb 25, '07 | Mar 25, '07 | Apr 22, '07 | May 20, '07 | Jun 1 |
|---|---|---|---|---|---|---|---|---|---|---|---|---|
| 9 | | 3 | ⊟ **Development** | **31 d** | **3/13/07** | **4/25/07** | | | | | | |
| 10 | | 3.1 | ⊟ **Sub System A** | **31 d** | **3/13/07** | **4/25/07** | | | | | | |
| 11 | | 3.1.1 | ⊟ **Sub System A Development** | **23 d** | **3/13/07** | **4/13/07** | | | | | | |
| 12 | 📷 | 3.1.1.1 | Sub System A Infrastructure Ready | 0 d | 3/13/07 | 3/13/07 | 8 | 3/13 | | | | |
| 13 | | 3.1.1.2 | Sub System A S/W Development | 20 d | 3/14/07 | 4/10/07 | 7 | | Aaron | | | |
| 14 | | 3.1.1.3 | Sub System A S/W Installation | 3 d | 4/11/07 | 4/13/07 | 13 | | farmadmin | | | |
| 15 | | 3.1.2 | Sub System A Unit Test | 8 d | 4/16/07 | 4/25/07 | 14 | | | Hagit Landman | | |
| 16 | | 3.1.3 | Sub System A Ready for Sub System Test | 0 d | 4/25/07 | 4/25/07 | 15 | | | 4/25 | | |
| 17 | | 3.2 | ⊟ **Sub System B** | **18 d** | **3/13/07** | **4/6/07** | | | | | | |
| 18 | | 3.2.1 | ⊟ **Sub System B Development** | **13 d** | **3/13/07** | **3/30/07** | | | | | | |
| 19 | | 3.2.1.1 | Sub System B Infrastructure Ready | 0 d | 3/13/07 | 3/13/07 | 8 | 3/13 | | | | |
| 20 | | 3.2.1.2 | Sub System B S/W Development | 10 d | 3/14/07 | 3/27/07 | 7 | | Hagit Landman | | | |
| 21 | | 3.2.1.3 | Sub System B S/W Installation | 3 d | 3/28/07 | 3/30/07 | 20 | | Ron | | | |
| 22 | | 3.2.2 | Sub System B Unit Test | 5 d | 4/2/07 | 4/6/07 | 21 | | Aaron | | | |
| 23 | 📷 | 3.2.3 | Sub System B Ready for Sub System Test | 0 d | 4/6/07 | 4/6/07 | 22 | | 4/6 | | | |
| 24 | | 4 | Sub System Test | 10 d | 4/26/07 | 5/9/07 | 16,23 | | | | | |
| 25 | | 5 | ⊟ **System Test** | **51 d** | **3/14/07** | **5/23/07** | | | | | | |
| 26 | | 5.1 | System Test Design | 10 d | 3/14/07 | 3/27/07 | 8 | | Developer | | | |
| 27 | | 5.2 | Testing Environment Ready | 0 d | 3/27/07 | 3/27/07 | 26FF | | 3/27 | | | |
| 28 | | 5.3 | System Test | 10 d | 5/10/07 | 5/23/07 | 27,24 | | | | | |
| 29 | | 6 | ⊟ **User Acceptance Test** | **73 d** | **3/14/07** | **6/22/07** | | | | | | |
| 30 | | 6.1 | User Acceptance Test Calendars | 10 d | 3/14/07 | 3/27/07 | 8 | | | | | |
| 31 | | 6.2 | User Acceptance Tests | 11 d | 5/24/07 | 6/7/07 | 28,30 | | | | | |
| 32 | | 6.3 | System Bug Fixes | 10 d | 6/8/07 | 6/21/07 | 31 | | | | | |
| 33 | | 6.4 | Go/No Go Decision | 1 d | 6/22/07 | 6/22/07 | 32 | | | | | |
| 34 | 🖼 | 7 | System Go Live | 2 d | 6/27/07 | 6/28/07 | 33FS+2 d | | | | | |

## To identify activities that represent deliverables:

1. Open the project in Project Professional.

2. Identify the activities that are deliverables and mark them. For example, "Detailed Design Document" is a deliverable.

3.  In Project Professional, from the **Collaborate** menu, select **Manage Deliverables**:

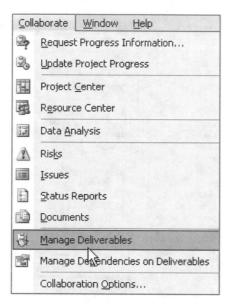

The **Deliverables** pane opens:

4.  Select a task that corresponds to a deliverable. In the example above, **Detailed Design Document** is a deliverable.

5.  Click **Add new deliverable...**. The **Add Deliverable** pane opens:

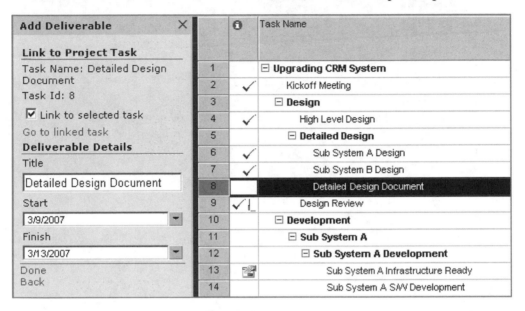

6.  Check the **Link to selected task** box.

7. Click **Done**. The deliverable is added to the **Deliverable** field of the **Deliverables** pane:

8. Repeat steps 4 to 7 for the rest of the deliverables.

9. Click **Save**, and then click **Publish**. The deliverables are now visible in the **Deliverables** list in the project workspace.

10. In the project workspace quick launch menu, click **Deliverables**:

The **Deliverables** page opens, displaying the deliverables list:

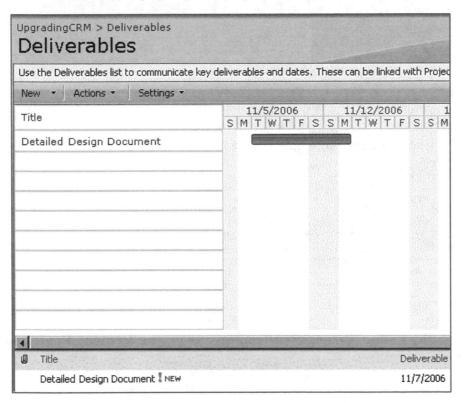

For other procedures related to deliverables, see the section on "Defining the Deliverable Management Plan".

## To assign team members to activities in the work plan:

When it has been determined which teams or team member will work on each task, you assign the resources to the tasks.

1. Launch Internet Explorer and open Project Web Access. The **Project Web Access** page opens.

2. In the quick launch menu, click **Project Center**:

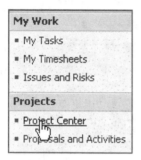

   The **Project Center** page opens.

3. Select the project:

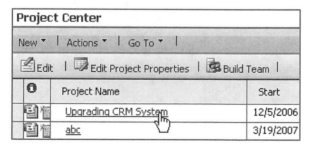

4. Click **Edit**. Project Professional launches. Click the **Project Professional** icon:

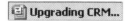

   Now you can see the project plan in Project Professional.

5. For each task, select a team member name from the drop-down list in the **Resource Names** column:

| WBS | Task Name | Duration | Start | Finish | Predecessors | Resource Names |
|-----|-----------|----------|-------|--------|--------------|----------------|
| 1 | Kickoff Meeting | 0 days | Tue 11/7/06 | Tue 11/7/06 | | Aaron Graves,farmadm |
| 2 | ⊟ **Design** | **12 days** | **Tue 11/7/06** | **Wed 11/22/06** | | |
| 2.1 | High Level Design | 2 days | Tue 11/7/06 | Wed 11/8/06 | 1 | Aaron Graves |
| 2.2 | ⊟ **Detailed Design** | **10 days** | **Thu 11/9/06** | **Wed 11/22/06** | | |
| 2.2.1 | Sub System A Design | 3 days | Thu 11/9/06 | Mon 11/13/06 | 3 | farmadmin ▾ |
| 2.2.2 | Sub System B Design | 5 days | Thu 11/9/06 | Wed 11/15/06 | 3 | Aaron Graves |
| 2.2.3 | Detailed Design Document | 5 days | Thu 11/16/06 | Wed 11/22/06 | 5,6 | farmadmin |
| 2.3 | Design Review | 0 days | Wed 11/22/06 | Wed 11/22/06 | 7 | Hagit Landman |
| 3 | ⊟ **Development** | **28 days** | **Thu 11/23/06** | **Mon 1/1/07** | | VB Team |

 **NOTE** You can select resources from the drop-down menu after you allocate the resources to the project. This is explained in the section on "Defining the Human Resource Management Plan".

### To build the team-level work plan:

Add more detailed activities at the team level. Since team-level work plans are more detailed, you or your team leader should provide a more detailed work plan, with more specific activities of shorter duration (so they will be easier to control).

### To allocate resources to resource types:

1. In Project Professional, from the **Tools** menu, select **Build Team from Enterprise...**:

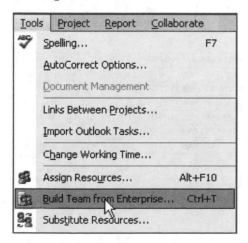

The **Build Team** dialog which opens contains two panes. The left one includes all the resources from the **Enterprise Resource Pool** according to your permissions, and the right pane includes the resources allocated to the project.

2. Select the resource type that you want to replace with a resource name (for example, replace the resource "farmadmin" with "Aaron"):

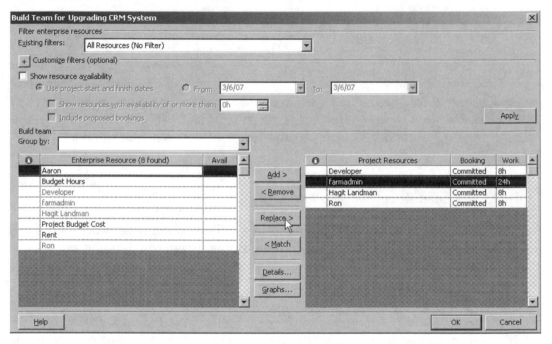

3. Click **Replace**, and then click **OK**. The system replaces "farmadmin" with "Aaron" in the project plan.

Before:

| | | | | | | |
|---|---|---|---|---|---|---|
| 2 | ⊟ **Design** | **12 days** | **Tue 11/7/06** | **Wed 11/22/06** | | |
| 2.1 | High Level Design | 2 days | Tue 11/7/06 | Wed 11/8/06 | 1 | Aaron Graves |
| 2.2 | ⊟ **Detailed Design** | **10 days** | **Thu 11/9/06** | **Wed 11/22/06** | | |
| 2.2.1 | Sub System A Design | 3 days | Thu 11/9/06 | Mon 11/13/06 | 3 | farmadmin |
| 2.2.2 | Sub System B Design | 5 days | Thu 11/9/06 | Wed 11/15/06 | 3 | farmadmin |
| 2.2.3 | Detailed Design Document | 5 days | Thu 11/16/06 | Wed 11/22/06 | 5,6 | farmadmin |
| 2.3 | Design Review | 0 days | Wed 11/22/06 | Wed 11/22/06 | 7 | farmadmin,Aaron Grav |

After:

| 2 | ⊟ **Design** | **12 days** | **Tue 11/7/06** | **Wed 11/22/06** | | |
|---|---|---|---|---|---|---|
| 2.1 | High Level Design | 2 days | Tue 11/7/06 | Wed 11/8/06 | 1 | Aaron Graves |
| **2.2** | ⊟ **Detailed Design** | **10 days** | **Thu 11/9/06** | **Wed 11/22/06** | | |
| 2.2.1 | Sub System A Design | 3 days | Thu 11/9/06 | Mon 11/13/06 | 3 | Aaron |
| 2.2.2 | Sub System B Design | 5 days | Thu 11/9/06 | Wed 11/15/06 | 3 | Aaron |
| 2.2.3 | Detailed Design Document | 5 days | Thu 11/16/06 | Wed 11/22/06 | 5,6 | Aaron |
| 2.3 | Design Review | 0 days | Wed 11/22/06 | Wed 11/22/06 | 7 | Aaron,Aaron Graves,H |

## To analyze the critical path:

This procedure displays the critical path.

1. In Project Professional, click the **Gantt Chart Wizard** button:

2. Follow the wizard's instruction. Click the **Critical path** box and click **Next**:

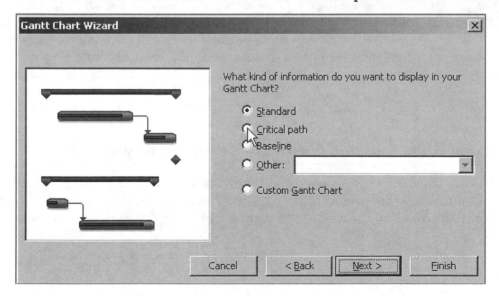

As soon as the wizard finishes formatting the view, the critical path is shown (in red) on the project Gantt chart:

| | ⓘ | WBS | Name | | | | | | | | | |
|---|---|---|---|---|---|---|---|---|---|---|---|---|
| | | | | uary | March | | | April | | | May | |
| | | | | M | E | B | M | E | B | M | E | B |
| 9 | | 3 | ⊟ **Development** | | | | | | | | | |
| 10 | | 3.1 | ⊟ **Sub System A** | | | | | | | | | |
| 11 | | 3.1.1 | ⊟ **Sub System A Development** | | | | | | | | | |
| 12 | 📝 | 3.1.1.1 | Sub System A Infrastructure Ready | | | 3/13 | | | | | | |
| 13 | | 3.1.1.2 | Sub System A S/W Development | | 3/14 | | | 4/10 | | | | |
| 14 | | 3.1.1.3 | Sub System A S/W Installation | | | | | 4/11 | 4/13 | | | |
| 15 | | 3.1.2 | Sub System A Unit Test | | | | | | 4/16 | 4/25 | | |
| 16 | | 3.1.3 | Sub System A Ready for Sub System T | | | | | | | 4/25 | | |
| 17 | | 3.2 | ⊟ **Sub System B** | | | | | | | | | |
| 18 | | 3.2.1 | ⊟ **Sub System B Development** | | | | | | | | | |
| 19 | | 3.2.1.1 | Sub System B Infrastructure Ready | | | 3/13 | | | | | | |
| 20 | | 3.2.1.2 | Sub System B S/W Development | | 3/16 | 3/29 | | | | | | |
| 21 | | 3.2.1.3 | Sub System B S/W Installation | | | 3/30 | 4/3 | | | | | |
| 22 | | 3.2.2 | Sub System B Unit Test | | | | 4/4 | 4/10 | | | | |

**NOTE** This is the basic, "out-of-the-box" way to see the critical path. Chapter 7 on monitoring and control will explain how to create a different view that will indicate which activity is critical and which activities should be checked as they are close to being critical.

3. Analyze the critical path and make changes as required.

## To fine-tune the high-level (contractual milestones)/master plan:

Analysis of the critical path, resource loading, or milestone dates might result in a need to make adjustments in the high-level (contractual milestones) or in the master plan (which in the case of a program is an integration of several projects).

For example, the goal of meeting a project end date earlier than the date shown on the critical path may require additional resources to be added to some activities and/or tasks to be started earlier than originally planned.

By making adjustments to resource availability or by reordering tasks, the critical path may be shortened.

Make incremental changes in project parameters (such as resourcing and task dependencies), noting the effect on the end date, until you are satisfied that the goal has been achieved.

## To approve the schedule:

When the project schedule is ready, send it to the steering committee for approval. Each project manager and team leader has to approve his or her plan as well.

Approvals should be saved under the **Project Approvals** list in the project workspace:

**Lists**
- Issues
- Risks
- Deliverables
- Calendar
- Tasks
- Stakeholders Matrix
- Requirements Matrix
- Project Approvals
- Communications Matrix
- Supplier Evaluation
- Closure Checklist

## To baseline the schedule:

When the project plans are approved, baseline the schedules.

1. In Project Professional, from the **Tools** menu, select **Tracking > Set Baseline...**:

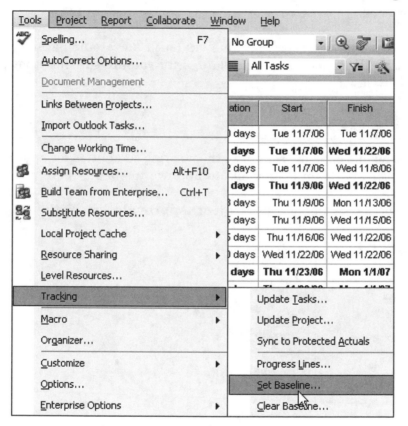

2. A baseline version of the schedule is stored, to which any further changes to the schedule can be compared.

## To define at what level activity types are reported:

Each forum needs to see a different view of the project plan. In Project Professional, in the sample **1 WBS Planning** view, flag the activities (in the relevant flag column, select **Yes** from the drop-down menu) to be shown to the steering committee, the activities to be shown at the program level, etc. The flags were defined in the section on "Building the Project Work Breakdown Structure".

## To define reporting views:

Define the views for each forum that was defined in the communication management plan: steering committee, project management, and team management.

The following example explains how to build the steering committee view. In this view, mainly high-level milestones are seen.

## Prerequisites

### To build the steering committee view in Project Professional:

This section explains how to build the view in a *different* way from that described in the section "To create the WBS view in Project Professional". Both ways are fine.

1.  Open Project Professional.
2.  From the **View** menu, select **Table: <table name> > More Tables...**:

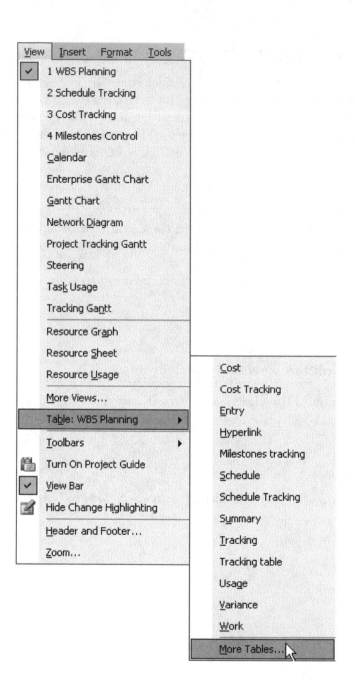

The **More Tables** dialog opens:

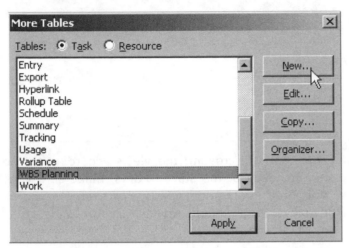

3. Click **New**. The **Table Definition** dialog opens:

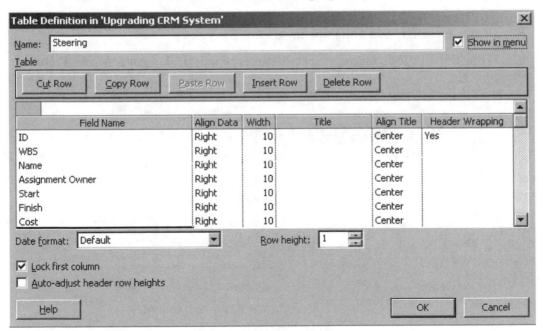

4. In the **Name** field, type the name of the table.

5. If this table is to appear in the menu, check the **Show in menu** box. This table will now appear in the **Tables** menu in Project Professional.

6. Fill in the fields you want to appear in the table. For example:
   ◆ ID
   ◆ WBS
   ◆ Name
   ◆ Assignment Owner
   ◆ Start
   ◆ Finish
   ◆ Cost

---

 **ATTENTION**    Since you are creating the views according to the different needs of the stakeholders, make sure you support their information needs. For example, the executive level usually needs mostly milestones instead of the most detailed plan.

---

7. Click **OK**.

8. In the message box that opens, click **Apply**.

9. From the **Project** menu, select **Filtered for: All Tasks > More Filters…**:

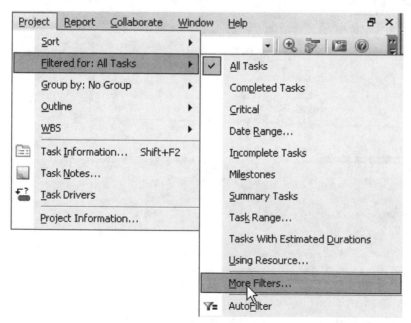

The **More Filters** dialog opens:

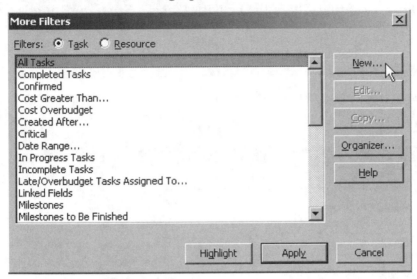

10. Click **New**. The **Filter Definition** dialog opens:

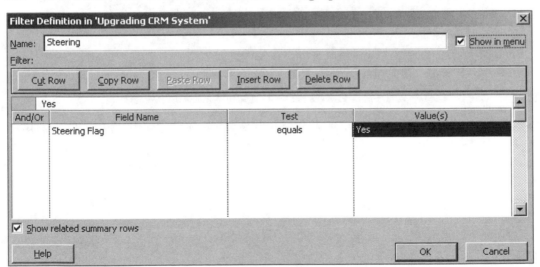

In the **Name** field, type the name of the filter.

11. Fill in the fields on the **Filter Definition** page. The example above shows the **Steering** view that filters the activities whose **Steering Flag** is set to **Yes**.

12. If this filter is to appear in the **Filters** menu in Project Professional, check the **Show in menu** box.

13. Click **OK**.

14. In the message box that opens, click **Apply**:

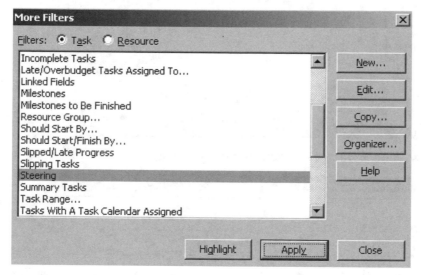

15. To create a view in Project Professional, from the **View** menu, select **More Views...**:

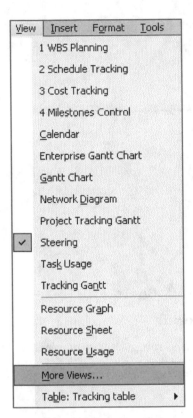

The **More Views** dialog opens:

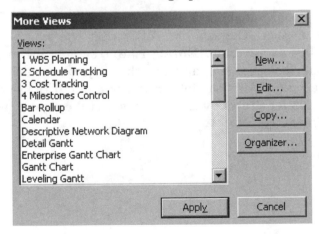

16. Click **New**. The **View Definition** dialog opens:

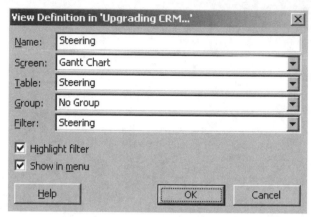

17. In the **Name** field, type "Steering".

18. From the **Screen** drop-down list, select **Gantt Chart**.

19. From the **Table** drop-down list, select **Steering**.

20. From the **Group** drop-down list, select the grouping that you want to use.

21. From the **Filter** drop-down list, select **Steering**.

22. Click **OK**. The view opens.

23. Add all the views defined in the communication management plan.

24. To copy the view to the global template:
    a. From the **Tools** menu, select **Organizer**. Verify that one side of the table displays **Global (+ non-cached Enterprise)** (the left side in the following example) and the other side displays the project in which the view was defined (the right side in the following example). If the screen does not look like this, under **Views available in**, select the right project from the drop-down menu.

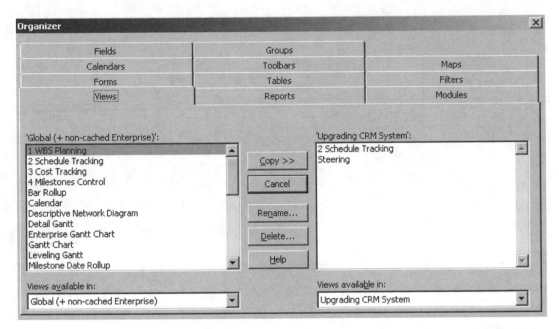

b. Copy the tables, fields, filters, and groups from the project side of the
   screen to the **Global** side of the screen by selecting the fields that you
   want to copy and clicking the **Copy** button in the middle between the
   two panes.

## Defining the Human Resource Management Plan

### Objectives

A detailed assessment of the resources required to undertake a project must be
performed. The required labor, equipment, and materials must be listed, and each
resource must be quantified. Finally, the human resource allocation must be
scheduled in order to provide the project manager and the team managers with
a complete view of the total amount of resources required for each stage of the
project.

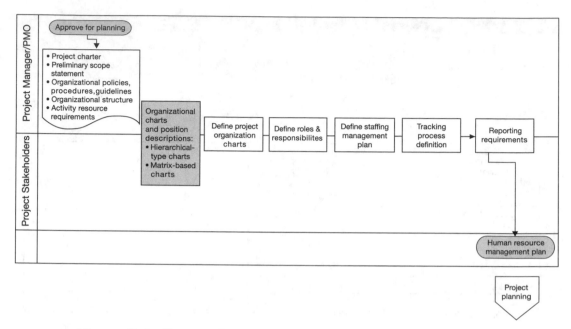

**Figure 5.4. Human Resource Management Plan Workflow**

The human resource management plan (see Figure 5.4) includes the definition of the roles and responsibilities for the program/project, staffing plan, training needs, team-building procedures, and recognition and rewards.

## Definition

**Staffing management plan**\*—The document that describes when and how human resource requirements will be met. It is contained in, or is a subsidiary plan of, the project management plan. The staffing management plan can be informal and broadly framed or formal and highly detailed, based on the needs of the project. Information in the staffing management plan varies by application area and project size.

---

\* Project Management Institute *A Guide to the Project Management Body of Knowledge (PMBOK® Guide)—Third Edition,* Project Management Institute, Inc., 2004. Copyright and all rights reserved. Material from this publication has been reproduced with the permission of PMI.

## Procedures

### To define program/project organization charts:

1. In Microsoft Office Visio, define the project organizational charts and organizational breakdown structure (OBS).

2. Get approval for the above charts from the steering committee.

3. Manage the above documents in the resource management plan folder of the project management plan document library. (To upload a document to a document library, see the procedure in Appendix A.6.)

### To define roles and responsibilities:

Define the project roles and responsibilities for each position in the project (for example, development team leader, quality assurance team leader, PMO, quality assurance team member, and so on).

For each position or group of positions (such as the development team members) create a Microsoft Word document that describes the roles and responsibilities of the position or group.

Upload the document to the roles and responsibilities document library in the project workspace:

**Documents**
- Project Documents
- Project Initiation
- Meeting Minutes
- Project Management Plan
- Glossary
- Procurement Management
- Quality Management
- Roles and Responsibilities
- Project Closure
- Project Schedules

To upload a document to a document library, see the procedure in Appendix A.6.

Manage the roles and responsibilities document in the resource management plan folder of the project management plan document library.

### To define tracking processes:

In the human resource management plan, define what reports and report views are required for each forum, based on the communication management plan requirements.

Define how resources will be tracked and the level of tracking. For example, at the team level, team members will be tracked by name or if a position is empty by position name (such as "experienced developer" or "senior developer"), but at the program level tracking will be by position (for example, the quality assurance team has one team leader, two experienced team members, and is missing two beginners).

### To create the human resource management plan:

1. Use a Microsoft Word document to define how human resources will be managed. A sample human resource management plan is available at http://office.microsoft.com/en-us/templates/results.aspx?qu=project&sc=4&av=ZWD.

2. Manage the plan in the resource management plan folder of the project management plan document library.

### To build the program/project team from the enterprise resource pool:

This procedure explains how to connect the project plan (in Project Professional) to the enterprise resource pool and to fill out the resource sheet.

1. Open the **Project Web Access** home page.

2. In the **Projects** section, select **Project Center**:

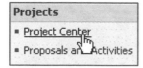

3. Select the project (in the example below, **Upgrading CRM System**):

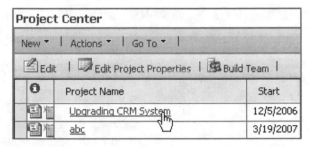

4. Click **Edit**:

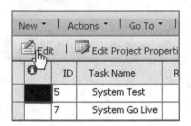

The project plan opens.

5. In Microsoft Project, from the **Tools** menu, select **Build Team from Enterprise...**:

The **Build Team for <Project Name>** dialog opens:

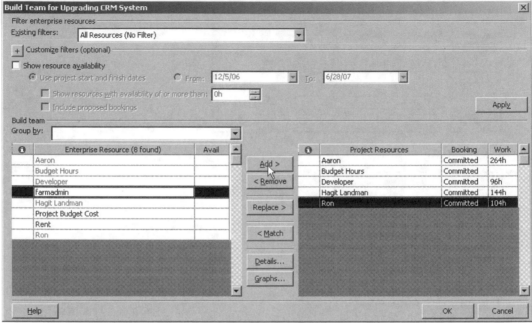

6. Add the relevant resources:

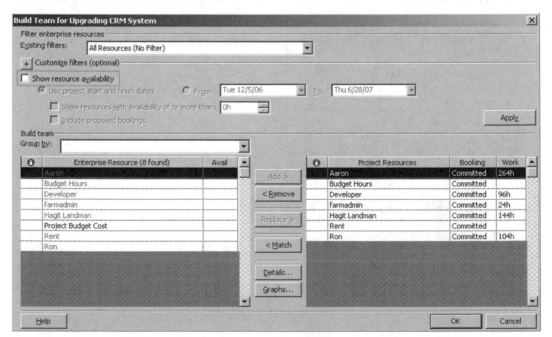

7. Check the **Show resource availability** box.

8. Make each resource either "Committed" to the project or "Proposed":

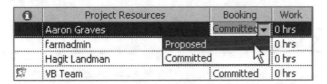

 ◆ **Committed**—A person who is "committed" consumes the allocated hours, and they are deducted from the work.
 ◆ **Proposed** —A person who is "proposed" does not influence the amount of allocated hours.

9. Click **OK**. The resources appear in the project's resource sheet:

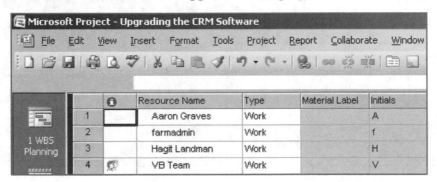

To view a resource's details, select the resource from the list and click **Details**:

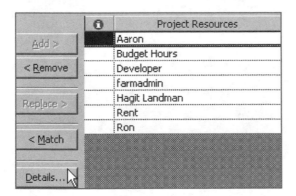

Add the information for the resource selected and click **OK**:

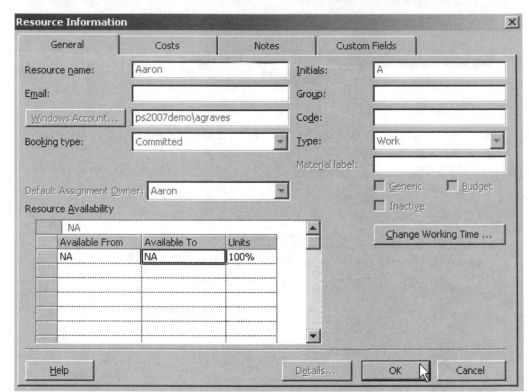

10. To view a resource's availability graph, click **Graphs...** on the **Build team...** screen:

11. The selected resource's availability graph will be displayed:

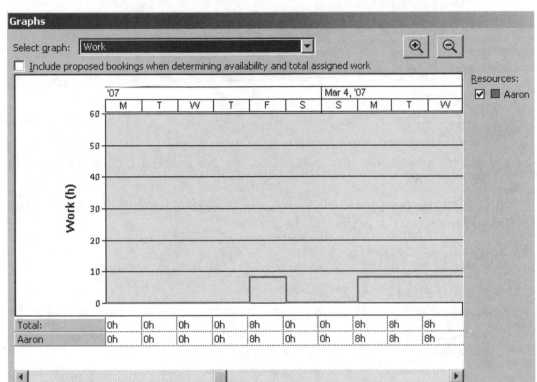

12. If the name of a resource is not yet known, select the team that you want to be a part of the project (for example, select "VB Team", "farmadmin", etc.).

## To assign team members to activities in the work plan:

After the project plan is ready and the activities are known, resources are assigned to the activities.

1. Open the **Project Web Access** home page.

2. In the **Projects** section, select **Project Center**:

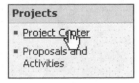

The following list opens:

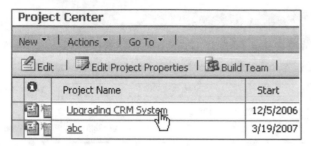

3. Select the project you are working on (in the example above, **Upgrading CRM System**).

4. Click **Edit**. Project Professional will open. Click the Project Professional button that appears at the bottom of the screen:

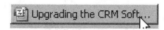

5. Assign resources to the project activities:

| ⓘ | WBS | Task Name | Duration | Start | Finish | Predecessors | Resource Names |
|---|---|---|---|---|---|---|---|
| | 1 | Kickoff Meeting | 0 days | Tue 11/7/06 | Tue 11/7/06 | | Aaron Graves,farma |
| | **2** | ⊟ **Design** | **1 day?** | **Tue 11/7/06** | **Tue 11/7/06** | 1 | |
| | 2.1 | High Level Design | 1 day? | Tue 11/7/06 | Tue 11/7/06 | | Aaron Graves |
| | 2.2 | Detailed Design | 1 day? | Tue 11/7/06 | Tue 11/7/06 | | Aaron Graves |
| | 2.3 | Design Review | 1 day? | Tue 11/7/06 | Tue 11/7/06 | | Aaron Graves |
| | **3** | ⊟ **Development** | **1 day?** | **Tue 11/7/06** | **Tue 11/7/06** | | |
| | **3.1** | ⊟ **Sub System A** | **1 day?** | **Tue 11/7/06** | **Tue 11/7/06** | | |
| | 3.1.1 | Sub System A De | 1 day? | Tue 11/7/06 | Tue 11/7/06 | | Hagit Landman |
| | 3.1.2 | Sub System A Ur | 1 day? | Tue 11/7/06 | Tue 11/7/06 | | Aaron Graves |
| | **3.2** | ⊟ **Sub System B** | **1 day?** | **Tue 11/7/06** | **Tue 11/7/06** | | farmadmin |
| | 3.2.1 | Sub System B De | 1 day? | Tue 11/7/06 | Tue 11/7/06 | | Hagit Landman |
| | 3.2.2 | Sub System B Ur | 1 day? | Tue 11/7/06 | Tue 11/7/06 | | VB Team |
| | 4 | Sub System Test | 10 days | Tue 11/7/06 | Mon 11/20/06 | | VB Team |
| | **5** | ⊟ **System Test** | **1 day?** | **Tue 11/7/06** | **Tue 11/7/06** | | |
| | 5.1 | System Test Design | 1 day? | Tue 11/7/06 | Tue 11/7/06 | | VB Team |
| | 5.2 | System Test | 1 day? | Tue 11/7/06 | Tue 11/7/06 | | VB Team |
| | **6** | ⊟ **User Acceptance Test** | **1 day?** | **Tue 11/7/06** | **Tue 11/7/06** | | |
| | 6.1 | User Acceptance Tes | 1 day? | Tue 11/7/06 | Tue 11/7/06 | | farmadmin |
| | 6.2 | User Acceptance Tes | 1 day? | Tue 11/7/06 | Tue 11/7/06 | | Aaron Graves |
| | 6.3 | System Bug Fixes | 1 day? | Tue 11/7/06 | Tue 11/7/06 | | Aaron Graves |
| | 7 | System Go Live | 0 days | Tue 11/7/06 | Tue 11/7/06 | | Hagit Landman |
| | 8 | sd | 1 day? | Tue 11/7/06 | Tue 11/7/06 | | |

## To define the staffing management plan:

1. Define the resource type that is needed for each activity, and check the availability of the existing resources.

2. In the human resource management plan, define the information that is required to control the staffing, such as number of resources allocated and where more staff is needed.

3. Manage the staffing management plan in Project Professional.

 RECOMMENDATION  When you open Project Professional (not from the server), choose the **Load Resource Summary Information** option. This way, you can see whether your resources are working on other projects and what their availability is.

4. Assign a resource by name (if known) or by team name (if the resource name is unknown) to each activity in the work plan. For the procedure, see the section on "Defining the Time Management Plan".

   After resources have been allocated to activities, you can see the allocation in Project Professional.

5. Open the project in Project Professional. Select **View > Resource Usage**:

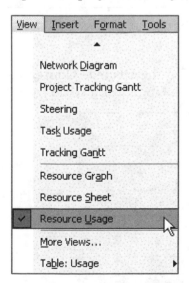

On the screen that follows, you can see the resources' assignments and allocations:

| | | | | | | | | |
|---|---|---|---|---|---|---|---|---|
| ⊟ **Aaron** | **1,512 h** | Work | 8h | 8h | 8h | 8h | 8h |
| Kickoff Meeting | 0 hrs | Work | | | | | |
| Sub System B D | 40 hrs | Work | | | | | |
| Detailed Design | 24 hrs | Work | 8h | 8h | | | |
| Sub System A S | 160 hrs | Work | | | 8h | 8h | 8h |
| Sub System B U. | 40 hrs | Work | | | | | |
| Sub System B re | 0 hrs | Work | | | | | |
| ⊞ Other projects a | 1,248 hrs | Work | | | | | |
| Budget Hours | | Work | | | | | |
| ⊟ Developer | 96 h | Work | | 0h | 8h | 8h | 8h |
| High Level Desi₁ | 16 hrs | Work | | | | | |
| Design Review | 0 hrs | Work | | 0h | | | |
| Sub System B in₁ | 0 hrs | Work | | 0h | | | |
| System Test De₂ | 80 hrs | Work | | | 8h | 8h | 8h |
| ⊞ Other projects a | 0 hrs | Work | | | | | |

In the **Resource Usage** view, assignments are displayed by resource. The example above shows that "Aaron" is overloaded in some periods (his name will appear in red) and that the position of "Developer" is still vacant and needs to be filled.

## To define the project manager or team manager view:

After the resources have been assigned to the activities in the project plan, you can present the resource usage in several views.

1. Open the project plan in Project Professional. Use the **Project Center** menu option and select the project (in the example below, **Upgrading CRM System**):

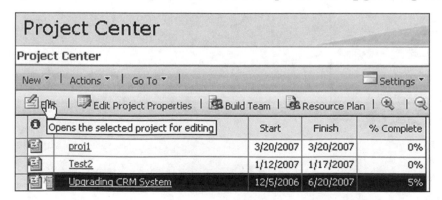

2. In Project Professional, from the **View** menu, select **Resource Usage**:

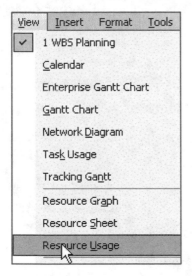

The following page opens:

| ⓘ | Resource Name | Work | Details | Nov 5, '06 | | | | | |
|---|---|---|---|---|---|---|---|---|---|
| | | | | S | S | M | T | W | T |
| ◇ 🖳 | ⊟ **VB Team** | **472 hrs** | Work | | | | 56h | 48h | 48h |
| | Design Review | 0 hrs | Work | | | | 0h | | |
| | Sub System A Infrastruc | 0 hrs | Work | | | | 0h | | |
| | Sub System A S/W Dev | 160 hrs | Work | | | | 8h | 8h | 8h |
| | Sub System A S/W Insta | 24 hrs | Work | | | | 8h | 8h | 8h |
| | Sub System A Unit Test | 40 hrs | Work | | | | 8h | 8h | 8h |
| | Sub System Test | 80 hrs | Work | | | | 8h | 8h | 8h |
| | System Test Design | 80 hrs | Work | | | | 8h | 8h | 8h |
| | Testing Environment Re | 0 hrs | Work | | | | 0h | | |
| | System Test | 80 hrs | Work | | | | 8h | 8h | 8h |
| | Go/NoGo Decision | 8 hrs | Work | | | | 8h | | |
| | ⊟ farmadmin | 0 hrs | Work | | | | 0h | | |
| | ⊞ Other projects and com. | 0 hrs | Work | | | | 0h | | |
| ◇ | ⊟ **Hagit Landman** | **168 hrs** | Work | | | | 32h | 24h | 24h |
| | Kickoff Meeting | 0 hrs | Work | | | | 0h | | |
| | Design Review | 0 hrs | Work | | | | 0h | | |
| | Sub System A Unit Test | 40 hrs | Work | | | | 8h | 8h | 8h |
| | Sub System B Developn | 80 hrs | Work | | | | 8h | 8h | 8h |
| | Sub System B Unit Test | 40 hrs | Work | | | | 8h | 8h | 8h |
| | Go/NoGo Decision | 8 hrs | Work | | | | 8h | | |
| | System Go Live | 0 hrs | Work | | | | 0h | | |
| | ⊞ Other projects and com. | 0 hrs | Work | | | | 0h | | |

This page shows the resource allocation (or overallocation, which will be displayed in red). You can also see if a resource is allocated to other projects. In the following example, "farmadmin" is allocated to other projects:

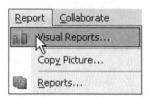

3. From the **Report** menu, select **Visual Reports...**:

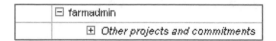

The **Visual Reports – Create Report** dialog opens:

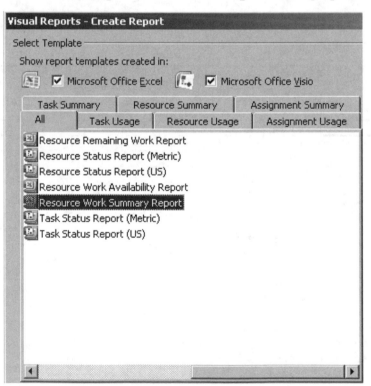

4. Select, for example, **Resource Work Summary Report**.

5. Click either **New Template...** to define a new template or **Edit Template...** to edit a template:

Add/remove fields and create the template according to the reports that you have defined.

6. Click **View** (at the bottom of this page). The report graph opens:

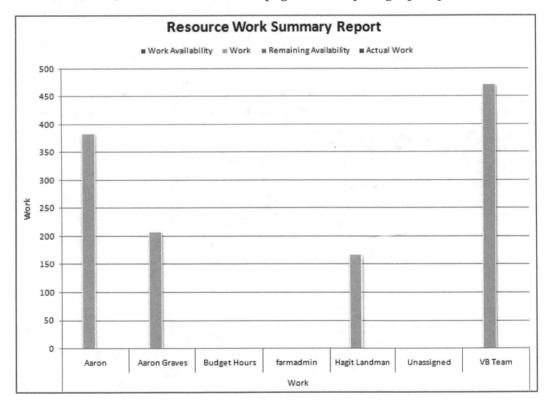

## To view the executive view:

1. Open the **Project Web Access** home page.

2. In the **Resources** section, select **Resource Center**:

3. Select an option for viewing the resources. For example, you may want to see a resource's assignments (assignments to "Aaron" in the following example):

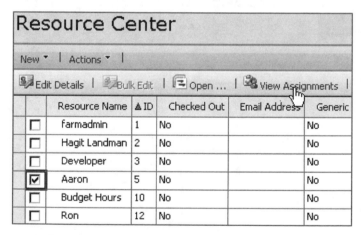

4. Click **View Assignments**:

| Task Name | Work | Remaining Work | Start | Finish | % Work C |
|---|---|---|---|---|---|
| ⊟ **Aaron** | **1,528h** | **1,484.8h** | **11/7/2006** | **4/12/2007** | |
| ⊟ **Upgrading CRM System** | **280h** | **280h** | **2/28/2007** | **4/12/2007** | |
| ⊟ **Upgrading CRM System** | **280h** | **280h** | **2/28/2007** | **4/12/2007** | |
| ⊟ **Design** | **80h** | **80h** | **3/2/2007** | **3/15/2007** | |
| ⊟ **Detailed Design** | **80h** | **80h** | **3/2/2007** | **3/15/2007** | |
| Sub System B Design | 40h | 40h | 3/2/2007 | 3/8/2007 | |
| Detailed Design Document | 40h | 40h | 3/9/2007 | 3/15/2007 | |
| ⊟ **Development** | **200h** | **200h** | **3/16/2007** | **4/12/2007** | |
| ⊟ **Sub System B** | **40h** | **40h** | **4/4/2007** | **4/10/2007** | |
| Sub System B Unit Test | 40h | 40h | 4/4/2007 | 4/10/2007 | |
| Sub System B Ready for Su | 0h | 0h | 4/10/2007 | 4/10/2007 | |
| ⊟ **Sub System A** | **160h** | **160h** | **3/16/2007** | **4/12/2007** | |
| ⊟ **Sub System A Developı** | **160h** | **160h** | **3/16/2007** | **4/12/2007** | |

5. From the **View** drop-down menu, select the view that you want to see:

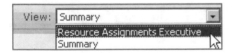

## Prerequisites

### To create the resource management plan document library:

For the procedure to create the resource management plan folder in the project management plan document library, see Appendix A.3 on creating a document library.

**To create the enterprise resource pool:**

1. On the **Project Web Access** (development environment) home page, select **Server Settings**:

2. In the **Enterprise Data** section, select **Resource Center**:

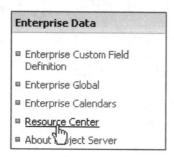

The **Resource Center** page opens:

3. Select **New > Resource**:

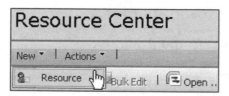

The following page opens:

| ⊟ **Type** | Type: |
|---|---|
| | [ Work ▾ ] |
| | ☐ Budget |
| | ☐ Generic |
| ⊟ **Identification Information**<br>The Display Name cannot contain square brackets or the server list separator | ☑ Resource can logon to Project Server |
| | * Display Name: |
| | [ farmadmin ] |
| | E-mail address: |
| | [ ] |
| | RBS: |
| | [ ] [...] |
| | Initials: |
| | [ f ] |
| | Hyperlink Name: |
| | [ ] |
| | Hyperlink URL: |
| | [ ] |
| | Account Status: |
| | [ Active ▾ ] |

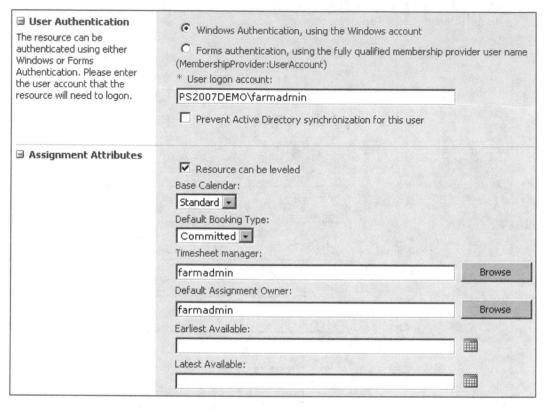

4. Fill in the relevant data for the resource, including **Security Groups**:

5. If the resource is from a team assignment pool, check the **Team Assignment Pool** box:

6. Click **Save**.

 The system allows only one member in the team assignment pool. Many resources can belong, for example, to the development team, but only one resource can have the **Team Assignment Pool** box checked. Once you build the project team and allocate the development team to the project, this resource will have the assignments of that team.

When building "named" resources, they must have the ability to connect to the server. This is granted by checking the **Resource can logon to Project Server** box:

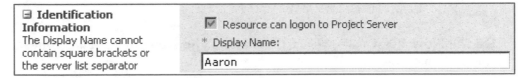

Now you will be able to see the resource on the **Resource Center** page:

## Resource Center

New ▾ | Actions ▾ |

📝 Edit Details | 📝 Bulk Edit | 📭 Open ... | 📖 View Assignments | 📖 View Availability |

| | Resource Name | ▲ ID | Checked Out | Email Address | Generic | Cost Center | Timesheet Manager |
|---|---|---|---|---|---|---|---|
| ☐ | farmadmin | 1 | No | | No | | farmadmin |
| ☐ | Hagit Landman | 2 | No | | No | | Hagit Landman |
| ☐ | Developer | 3 | No | | No | | Developer |

## To create the executive view:

1. In Project Web Access (development environment), select **Server Settings**:

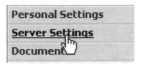

2. On the **Server Settings** page, under the **Look and Feel** section, select **Manage Views**:

On the **Manage Views** page, select **New View**:

3. On the **New View** page, select the **View Type** (**Resource Assignments** in the example below):

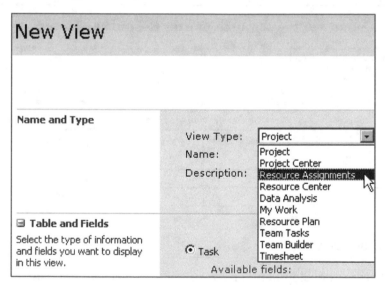

4. Fill in the **Name** of the view:

| Name and Type | View Type: | Resource Assignments |
|---|---|---|
| | Name: | Resource Assignments Executive |
| | Description: | Resource Assignments Executive view |

5. Define the view's parameters (tables and fields to be shown, format view, filters, and security categories) on the **New View** page.

6. Click **Save**.

## Defining the Cost Management Plan

### Objectives

The cost management plan describes how the project costs will be managed. It identifies the processes and procedures used to manage costs throughout the project's life cycle. This plan summarizes the approach to cost budgeting. It describes the cost tracking procedures and defines how the variances will be addressed.

The costs of the required labor, equipment, and materials are calculated, as well as the total cost of undertaking each activity within the project plan. These calculations are performed in this stage.

At the end of the cost management plan definition, the cost baseline is set.

### Procedures

#### To define budget and cost rules:

1. Define the project budget.

2. Define units of measurement for each resource type. For example, work should be measured in person-hours, person-days, or person-months. For multinational programs, currencies and average exchange rates must be defined.

3. Define the budget codes for the activities and the actual cost accumulation rules.

#### To plan costs using Project Professional:

1. Verify that all the relevant resources and resource types are assigned to the project plan.

2. Open the **Project Web Access** home page.

3. In the **Projects** section, select **Project Center**:

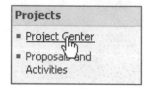

4. Open the project (in the following example, **Upgrading CRM System**) for editing in Microsoft Project:

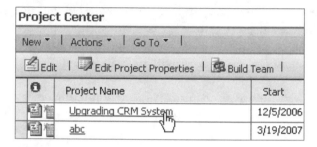

5. Add all budget and cost resources to the project plan in Project Professional.

---

◆ A cost-type resource allows you to follow the project's total cost. To the budget cost you allocate a sum which is the project's total budget.

◆ A budget-type resource allows you to compare the planned budget to the actual cost and actual work. To the budget work you allocate the sum of hours which is the project's budget.

---

6. From the **Tools** menu, select **Build Team from Enterprise...**:

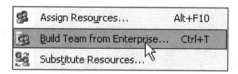

The **Build Team** dialog opens:

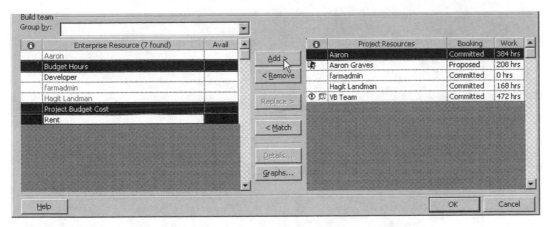

7. Select the required resources. In the example above, **Budget Hours**, **Project Budget Cost**, and **Rent** are selected.

8. To view a resource's type, double-click on that resource.

9. Click **Add**.

10. Click **OK**.

11. Allocate the resources in the **Resource** column by selecting them. In the following example, the resource **Rent** was allocated to the **Development** task and the resource **Budget Hours** was allocated to the project summary task:

| | | | | | | | |
|---|---|---|---|---|---|---|---|
| ⊟ **Upgrading the CRM Software** | **20 days** | ######## | ######## | **1,232 hrs** | **$0.00** | | **Budget Ho** ▾ |
| Kickoff Meeting | 0 days | Tue 11/7/06 | Tue 11/7/06 | 0 hrs | $0.00 | ,Hagit Landman | in,Hagit Landman |
| ⊟ **Design** | **5 days** | **Tue 11/7/06** | **Mon 11/13/06** | **120 hrs** | **$0.00** | | |
| High Level Design | 2 days | Tue 11/7/06 | Wed 11/8/06 | 16 hrs | $-00 | | Aaron Graves |
| ⊟ **Detailed Design** | **5 days** | **Tue 11/7/06** | **Mon 11/13/06** | **104 hrs** | **$0.00** | | |
| Sub System A Design | 3 days | Tue 11/7/06 | Thu 11/9/06 | 24 hrs | $0.00 | Aaron | Aaron |
| Sub System B Design | 5 days | Tue 11/7/06 | Mon 11/13/06 | 40 hrs | $0.00 | Aaron | Aaron |
| Detailed Design Document | 5 days | Tue 11/7/06 | Mon 11/13/06 | 40 hrs | $0.00 | Aaron | Aaron |
| Design Review | 0 days | Tue 11/7/06 | Tue 11/7/06 | 0 hrs | $0.00 | ,Hagit Landman | ndman,VB Team |
| ⊟ **Development** | **20 days** | **Tue 11/7/06** | **Mon 12/4/06** | **608 hrs** | **$0.00** | | Rent |

 The budget resources can be assigned only to the project summary task.

12. On the **Resource Usage** page, add the amounts of **Budget Cost** and **Budget Work** (hours):

| ⓘ | Resource Name | Cost | Budget Cost | Budget Work |
|---|---|---|---|---|
| | ⊟ Budget Hours | | | 1,000 hrs |
| | *Upgrading the C* | | | *1,000 hrs* |
| | ⊟ Project Budget Cost | | $70,000.00 | |
| | *Upgrading the C* | | *$70,000.00* | |
| | ⊟ Rent | $80,000.00 | | |
| | *Development* | $80,000.00 | | |

13. Ensure that all resources have a rate per measurement unit.
   a. In Microsoft Project, from the **Project** menu, select **Resource Sheet**:

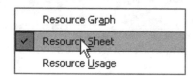

   b. Double-click on the resource (in the following example, "Aaron") to which you want to assign a rate per hour. The **Resource Information** dialog opens:

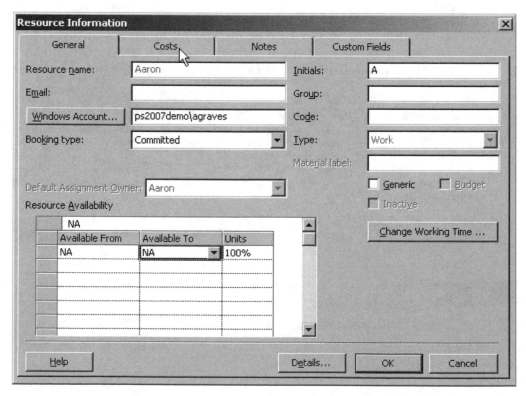

c. Select the **Costs** tab. The **Costs** page opens:

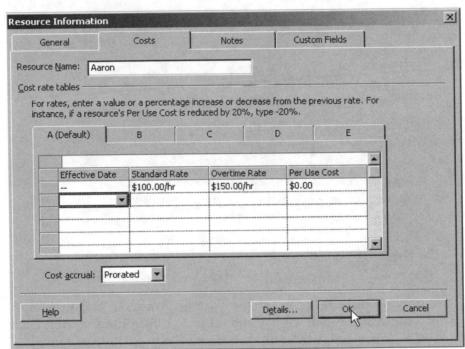

d. Enter the rates (up to five types).

e. Click **OK**. After the costs are associated with the project plan, you can see the cost of the project:

| | ⓘ | WBS | Name | Duration | Start | Finish | Work | Cost |
|---|---|---|---|---|---|---|---|---|
| 0 | | 0 | ⊟ Upgrading CRM System | 20 days | ######### | ######### | 1,232 hrs | $222,960.00 |

14. Verify that all the work hours and materials allocated to the activities are correct.

## To define earned value rules:

1. Define the formula to be used for calculating earned value in the program/project (because there are several formulas for calculating earned value). You can use the Project Professional Reports tool to calculate earned value.

2. Open the project in Project Professional.

3. Select **Tools > Options**.

4. In the **Calculation** folder, select **Earned Value**:

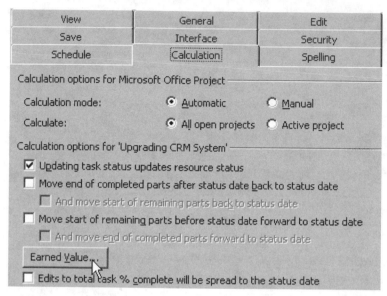

5. In the following screen, select the formula from the **Default task Earned Value method** drop-down list and select the baseline from the **Baseline for Earned Value calculations** drop-down list:

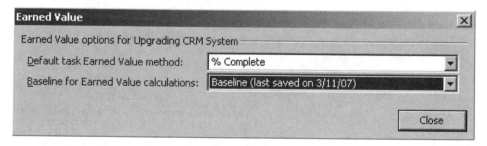

## To define reporting formats in Project Professional:

1. Open the project in Project Professional.

2. From the **Report** menu, select **Visual Reports...**:

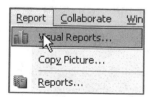

The **Visual Reports – Create Report** dialog opens:

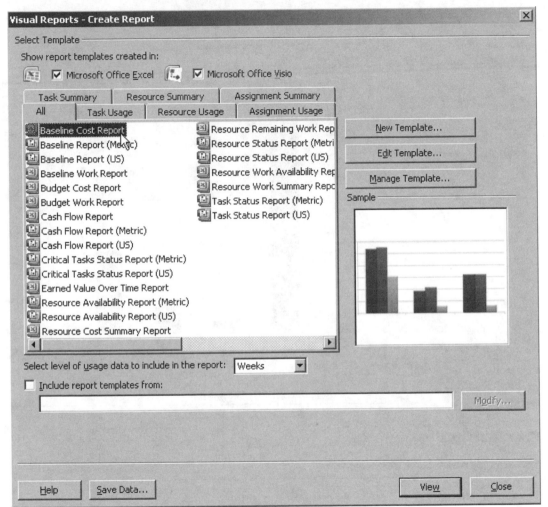

3. Select the type of report you want to produce.

4. Edit the template if you need to make changes by selecting **View**:

5. The report defined is created (in the following example, **Baseline Cost Report**):

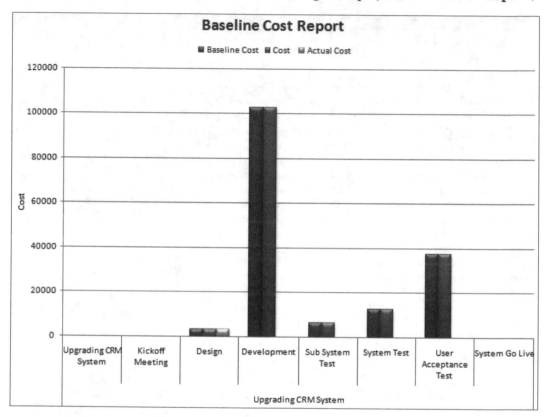

## Prerequisites

**To add a new cost resource:**

1. Open the **Project Web Access** home page.

2. In the **Resources** section, select **Resource Center**:

3.  On the **Resource Center** page, from the **New** menu, select **Resource**:

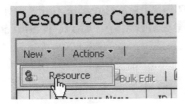

The **New Resource** page opens:

## New Resource

\* indicates a required field

Save    Cancel

⊟ **Type**

Type:
Work ▾

☐ Budget

☐ Generic

⊟ **Identification Information**
The Display Name cannot contain square brackets or the server list separator

☐ Resource can logon to Project Server
\* Display Name:

Rent

E-mail address:

RBS:

...

Initials:

4.  From the **Type** drop-down list, select **Cost**:

⊟ **Type**

Type:
Work ▾
Work
Material
Cost

5. In the **Display Name** field, type "Rent" (for example).

6. Click **Save**. The new resource appears on the **Resource Center** page in the **Resource Name** column. You can see **Work** resources and **Cost** resources:

| | ▲ Resource Name | ID | Checked Out | Email Address | Generic | Cost C |
|---|---|---|---|---|---|---|
| | ⊟ **Work** | | | | | |
| ☐ | Aaron | 5 | No | | No | |
| ☐ | Developer | 3 | No | | No | |
| ☐ | farmadmin | 1 | No | | No | |
| ☐ | Hagit Landman | 2 | No | | No | |
| | ⊟ **Cost** | | | | | |
| ☐ | Rent | 9 | No | | No | |

## To add a budget resource:

1. On the **Resource Center** page, from the **New** menu, select **Resource**.

2. On the **New Resource** page, specify the resource **Type** as **Work** and check the **Budget** box:

3. Repeat steps 1 and 2, but in step 2 select the resource **Type** as **Cost**:

Two new items appear on the **Resource Center** page in the **Resource Name** column:
   ◆ **Budget Hours** is listed under **Work** resources
   ◆ **Project Budget Cost** is listed under **Cost** resources

Resource Center

| | ▲ Resource Name | ID | Checked Out | Email Address | Generic | Cost Center | Timesheet |
|---|---|---|---|---|---|---|---|
| | **⊟ Work** | | | | | | |
| ☐ | Aaron | 5 | No | | No | | Aaron |
| ☐ | Budget Hours | 10 | No | | No | | |
| ☐ | Developer | 3 | No | | No | | Developer |
| ☐ | farmadmin | 1 | No | | No | | farmadmin |
| ☐ | Hagit Landman | 2 | No | | No | | Hagit Landma |
| | **⊟ Cost** | | | | | | |
| ☐ | Project Budget | 11 | No | | No | | |
| ☐ | Rent | 9 | No | | No | | |

## Defining the Quality Management Plan

### Objectives

Quality is defined as conformance to requirements and fitness for use. This means that the project must deliver what was required and that the products must satisfy the actual needs.

The quality management plan (see Figure 5.5) is developed in order to ensure that the project deliverables meet the customer requirements. This plan lists in detail the quality targets to be achieved and the quality assurance and control activities performed in the project. It identifies the techniques and standards to be used. The plan identifies who on each team or in a company is responsible for quality. It also describes the project manager's responsibilities in the quality area.

### Procedures

The project manager and quality manager include in the quality management plan items such as:

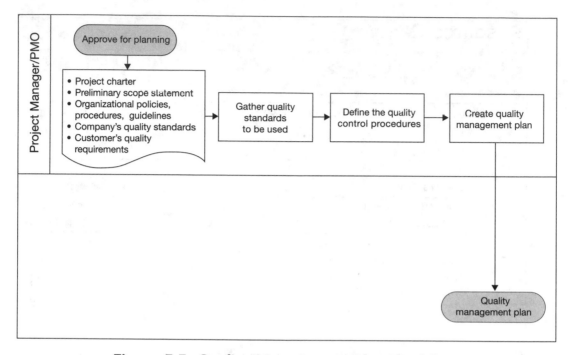

**Figure 5.5. Quality Management Plan Workflow**

◆ Measures of quality performance

◆ Benefit/cost analysis

◆ Cost of quality

The quality management plan identifies the quality standards to be used in the program/project and describes how these standards will be met. It also defines the quality gates and specifies how to incorporate them in the program/project schedule.

## To gather quality standards to be used in the program/project:

1. Gather the quality standards to be used in the program/project from:
   ◆ The requirements matrix
   ◆ Quality standards used in the company

2. Upload the relevant documents to the quality management document library. For the procedure, see Appendix A.6 on uploading a document to a document library.

## To create quality checklists:

Create quality checklists for delivery acceptance and for decision making regarding moving through quality gates.

## To create the quality management plan:

Create and define the quality management plan, and upload it to the project management plan document library. For the procedure, see Appendix A.6 on uploading a document to a document library.

An example of a quality management plan can be found at http://office.microsoft. com/en-us/templates/results.aspx?qu=project&sc=4&av=ZWD.

## Prerequisite

### To create the quality management document library:

Follow the procedure in Appendix A.3 for creating a document library.

# Defining the Risk Management Plan

## Objectives

Risk management (see Figure 5.6) is a critical sub-process within the project life cycle. In order to meet risks effectively, all foreseeable project risks must be identified and rated in terms of their probability of occurrence and their potential impact on the project.

Risks are prioritized, and a set of actions are identified to reduce the probability of occurrence of each risk and its impact on the project should that risk occur.

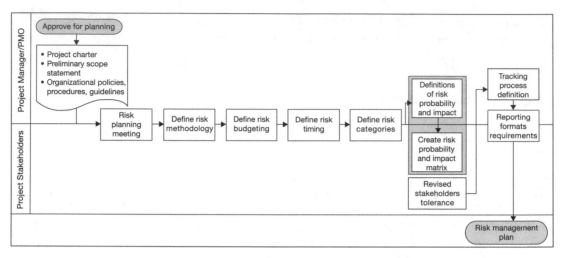

**Figure 5.6. Risk Management Plan Workflow**

## Procedures

### To host the risk planning meeting:

1. Schedule the risk planning meeting.

2. Log the risks discussed in that meeting in the risks log.

### To define the risk methodology:

1. Define the risk methodology to be used in the program/project. For example:
   ◆ Define the risk thresholds (what grade of risk is considered "red", what is considered "yellow", and what is considered "green").
   ◆ Define the risk matrix (whether severity × probability is 5 × 5 or 3 × 3).
   ◆ Define what types of risks will be escalated.
   ◆ Define what risks will be ignored.

2. Record the above definitions in the risk management plan.

### To define risk budgeting:

1. Define the budget allocated to deal with risks.

2. Record this definition in the risk management plan.

## To define risk timing:

1. Define the time frames for risk resolution.

2. Record these definitions in the risk management plan.

## To define risk categories:

1. Define risk categories for the program/project: time, technology, cost, development, etc.

2. Record these definitions in the risk management plan.

## To define the risk escalation procedure:

1. Define what risk types are shown at each level of reporting.

2. For each risk level of reporting, define whether the risk is handled within a team, project, program, or by the steering committee.

3. Record these definitions in the risk management plan.

## To update the risks log:

1. In the project workspace, in the **Lists** section, select **Risks**:

   The **Risks** page opens.

2. Click **New**:

The **Risks: New Item** page opens:

UpgradingCRM > Risks > New Item
## Risks: New Item

|  |  | OK | Cancel |

📎 Attach File | Link Items      * indicates a required field

| | |
|---|---|
| **Title** * | |
| **Owner** | |
| **Assigned To** | |
| **Status** | (1) Active |
| **Category** | (2) Category2 |
| **Due Date** | ▦ 12 AM ▾ 00 ▾ |
| **Probability** * | 0   % |
| **Impact** * | 5 <br> The magnitude of impact should the risk actually happen |
| **Cost** | 0 <br> The cost impact should the risk actually happen |

3. Fill in the relevant fields.

4. Click **OK**.

## To view the risks log:

1. In the project workspace, in the left pane under **Lists**, select **Risks**:

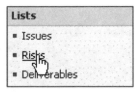

**Lists**
- Issues
- Risks
- Deliverables

The risks log opens.

2. In the **View** menu on the right-hand side, select the risks view that you want:

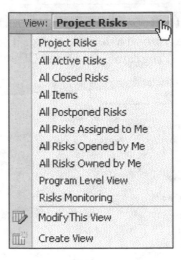

## Prerequisites

### To change category values in the risk category column:

1. Change the list of values in the risk category column to the following (for example):
   - ◆ Time
   - ◆ Cost
   - ◆ Technology
   - ◆ Development
   - ◆ Quality assurance
   - ◆ Other

2. In the project workspace, in the left pane under **Lists**, select **Risks**:

For the procedure to modify an existing column, see Appendix A.22.

## To add the reporting level column in the risks list:

Create a new column named "Reporting level." For the type of information in this column, select the **Choice** box. The values to choose from are defined under **Type each choice on a separate line** (Team, Project, Program, Steering, Other):

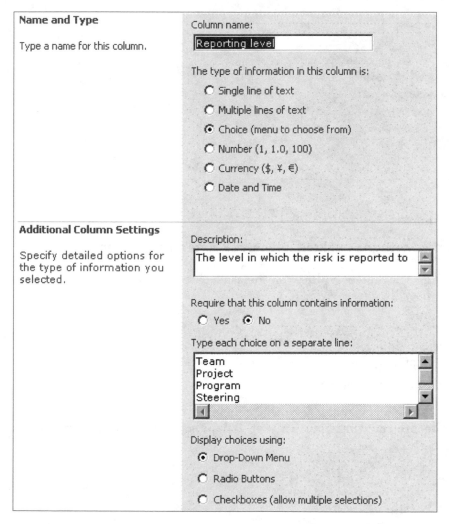

For the procedure, see Appendix A.9 on adding a choice column to a list.

## To create reporting views:

Create a view for each reporting level, with reporting level as a filter.

Suppose there are two types of risk at the project level and at the program level. We need to create a view for program-level risk reporting and a view for project-level risk reporting. The screen shot below shows the program-level view:

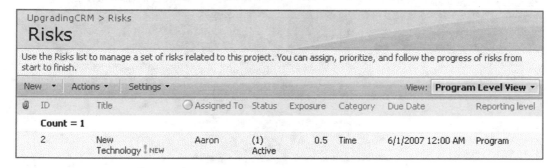

For the procedure to create a list view, see Appendix A.21.

# Defining the Communication Management Plan

The communication management plan includes the information to be provided to the project stakeholders to keep them informed of project progress. All stakeholders are listed, and their requirements for information are clearly identified. A schedule of communication events and activities is laid out to ensure that the necessary information is communicated to the right people at the right time.

The communication/governance structure shows the formal communication channels of the different levels of the program/project and decision making. Figure 5.7 depicts this structure and information flows.

Figure 5.8 depicts the workflow of the communication management plan definition.

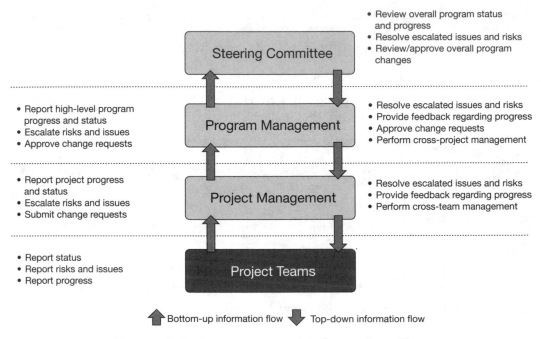

**Figure 5.7. Structures and Information Flows**

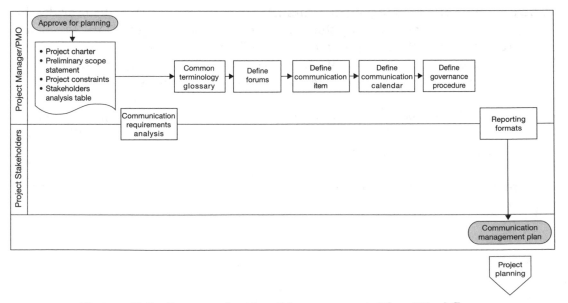

**Figure 5.8. Communication Management Plan Workflow**

## Objectives

◆ To support *top-down communication* flow so that the information reaches all employees affected by the project

◆ To brand and promote the project within the organization through *internal marketing*

◆ To ensure awareness and understanding of the current project status by the key stakeholders

◆ To support the client with accurate, detailed, and well-timed information

◆ To demonstrate commitment of the key sponsors to the project goals

◆ To build support for, and internal ownership of, the changes brought about by the project

◆ To manage impacts, concerns, and expectations up front (to not allow time for rumors to spread)

◆ To involve stakeholders in the change rather than just inform them of it

◆ To promote the benefits of the change

◆ To overcome potential barriers and issues

## Procedures

Define communication forums and fill out the communication/meeting matrix.

## To fill out the communication matrix:

1. In the **Lists** section, select **Communication Matrix**:

The **Communication Matrix** page opens:

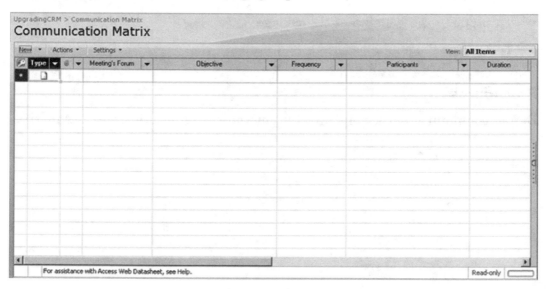

2. Click **New**:

The **Communication Matrix: New Item** page opens:

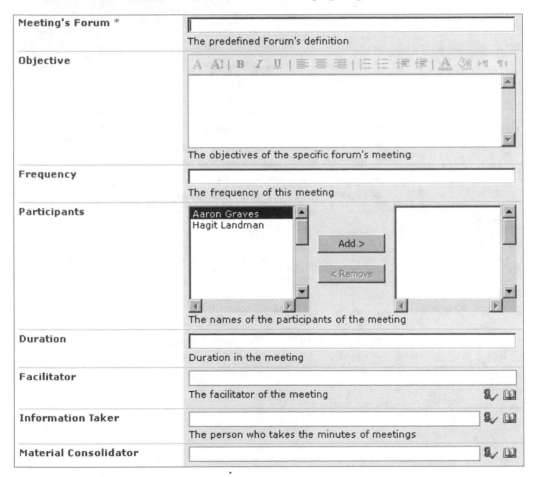

3.  Fill in the forum details.

4.  Click **OK**.

5.  Repeat steps 2 to 4 for each forum you want to enter. Table 5.5 is an example of a completed communication matrix.

### Table 5.5. Sample Communication Matrix

| Meeting Category | Objective | Frequency |
|---|---|---|
| Executive sponsors | ◆ Information alignment<br>◆ Review overall program progress in line with the contract<br>◆ Address any escalated issues and action items from the steering committee | Once a quarter |
| Steering committee | ◆ Review overall program status and progress<br>◆ Resolve escalated issues and risks<br>◆ Review/approve overall program changes | Once a month |
| Program status review meeting | ◆ Report high-level program progress and status<br>◆ Escalate risks and issues<br>◆ Resolve escalated issues and risks<br>◆ Approve change requests<br>◆ Provide feedback regarding progress | |
| Seller internal program meeting | | |
| Seller project status review meeting | | |
| Project-level meeting | ◆ Report project progress and status<br>◆ Escalate risks and issues<br>◆ Submit change requests | Once a week |

## Table 5.5. Sample Communication Matrix (continued)

| Participants | Time | Facilitator | Information Taker | Material Consolidator |
|---|---|---|---|---|
| ◆ Customer CEO<br>◆ Seller CEO | 30 min | Program lead | | Seller |
| Steering committee members | 2 hr | PMO director | Customer's PMO | Seller's program manager + customer's program manager + PMO |
| Program management members (both seller and customer) | 2 hr | PMO | | |
| Individual project organization | As needed | Individual project manager | Project members | Meeting initiator |

### To define area reports and the views for each reporting level:

1. Define the reporting requirements that are needed from each area (for example, risk reporting) for each reporting level or forum and incorporate them in each area plan.

2. Document the reports and views in the communication management plan (add them to the Microsoft Word document).

### To define the escalation procedure:

1. Define the escalation procedure for each forum. The procedure must state, for example, what type of risks will be handled at the project management forum and what will be escalated to the steering committee level.

2. Document the escalation procedure in the communication management plan (add it to the Microsoft Word document).

### To upload the communication management plan to the project workspace:

When the communication management plan document is ready, upload it to the project workspace in the communication management plan folder in the project management plan document library. For the procedure, see Appendix A.6 on uploading a document to a document library.

### To prepare the project glossary:

Prepare the project glossary documents (for example, "A to E", "F to K", etc.) and upload them to the glossary document library in the documents folder. For the procedure, see Appendix A.6 on uploading a document to a document library.

## Prerequisites

The prerequisites for this task are:

◆ The communication matrix, using the data in Table 5.6

◆ The glossary document library

## Table 5.6. Building the Communication Matrix

| Field Name | Description | Field Type |
|---|---|---|
| Meeting Forum | Predefined forums for the meetings | Single line of text |
| Objective | The meeting objectives and the level of the items discussed in the meeting | Multiple lines of text |
| Frequency | Frequency with which the forum is held | Single line of text |
| Participants | The forum members | Lookup table—Stakeholders Matrix (allows multiple values) |
| Time | Length of the meeting | Single line of text |
| Facilitator | Facilitator of the meeting | Person or group |
| Information Taker | The person responsible for the minutes of the meeting and capturing the meeting items | Person or group |
| Material Consolidator | The person responsible for consolidating the material for the forum | Person or group |

## To create the communication matrix:

1. In the project workspace, from the **Site Actions** menu, select **Create**:

2. In the **Custom Lists** section, select **Custom List in Datasheet View**:

The **New** page opens:

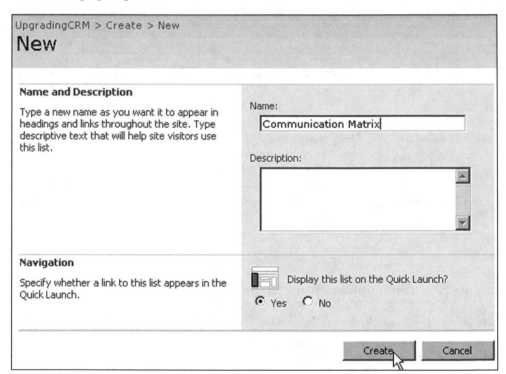

3. In the **Name** field, type "Communication Matrix".

4. In the **Description** field, type a short description of the communication matrix.

5. Click **Create**. The **Communication Matrix** page opens:

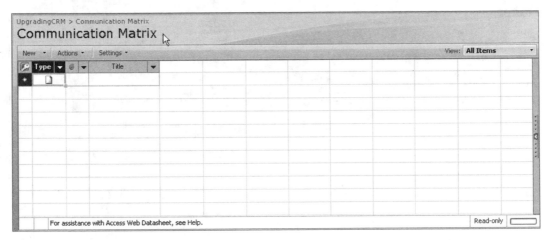

a. To change the **Title** column name, right-click on the name.

b. From the menu that pops up, select **Edit/Delete Column...**:

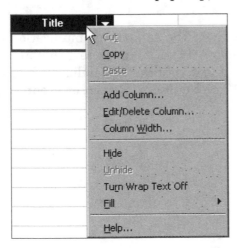

The **Change Column: Communication Matrix** page opens:

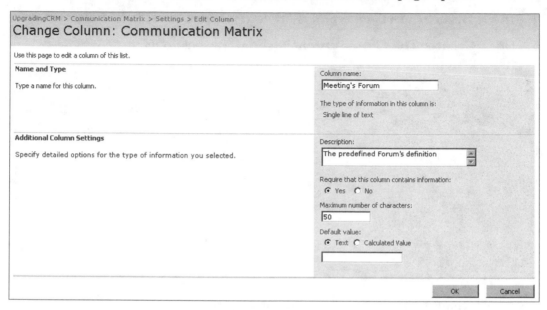

c.   Change the column's parameters according to the sample communication matrix above and click **OK**.

6.   Add all the required columns according to the sample communication matrix above. For the procedure, see Appendix A.11 on adding a text column, Appendix A.12 on adding a multiple lines of text column, Appendix A.13 on adding a lookup column, and Appendix A.17 on adding a "person or group" column.

The completed communication matrix should look as follows:

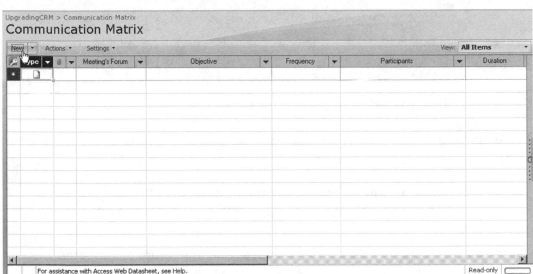

## To create the glossary document library:

For the procedure, see Appendix A.3 on creating a document library.

# Defining the Deliverable Management Plan

## Objectives

The deliverable management plan ensures that the deliverables of the program are:

◆ Identified

◆ Created, filed, changed, tracked, and archived in a consistent and transparent manner

◆ Delivered to the right party on the customer side

◆ Compliant with the quality standards set for the program/project

◆ Compliant with the company's quality control standards/processes

◆ Traceable, which means that any changes to deliverables within the scope of the program, and the impact of those changes on related deliverables, are tracked

◆ Easily retrieved by stakeholders

There are three types of deliverables, and each must be clearly identifiable in the plan:

◆ **Management deliverables**—Produced as part of the management and control of the project or program (for example, project management plan)

◆ **Specialist deliverables**—Products that make up, or are used in, the delivery of the final deliverable (for example, detailed design)

◆ **Quality deliverables**—Produced for or by the quality process (for example, the quality gates)

Figure 5.9 depicts the workflow of the deliverable management plan definition.

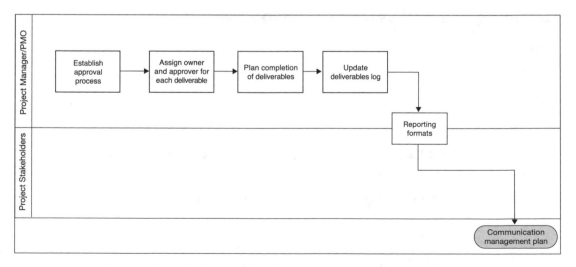

**Figure 5.9. Deliverable Management Plan Workflow**

## Procedures

### To define program/project deliverables:

The program/project deliverables were added to the project plan while building the project schedule (time management in this chapter).

In the project plan, identify the deliverables as deliverables. In the project workspace under **Lists**, select **Deliverables**:

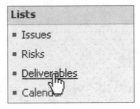

The **Deliverables** page opens:

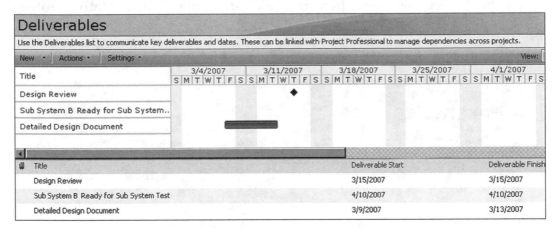

The deliverables that were identified in the project plan are displayed. You can add more deliverables by selecting **New > New Item**. The **Deliverable: New Item** page will open. Fill in the relevant data for the deliverable.

## To define the documentation deliverable management procedure:

1. Define the deliverables that must be produced within the program/project scope.

2. Define the deliverable owners, reviewers, and approvers; plans to deliver; and the approval process.

3. Document this procedure in the deliverables management plan and upload it to the project workspace under the project management plan document library.

## To update the deliverables log:

After the deliverables are identified, allocated, and their delivery dates are set, fill in the deliverables log.

1. In the project workspace, from the quick start menu, select **Deliverables**.

2. Enter the above deliverables in the deliverables list.

3. In the project workspace, select **Deliverables**. The **Deliverables** page opens:

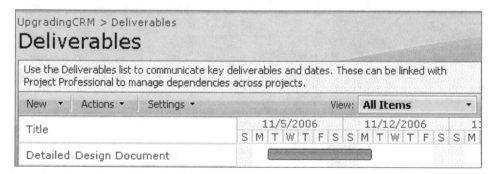

4. Select **New**. The **Deliverables: New Item** page opens:

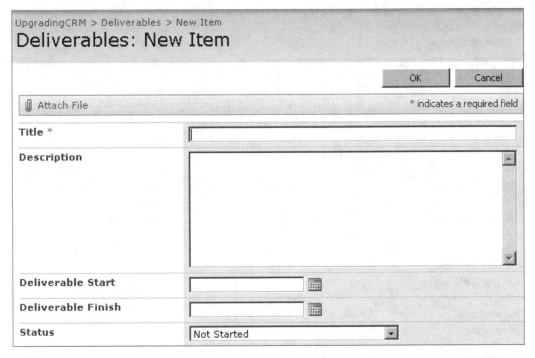

5. On the **Deliverables: New Item** page, fill in the details for the deliverable according to the information in Table 5.7.

6. Click **OK**.

7. Repeat steps 3 to 6 for all the deliverables identified.

## Table 5.7. Deliverables Information

| Field Name | Description |
| --- | --- |
| Title | Name of the deliverable |
| Description | A brief description of the document |
| Deliverable Start | Date the work on the deliverable starts |
| Delivery Due Date | Planned due dates according to the work plan |

## Table 5.7. Deliverables Information (continued)

| Field Name | Description |
| --- | --- |
| Type | Spec, report, etc. |
| Status | Status of the delivered document |
| Project | Project responsible for the deliverable (if there are several projects within a program) |
| Deliverable Owner | Name of the person responsible for producing the deliverable |
| Deliverable Source (Party) | Party responsible for the deliverable (company, client, or third party) |
| People Working on the Deliverable | Names of those involved in the deliverable, along with their roles |
| Deliverable Reviewers | Names of those who review the deliverable, along with their roles |
| Deliverable Approvers | Names of those who approve the deliverable, along with their roles |
| Milestone Dependency | Key milestones whose completion depends on the deliverable |
| Location | Reference to the deliverable file location |
| Distribution List | List of those persons the deliverable will be issued to and its amendments forwarded to as a matter of course; these are the holders of official copies |
| Cross-reference to the Change Requests Log | Changes that impact the deliverable, and the status of incorporating those changes into the deliverable |
| Cross-reference to the Issues Log | Issues that impact the deliverable, and the status of incorporating those issues into the deliverable |

## Prerequisite

A prerequisite to this task is the creation of the deliverables list. Table 5.8 is a sample deliverables list.

**Table 5.8. Sample Deliverables List**

| Field Name | Description | Field Type |
|---|---|---|
| Title | Name of the deliverable | Single line of text |
| Description | A brief description of the document | Multiple lines of text |
| Deliverable Start | Date the work on the deliverable starts | Date/time field |
| Delivery Due Date | Planned due dates according to the work plan | Date |
| Type | Spec, report, etc. | Choice (value list) |
| Status | Status of the delivered document | Choice (value list): <br>◆ Not Started <br>◆ Started <br>◆ In Editing <br>◆ Draft for Circulation—First Iteration <br>◆ Draft for Circulation—Second Iteration <br>◆ Approved <br>◆ Baseline <br>◆ Delivered |
| Project | Project responsible for the deliverable (if there are several projects within a program) | Single line of text |
| Deliverable Owner | Name of the person responsible for producing the deliverable | Lookup to the "Stakeholder Name (linked item)" field in the stakeholders matrix (allow multiple values) |

**Table 5.8. Sample Deliverables List (continued)**

| Field Name | Description | Field Type |
|---|---|---|
| Deliverable Source (Party) | The party responsible for the deliverable (company, client, or third party) | Choice (value list) |
| People Working on the Deliverable | Names of those involved in the deliverable, along with their roles | Lookup to the "Stakeholder Name (linked to item)" field in the stakeholders matrix |
| Deliverable Reviewers | Names of those who review the deliverable, along with their roles | Lookup to the "Stakeholder Name (linked to item)" field in the stakeholders matrix |
| Deliverable Approvers | Names of those who approve the deliverable, along with their roles | Lookup to the "Stakeholder Name (linked to item)" field in the stakeholders matrix |
| Milestone Dependency | Key milestones whose completion depends on the deliverable | Link to the milestone activities in Project Professional |
| Location | Reference to the deliverable file location | Link to the file stored on the server |
| Distribution List | List of those persons the deliverable will be issued to and its amendments forwarded to as a matter of course; these are the holders of official copies | Lookup to the "Stakeholder Name (linked to item)" field in the stakeholders matrix (allow multiple values) |
| Cross-reference to the Change Requests Log | Changes that impact the deliverable, and the status of incorporating those changes into the deliverable | Link to the requirements matrix stored on the server |
| Cross-reference to the Issues Log | Issues that impact the deliverable, and the status of incorporating those issues into the deliverable | Link to the issues log on the server |

## To create the deliverables list:

1. In the project workspace, update the deliverables list to include the fields that appear in the sample deliverables list in Table 5.8. The deliverables list is in the project workspace on the left pane under **Lists**:

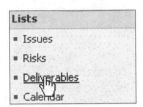

2. Add the required columns to the list. For the procedure, see Appendix A.9 on adding a choice column to a list, Appendix A.11 on adding a text column, Appendix A.12 on adding a multiple lines of text column, Appendix A.13 on adding a lookup column, Appendix A.17 on adding a "person or group" column, and Appendix A.18 on adding a date column.

# Defining the Procurement Management Plan

## Objectives

The procurement management plan describes the procurement process for the project:

◆ Make or buy decisions—which items will be outsourced and which will be produced in-house

◆ Possible suppliers

◆ Time frames

◆ Methods of supplier monitoring (types of reports, etc.)

The procurement management plan can include:

◆ The type of contracts to be used (for example, fixed cost, time and materials, etc.)

◆ Supplier evaluation criteria

- ◆ Supplier quality assurance demands

- ◆ Supplier reporting procedures

- ◆ Procurement monitoring and control procedures

- ◆ Training issues

- ◆ Infrastructure required to install suppliers' products

- ◆ Terms and conditions for suppliers

## Procedures

### To create the procurement management plan:

Create the procurement management plan and upload it to the project management plan document library. For the procedure, see Appendix A.6 on uploading a document to a document library.

### To fill out the supplier evaluation criteria list:

Define the areas of supplier evaluation and the weighting (level of importance) for each area that best suits your business requirements.

1. On the project home page under **Lists**, select **Supplier Evaluation**:

2. On the following screen, select **New > New Item**:

3. On the **Supplier Evaluation: New Item** screen, fill in the **Subject** and the **Weight**:

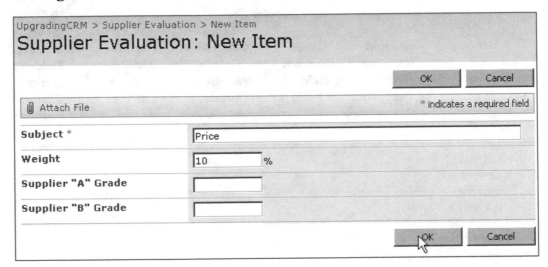

4. Repeat steps 2 to 3 for all the relevant subjects to evaluate your suppliers. Include the resulting table in the procurement management plan document.

## Prerequisites

### To create the procurement management plan folder:

Create the procurement management plan folder under the project management plan document library. For the procedure, see Appendix A.3 on creating a document library.

### To build the supplier evaluation table:

1. Define the evaluation criteria in a datasheet. For the procedure, see Appendix A.7 on creating a new list.

2. Place the list in the procurement management plan folder, under the project management plan document library.

Table 5.9 is a sample supplier evaluation table.

### Table 5.9. Sample Supplier Evaluation Table

| Text Field | Weight (Number Field = Percent) | Suppler "A" | | Suppler "B" | |
| --- | --- | --- | --- | --- | --- |
| | | Grade (Number Field = 1–10) | Score (Calculated Field = Weight × Grade) | Grade (Number Field = 1–10) | Score (Calculated Field = Weight × Grade) |
| Management | | | | | |
| Project Management | | | | | |
| Quality System | | | | | |
| Competency to Requirement "A" | | | | | |
| Competency to Requirement "B" | | | | | |
| … | | | | | |
| … | | | | | |
| Total | | | | | |

# Setting the Baseline

## Objective

◆ To set the baseline for the project plans and costs, so that planned vs. actual can be tracked

## Definition

**Baseline**\*—The approved time-phased plan (for a project, a work breakdown structure component, a work package, or a schedule activity), plus or minus approved project scope, cost, schedule, and technical changes. It generally refers to the current baseline, but may refer to the original or some other baseline. It is usually used with a modifier (e.g., cost baseline, schedule baseline, performance measurement baseline, technical baseline).

## Procedure

Once all the activities and all the costs associated with the program/project are in the project plan, and after the steering committee has approved the project management plan, the baseline must be set.

---

\* Project Management Institute *A Guide to the Project Management Body of Knowledge (PMBOK® Guide)—Third Edition,* Project Management Institute, Inc., 2004. Copyright and all rights reserved. Material from this publication has been reproduced with the permission of PMI.

## To set the baseline:

1. In Microsoft Project, from the **Tools** menu, select **Tracking > Set Baseline...**:

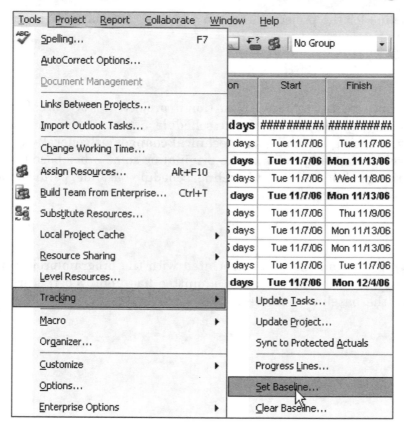

This action sets the baseline for the timeline, resource assignments, budget, and costs.

2. From this point on, you can track planned parameters vs. actual parameters.

## Prerequisites

This task is built into the application. No adaptations or configurations are needed. There are no prerequisites for it.

# Execution Process

The execution process follows the planning process. Most of the project/program work is performed in the execution process; therefore, this process usually uses the most resources in the project life cycle.

The execution process consists of the procedures to complete the work defined in the planning process. During this process, the deliverables are produced and delivered to the customers.

The process starts with the project execution kickoff meeting, which is used to describe the project to all of the team members.

## Overview

In this process, the execution of the project management plan leads to the production of the program/project deliverables and their delivery to the client for sign-off.

This phase also requires meeting stakeholders' expectations.

The main outputs of the execution process are:

◆ Deliverables as defined in the program/project scope statement

◆ Implemented change requests

◆ Reports

## Workflow

To provide a solution that meets the requirements that are defined for the execution process, the features/functions listed in Table 6.1 must be implemented.

**Table 6.1. Execution Feature/Function Processes**

| Requirement | Solution Feature/ Function Guidelines | Relevant Procedure |
|---|---|---|
| **Integration Management** | | |
| Hold the project execution kickoff meeting | ◆ Use Microsoft Word to create the minutes of meeting document<br>◆ Use Windows SharePoint Services to open the meeting workspace (optional) | "To conduct the project execution kickoff meeting" |
| **Scope Management** | | |
| Manage change requests | Use the Windows SharePoint Services list to manage the change requests log | "To manage change requests" |
| Report change request status | Use the Windows SharePoint Services list to manage the change requests log | "To report change request status" |

## Table 6.1. Execution Feature/Function Processes (continued)

| Requirement | Solution Feature/ Function Guidelines | Relevant Procedure |
|---|---|---|
| Create, manage, and deliver the program/ project document deliverables | Use the Windows SharePoint Services list to manage deliverables | "To execute the document deliverables management plan" |
| Create, manage, and deliver the program/ project deliverables | Use the Windows SharePoint Services list to manage deliverables | "To create the program/ project deliverables (not documentation)" |

**Time Management**

| | | |
|---|---|---|
| View and manage assignments that were supposed to be completed in the previous reporting period | Use Windows SharePoint Services to report task status | "To view and manage assignments" |
| Approve/disapprove reported tasks | Use Windows SharePoint Services to approve/disapprove tasks | "To approve/disapprove reported tasks" |
| Define the method of progress reporting for the project | Use Project Professional to define the method of progress reporting | "To define the method of progress reporting" |
| Review impact on the project schedule | Use Project Professional to review the impact | "To review impact on the project schedule" |
| Report schedule progress | Use Project Professional to report progress | "To report schedule progress" |

**Cost Management**

| | | |
|---|---|---|
| Collect the project costs and expenses | Use Project Professional to collect all costs and expenses | "To collect project costs and expenses" |

## Table 6.1. Execution Feature/Function Processes (continued)

| Requirement | Solution Feature/ Function Guidelines | Relevant Procedure |
|---|---|---|
| **Quality Management** | | |
| Perform quality audits and report quality progress | Use the Windows SharePoint Services document list to document quality reports | "To perform quality audits and report quality progress" |
| **Human Resource Management** | | |
| Perform orientation and coaching for new team members | Use the Windows SharePoint Services document list to store the orientation kit | "To orient and coach new team members" |
| Communicate new and/or changed assignments | | "To communicate new and/or changed assignments" |
| Develop the project team | | "To develop the project team" |
| Manage human resources | Use Windows SharePoint Services to save all roles and responsibilities documents | "To manage human resources" |
| Perform team-building activities | | "To build the project team" |
| **Communication Management** | | |
| Manage the communication management plan and distribute information | Use the Windows SharePoint Services announcements feature to add announcements | "To add announcements to the project home page" |
| Manage the project event calendar | Use the Windows SharePoint Services calendar to manage the project activities | "To manage the project calendar of events" |

### Table 6.1. Execution Feature/Function Processes (continued)

| Requirement | Solution Feature/ Function Guidelines | Relevant Procedure |
|---|---|---|
| Manage action items | Use the Windows SharePoint Services lists to manage action items | ◆ "To log action items" <br> ◆ "To report action item status" |
| **Risk Management** | | |
| Log new risks | Use the Windows SharePoint Services risks list to log new risks | "To log a new risk" |
| Assess risks | Use the Windows SharePoint Services risks list to assess risks | "To assess risks" |
| Manage risks | Use the Windows SharePoint Services risks list to manage risks | "To manage risks" |
| Manage the risk mitigation plans | Use the Windows SharePoint Services risks list to manage risks | "To manage mitigation plans" |
| Escalate risks | Use the Windows SharePoint Services risks list to escalate risks | "To escalate risks" |
| Report risk status | Use the Windows SharePoint Services risks list to report risks | "To report risk status" |
| **Issues Management** | | |
| Upgrade risks to issues | Use the Windows SharePoint Services issues list to manage issues | "To upgrade a risk to an issue" |
| Open new issues | Use the Windows SharePoint Services issues list to view the issues log | "To open a new issue" |
| View the issues log | Use the Windows SharePoint Services issues list to manage issues | "To view the issues log" |

**Table 6.1. Execution Feature/Function Processes (continued)**

| Requirement | Solution Feature/ Function Guidelines | Relevant Procedure |
|---|---|---|
| **Procurement Management** | | |
| Receive sellers' responses | Use the Windows SharePoint Services document library to save responses | "To receive suppliers' responses" |
| Select sellers | Use the Windows SharePoint Services lists to log the evaluation criteria | "To select sellers using the supplier evaluation table" |
| Issue purchase orders | Use the Windows SharePoint Services document library to save purchase orders | "To issue a purchase order" |
| Manage sellers | Use the Windows SharePoint Services document library to save the supplier progress reports | "To manage suppliers" |

# Directing and Managing Project Execution

The project manager directs and manages execution of the project, to develop the product or service that the project was commissioned to deliver, according to the scope statement (including approved change requests).

This process uses all of the plans, schedules, procedures, and templates that were prepared, agreed to, and baselined in the course of the planning process.

The project manager, team leads, and team members are responsible for:

- ◆ Handling unpredicted events
- ◆ Reporting progress on the schedule
- ◆ Reporting costs
- ◆ Managing and tracking risks

◆ Developing the project team

◆ Delivering information to the project stakeholders

◆ Keeping records and reports to be used for lessons learned and project closure

## Definitions

◆ **Design review\* (technique)**—A management technique used for evaluating a proposed design to ensure that the design of the system or product meets the customer requirements or to assure that the design will perform successfully, can be produced, and can be maintained.

◆ **Document inspection**—Each document is thoroughly inspected by one or more reviewers, who then convey their comments to the author.

◆ **Code inspection**—Every program module's source code is carefully inspected by a team leader or a senior programmer, prior to the start of unit testing.

◆ **Document approval**—Every document is approved by the author's supervisor; some documents require the approval of additional managers. The people who approve a document should either review it themselves or delegate the review to a competent person.

## Integration Management: Kickoff Meeting

### Objectives

The project execution kickoff meeting is the start of the execution phase. It serves to orient the project team members and to familiarize them with the project terminology and with the procedures that were defined in the project management plan. It is important that the project stakeholders are familiar with the procedures defined and know exactly what is expected of them.

---

\* Project Management Institute *A Guide to the Project Management Body of Knowledge (PMBOK® Guide)—Third Edition,* Project Management Institute, Inc., 2004. Copyright and all rights reserved. Material from this publication has been reproduced with the permission of PMI.

## Procedure

**To conduct the project execution kickoff meeting:**

1. Publish the agenda a week prior to the meeting. There is a sample agenda in the execution meetings folder of the meeting minutes document library:

2. Conduct the meeting.

3. As soon as the meeting is over, publish the minutes. There is a template for minutes of meetings in the meeting minutes document library.

4. Upload the minutes to the execution meetings folder.

5. Send the link to the minutes to the relevant stakeholders.

---

 You can also manage meetings by creating a meeting workspace. For the procedure to create a workspace, see the "Communication Management" section of this chapter.

---

## Prerequisites

There are two prerequisites for the above procedure: creating a document library, agenda template, and the minutes of meeting template and giving stakeholders permission to access the project home page.

**To create the execution meetings document library:**

1. In the meeting minutes document library, create a new folder for execution meetings:

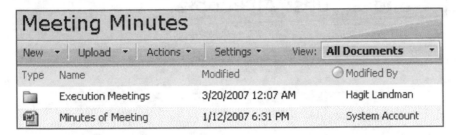

For the procedure to create a new folder in an existing document library, see Appendix A.23.

2. Create a template for the agenda for the kickoff meeting and upload it to the execution meetings folder.

3. Create a template for minutes of meeting and upload it to the execution meetings folder.

**To set up access rights to the project web site for team members:**

Ensure that all project stakeholders, including team members as appropriate, have access to the project home page.

1. In the project workspace, select **People and Groups** from the left pane:

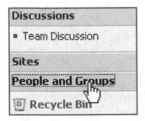

On the **People and Groups: All People** page, you can see who has access to the project workspace.

2. If you need to add a person or a group, on the **People and Groups: All People** page, select **New**:

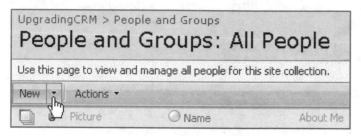

The **Add Users** page opens:

UpgradingCRM > Site Settings > Permissions > Add Users

## Add Users: UpgradingCRM

Use this page to give new permissions.

**Add Users**

You can enter user names, group names, or e-mail addresses. Separate them with semicolons.

Add all authenticated users

Users/Groups:

**Give Permission**

Choose the permissions you want these users to have. You can add users to a SharePoint group (which is already assigned to a permission level), or you can add users individually and assign them to a specific permission level.

SharePoint groups are recommended as they allow for ease of permission management across multiple sites.

Give Permission

○ Add users to a SharePoint group

(none) ▾

● Give users permission directly

☐ Full Control - Has full control.

☐ Design - Can view, add, update, delete, approve, and customize.

☐ Contribute - Can view, add, update, and delete.

☐ Read - Can view only.

☐ Web Administrators (Microsoft Office Project Server) - Users who have Manage Windows SharePoint Services permission in Microsoft Office Project Server.

☐ Project Managers (Microsoft Office Project Server) - Users who have published this project or who have Save Project permission in Microsoft Office Project Server.

☐ Team members (Microsoft Office Project Server) - Users who have assignments in this project in Microsoft Office Project Server.

3. Fill in the name of the person or group to be added and check the permission you want to grant them.

4. Click **OK**.

## Scope Management

### Managing Change Requests

Normally, change requests are initiated by the client, who describes a problem or proposes a change or enhancement.

Change requests are made and approved according to the procedure defined in the project management plan. They should be logged as soon as possible after initiation.

### *Definition*

**Change request control board**—A group of people, usually customer's and seller's representatives, who are responsible for approving/disapproving change requests.

### *Objective*

◆ To manage changes to the project scope and project schedule

### *Procedures*

### To manage change requests:

1. Open Project Web Access.

2. Select the project workspace.

3. In the **Lists** section of the quick launch menu, select **Requirements Matrix**:

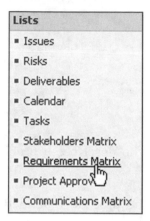

4. Select the **Change Requests Log** view:

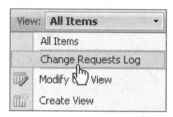

The **Change Requests Log** opens:

## Requirements Matrix

New ▾ | Actions ▾ | Settings ▾

| CR ID | Title | Description | Current Status | Current Status Date | Requirement Origin |
|-------|-------|-------------|----------------|---------------------|--------------------|
| CR1 | Add Type A Functionality | A functionality | Pending | 3/8/2007 | RFP; Change Request |
| CR2 | Add multi users functionality | Add multi users | Approved | 3/8/2007 | Change Request |

5. For each new change request:
   a. From the **New** drop-down list, select **New Item**:

   The **Requirements Matrix: New Item** page opens.
   b. Enter all known relevant data:

UpgradingCRM > Requirements Matrix > New Item

## Requirements Matrix: New Item

|  | OK | Cancel |

📎 Attach File                                    * indicates a required field

| **Title *** | |
| **Description** | A A̅ \| B I U̲ \| ☰ ☰ ☰ \| ☰ ☰ ⊞ ⊞ \| A ◈ ▸¶ ¶◂ |
| | |
| **Requirements Type** | ☑ Technical |
| | ☐ Management |
| | ☐ Finance |
| | ☐ QA |
| | Type the requirements |
| **Relevant Stakeholder** | Aaron Graves / Hagit Landman     [Add >]  [< Remove] |
| | Point of contact to provide responses |
| **Requirement Origin** | ☐ RFP |
| | ☐ RFI |
| | ☐ SOW |
| | ☑ Change Request |

6. Click **OK**. Each change request is subject to an impact assessment, in which its cost and benefits are evaluated.

7. As the request progresses through the various stages of evaluation, update its status.

   Following approval of the change request by the change request control board (or other approver as defined in the project management plan), the work is planned, scheduled, and carried out.

8. When the work has been completed, change the change request status to **Closed**:

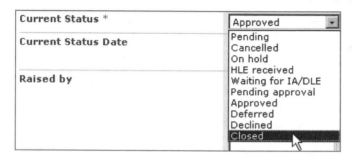

9. Continue maintaining and updating the status of all of the change requests in the change requests log view of the requirements matrix.

### To report change request status:

1. In the requirements matrix, select the **Change Requests Report** view:

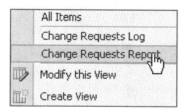

2. The report log opens:

3. To analyze the report, from the **Actions** drop-down list, select **Export to Spreadsheet**:

4. Perform the analysis you want in Excel.

5. Distribute the report to the relevant stakeholders.

### *Prerequisite*

A prerequisite for the above procedures is creation of the change requests report view.

## To create the change requests report view:

1. Open Project Web Access (development environment).

2. Select the project workspace.

3. In the **Lists** section of the quick launch menu, select **Requirements Matrix**.

4. Create a view for the change requests report. Select appropriate fields. Follow the definition of the report as described in the project management plan. For example, the following fields would appear in the view:
   ◆ **Requirement Type**
   ◆ **Relevant Stakeholder**
   ◆ **Responsible Department**
   ◆ **Requirement Compliance**
   ◆ **Current Status**
   ◆ **Change Request Owner**
   ◆ **Priority**
   ◆ **Target Date**
   ◆ **Version**

   For the procedure to create a list view, see Appendix A.21.

5. Select the fields you want to use to sort change requests. For example, select **Priority**, then **Current Status**.

6. Filter the report to include only those requirements that come from change requests:

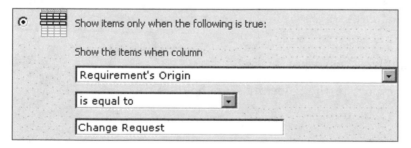

7. To select one or more fields as the source of totals in the report view, from the **Totals** drop-down list next to each field select the type of total to be used. The following example includes the number of change requests for each status and the number of change requests of each priority value:

| Totals | Column Name | Total |
|---|---|---|
| Select one or more totals to display. | CR Owner | None ▾ |
| | Current Status | Count ▾ |
| | Priority | Count ▾ |
| | Requirement Compliance | None ▾ |
| | Target Date (Average supported in datasheet view only) | None ▾ |
| | Version | None ▾ |

8. Click **Save**.

## Managing Deliverables

The main goal of this sub-process is to create, manage, and deliver program/ project deliverables.

In the planning process, the steering committee defined the deliverables and the deliverable acceptance process. The project manager ensures that the program/ project deliverables are produced only as defined in the project scope.

Any deviation from the original scope is handled as a change request. All accepted change requests become part of the project scope and are delivered with the project deliverables.

### *Objectives*

◆ To ensure that the deliverables are produced, managed, and tracked

◆ To ensure that document deliverables are:
   ◇ Defined and produced within the program scope
   ◇ Identified, created, filed, changed, and archived in a consistent and transparent manner
   ◇ Delivered to the right party on the customer side
   ◇ Compliant with the quality standards/processes
   ◇ Clearly identified with the software or product versions in use
   ◇ Traceable, such that any changes to deliverables within the scope of the program, and the impact of those changes on related deliverables, are tracked
   ◇ Easily retrieved by stakeholders

◆ To maintain up-to-date records that contain relevant pieces of information

◆ To control changes to the deliverables by ensuring that changes are approved

◆ To audit the records to ensure that they contain the authorized deliverables and only those deliverables

## Procedures

### To execute the document deliverables management plan:

1. Add a line to the deliverables list when:
   ◆ A new document is created
   ◆ A document is delivered to the client

2. When changes are made, update the document deliverable status in the deliverables list as follows:
   ◆ The draft document is submitted for review and the deliverable is forwarded to the PMO to start the review and approval process. Change status to **Started**.
   ◆ The deliverable is distributed to reviewers and approvers. The **Draft for Circulation** status is confirmed and the deliverable is circulated to reviewers for the first round of comments and feedback. Change status to **Draft for Circulation—First Iteration**.
   ◆ The deliverable is reviewed and comments are returned. The comments on the deliverable are forwarded to the PMO.
   ◆ All comments are collated, aggregated, filed, and forwarded to the owner. Change status to **In Editing**.
   ◆ The deliverable owner either arranges for the deliverable to be amended in line with the comments or responds to the comments.
   ◆ The deliverable is received by the PMO. Response to comments is confirmed, and the deliverable is circulated to reviewers for the second round of comments and feedback. Change status to **Draft for Circulation—Second Iteration**.
   ◆ Remaining comments from the second iteration are discussed directly with the reviewers/approvers, and the revisions are agreed upon.
   ◆ Final submission for sign-off.
   ◆ The approver signs off on the deliverable and returns it to the PMO. Change status to **Approved**.
   ◆ The deliverable is completed, filed as approved, and the team is notified of its status and location in the knowledge base. Change status to **Baseline**.

◆ The deliverable is delivered to the other party, and its receipt is acknowledged. Change status to **Delivered**.

3. Report significant deviations from the plan.

4. Track all documents that require client approval. If a document does not receive client approval, include reservations, objections, and review comments in the documentation plan.

5. Notify all the groups affected by the relevant changes.

## To create the program/project deliverables (not documentation):

1. Check the requirements matrix to see that all committed to and agreed upon deliverables are created. Manage the deliverables; verify that they are in accordance with the requirements, that they fit the agreed-upon standards, and so on.

2. Check regularly that only what was required is being delivered and no extras. Handle an extra or out-of-scope requirement as a change request.

3. Update the deliverable status table and the project schedule.

## Prerequisites

There are no prerequisites for these procedures (lists and logs were created in the planning process).

# Time Management: Project Schedule

Program time and schedule management includes the processes that ensure the timely completion of the program. The execution process ensures that the schedules are tracked and updated, tasks are assigned and monitored, schedules are reported, and issues are escalated when necessary.

## Objectives

◆ To ensure that both management and the team members know and understand the status of the program (management through integrated high-level plans and team members through detailed, team-level work plans)

◆ To ensure that the PMO checks the interdependencies between the project plans of the teams to verify that they are aligned

◆ To ensure that the client receives a report to verify that the program is on track

◆ To ensure that the project plans shows a flag to indicate critical risks and issues

## Workflow

Figure 6.1 depicts the execution process time management workflow.

## Procedures

### To view and manage assignments:

As soon as the project plan is published to the server by the project manager, each team member receives a message regarding his or her tasks. Each team member can see those tasks on the **Project Web Access** home page.

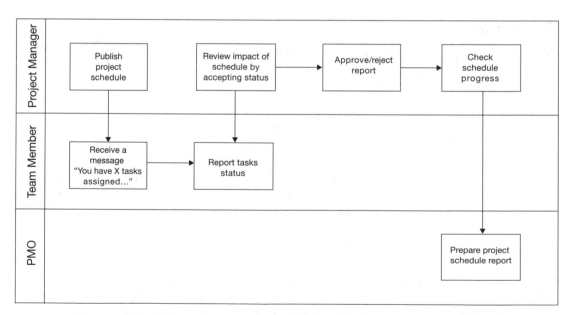

**Figure 6.1. Execution Process Time Management Workflow**

The following procedure is for team members to view and manage assignments that were supposed to be completed in the previous reporting period.

1. To see tasks, either select **My Tasks** from the **My Work** menu or under **Reminders > Tasks** click the **<#> new tasks** link:

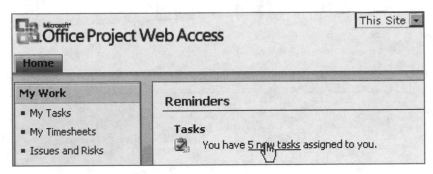

The tasks assigned are displayed:

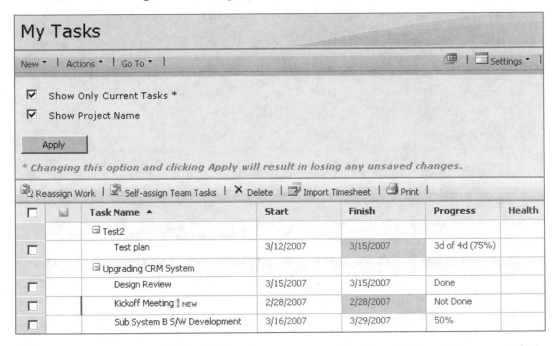

2. In the **Progress** field, define the progress of each activity. Dates past their **Finish** date will appear in pink. The reporting for each activity is according to its definition.

3   The progress for an activity is updated by updating the actual hours. To update the **Test plan** activity, for example, click the **Progress** field for that activity. The **Actual Hours** window opens:

◄ **3/26/2007 > 4/2/2007** ►

| | Mon 26 | Tue 27 | Wed 28 | Thu 29 | Fri 30 | Sat 31 | Sun 01 |
|---|---|---|---|---|---|---|---|
| Work | 0h | 0h | 0h | 0h | 0h | 0h | 0h |
| Actual Work | 0h | 0h | 0h | 0h | 0h | 0h | 0h |
| Overtime | 0h | 0h | 0h | 0h | 0h | 0h | 0h |

*...g this option and clicking Apply will result in losing any unsaved changes.*

| ...h Work | 🖉 Self-assign Team Tasks | ✖ Delete | 🖾 Import Timesheet | 🖨 Print |

| Task Name ▲ | Start | Finish | Progress | Health |
|---|---|---|---|---|
| ⊟ Test2 | | | | |
|    Test plan | 3/12/2007 | 3/15/2007 | 3d of 4d (75%) | |
| ⊟ Upgrading CRM System | | | | |

4.   Report the **Actual Work** (in hours) for the **Progress** field:

| | Mon 26 | Tue 27 | Wed 28 | Thu 29 | Fri 30 | Sat 31 | Sun 01 |
|---|---|---|---|---|---|---|---|
| Work | 8h | 8h | 0h | 0h | 0h | 0h | 0h |
| Actual Work | 8h | 8h | 0h | 0h | 0h | 0h | 0h |
| Overtime | 0h | 0h | 0h | 0h | 0h | 0h | 0h |

As soon as the hours are reported, the field is updated:

| ⊟ Test2 | | | |
|---|---|---|---|
|    Test plan | 3/12/2007 | 3/15/2007 | 5d of 5d (100%) |

Activities that have zero duration should be reported as **Done** or **Not Done**:

| ⊟ Upgrading CRM System | | | |
|---|---|---|---|
|    Design Review | 3/15/2007 | 3/15/2007 | Done |
|    Kickoff Meeting ! NEW | 2/28/2007 | 2/28/2007 | Not Done ▼ |
|    Sub System B S/W Development | 3/16/2007 | 3/29/2007 | Not Done / Done |

For activities that should be reported by percent of completion, the percent of completion must be entered:

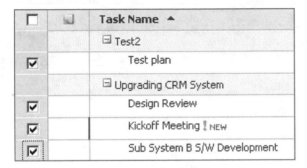

| ⊟ Upgrading CRM System | | | |
|---|---|---|---|
| Design Review | 3/15/2007 | 3/15/2007 | Done |
| Kickoff Meeting ! NEW | 2/28/2007 | 2/28/2007 | Not Done |
| Sub System B S/W Development | 3/16/2007 | 3/29/2007 | 60% |

Select tasks to submit to the team leader or the project manager to approve:

| ☐ | ✎ | **Task Name** ▲ |
|---|---|---|
| | | ⊟ Test2 |
| ☑ | | Test plan |
| | | ⊟ Upgrading CRM System |
| ☑ | | Design Review |
| ☑ | | Kickoff Meeting ! NEW |
| ☑ | | Sub System B S/W Development |

5.  Click **Submit Selected**:

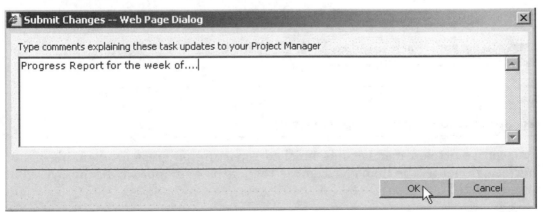

6.  Alternatively, click **Save All** (to save the updates but not submit them yet).

7.  Optionally, add comments to the report:

| 🔲 **Submit Changes -- Web Page Dialog** | ✕ |
|---|---|

Type comments explaining these task updates to your Project Manager

Progress Report for the week of....|

OK    Cancel

8. Click **OK**.

9. Optionally, reassign the task. On the **My Tasks** page, select:

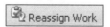

10. The **Task Reassignment** screen opens:

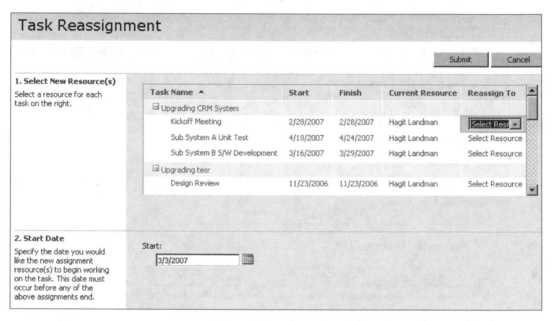

11. Select the resource to which you want to reassign the task.

12. Click **Submit**.

>  Each resource must be able to see his or her tasks and assignments and report progress.

## To approve/disapprove reported tasks:

As soon as a team member has finished reporting progress or changing his or her assignments, the manager can see the status and approve/disapprove what was reported.

On the **Project Web Access** home page, the following message notifies you of the updates: **You have X task update from resources pending your approval**:

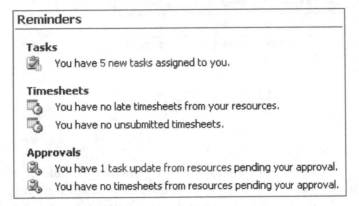

1. In the left pane on that page, go to **Approvals**. In the **Approvals** section, click **Task Updates**:

The **Task Updates** page opens:

| ⓘ | Name | Assigned To | Type | Sent | % Complete | Work |
|---|---|---|---|---|---|---|
| | ⊟ **Sub System B Development** | | **Task update** | **NA** | | **80h** |
| | Sub System B S/W Development | Hagit Landma | Task update | '26/2007 | 60% | 80h |

This page lists the tasks reported by a manager's employees. In example above, the **Sub System B S/W Development** activity, reported by an employee, appears in the **Name** column.

2. Select the relevant tasks and click **Preview** on the toolbar:

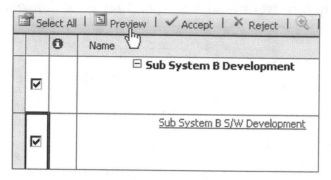

The **Approval Preview** page opens. You can see the effect of the reporting on the plan. You can see the previous duration and the updated one and the previous start/finish and the updated ones. This shows you what will happen if you approve what was reported.

3. On the right hand-side, select the view that will help you decide whether to accept or reject the updates (in the example below, **Project Tracking w. Indicators**):

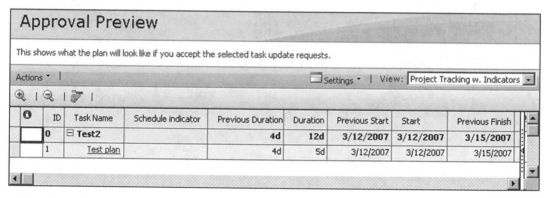

4. Select **Close** at the bottom of the page.

5. You will return to the **Task Updates** page.

6. On the toolbar, click **Accept** or **Reject** to approve or disapprove the task reporting:

The **Confirmation** dialog opens. Here you can add comments:

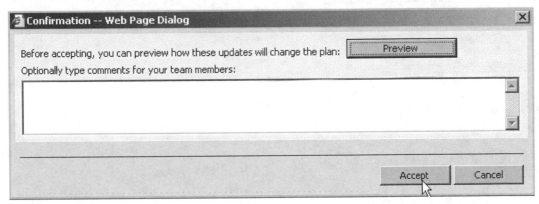

7. Optionally, click **Preview** to preview the plan or add comments.

8. Click **Accept**.

## To define the method of progress reporting:

Each resource must be able to see his or her tasks and assignments and report progress. The tasks must be updated in the project schedule.

The reports are produced according to the reporting method: percent complete, actual periodic hours (monthly, weekly, daily, etc.), or other.

You can change the way your resources report their actual work on the project.

 You can change the progress reporting method only if this action is enabled by the server administrator.

1. From the project center, open the project schedule.

2. In Project Professional, from the **Collaborate** menu, select **Collaboration Options...**:

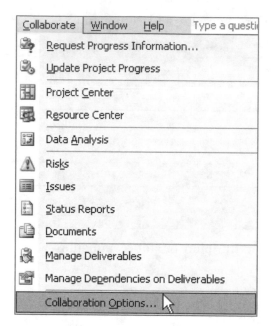

3. Select the **Collaborate** tab:

| View | General | Edit | Calendar |
|------|---------|------|----------|
| Save | Interface | Security | |
| Schedule | Calculation | Spelling | Collaborate |

Collaboration options for 'Upgrading the CRM Software'

Project Server URL: 'http://ps2007demo/DEV/'

Identification for Project Server: Windows user 'PS2007DEMO\hlandman'

Workspace URL: 'http://ps2007demo/DEV/UpgradingCRM'

☑ Allow resources to reassign tasks using Project Server

Method that resources should use to report progress on tasks:
   ○ Use the default method set on Project Server:
      This is currently set to 'Percent of Work Complete'

Always use a specific method of progress reporting for this project:
   ◉ Percent of Work Complete
   ○ Actual Work Done and Work Remaining
   ○ Hours of work done per period

4. Select the required method of progress reporting for the project.

5. Click **OK**.

## To review impact on the project schedule:

After all the reports are approved, you must check the overall status of the project schedule in Project Professional.

1. Open the project center.

2. Open the project in Project Professional.

3. From the **View** menu, select the tracking view for the project (in the example below, **Project Tracking Gantt**):

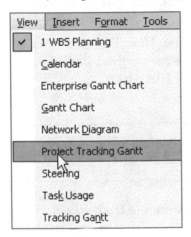

4. Analyze the Gantt chart displayed. Check if there is a difference in the activity reporting from the last report. Check the current status vs. baseline. You can see the difference by checking the predefined schedule indicators. In the following example, there is a schedule indicator that implies that the project is slightly behind compared to the baseline:

| | ⓘ | Task Name | Schedule indicator | Critical path candidate | Duration | Start | Finish | Total Slack | vember 11/5 \| 11/12 \| 11/19 \| 11/26 \| 12/3 | Decem |
|---|---|---|---|---|---|---|---|---|---|---|
| 3 | ✓ | High Level Design | ✓ | ✓ | 2 d | 11/7/06 | 11/8/06 | 0 d | ⬛ 100% | |
| 4 | | ⊟ **Detailed Design** | ☹ | ☺ | **11 d** | **11/9/06** | **11/23/06** | **51 d** | ▬▬▬▬ 94% | |
| 5 | ✓ | Sub System A Design | ✓ | ✓ | 3 d | 11/9/06 | 11/13/06 | 0 d | ▬ 100% | |
| 6 | | Sub System B Design | ☹ | ☺ | 6 d | 11/9/06 | 11/16/06 | 55.75 d | ▬ 90% | |
| 7 | 🗄 | Detailed Design | ☹ | ☺ | 5 d | 11/17/06 | 11/23/06 | 51 d | ▬ 95% | |
| 8 | ✓ | Design Review | ✓ | ✓ | 0 d | 11/23/06 | 11/23/06 | 0 d | ◆ 11/23 | |
| 9 | | ⊟ **Development** | ☹ | ⬤ | **28 d** | **11/23/06** | **1/2/07** | **0 d** | ▼ | |
| 10 | | ⊟ **Sub System A** | ☹ | ☺ | **28 d** | **11/23/06** | **1/2/07** | **23 d** | ▼ | |

In the above view, there are two bars for each activity:

◆ **Baseline** (bottom line)—Baseline Start to Baseline Finish (In these fields, you see the current baseline. If there was an original baseline, you can see it in **Baseline Start1** and **Baseline Finish1**.)

◆ **Current** (top line)—Start to Finish

---

**RECOMMENDATION**

Add another bar showing the previously reported schedule (**Start1** and **Finish1**).

---

5. Check for activities denoted by ◆. This icon means that an activity is not going to make the deadline set for it.

6. Analyze the critical path. You can use the critical path candidate indicators (as in the above example) to check the activities that are on the critical path or will be on the critical path. You can also check the total slack of the activities. Activities with total slack of zero or less than zero should be treated first, and then the activities that are candidates to be on the critical path should be checked.

7. Analyze the deliverables. Verify that the deliverables are delivered and accepted as was planned. If you anticipate the possibility of a change in a deliverable, report that possibility to the relevant stakeholder(s).

8. If required, consolidate project plans into one program.

9. As soon as the project plan is analyzed and the required changes are made, check if the changes made to the plan require approval from stakeholders. For example, a change to a deliverable due date must be agreed to by the relevant stakeholder.

10. If required, escalate changes.

11. Save the project schedule.

## To report schedule progress:

Save and publish the project plan in Project Professional.

## To prepare the project plan for the next reporting period:

As soon as the project plan is approved for the reported period, the reported project plan must be archived. The schedule is saved locally because the server does not save the history of the project plans. After saving, the resulting file is uploaded to the project home page, to a library defined for it.

1. Save the project plan as a file by clicking on **Save As...**:

The **Save to Project Server** dialog is displayed:

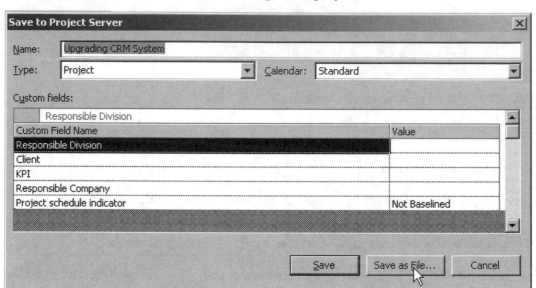

2. Click **Save as File...**.

3. Give the file the name of the project and the revision number or date, so that you will be able to locate the file in the future.

4. Copy the **Start/Finish** columns (current report) to **Start1/Finish1** (previous report) to enable comparison in the next report. To do so, as soon as the project is saved to a file, close the file and open the project from the project center. Once the project is opened, select **Tools > Tracking > Set Baseline...**:

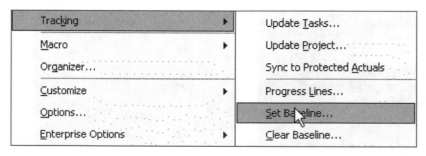

5.  In the **Set Baseline** dialog, select the **Set interim plan** option button. This copies the columns (unless a macro for copying columns was defined):

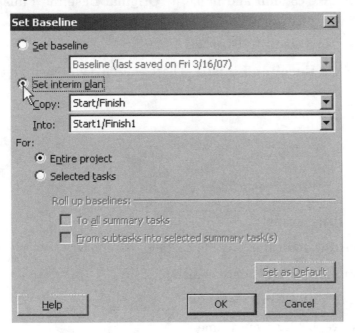

6.  Click **OK**.

## To save the new baseline:

Sometimes during the project life cycle, there is a need to change the baseline that was established in the planning phase. The need might arise for various reasons. For example, a supplier might surprise you and deliver the hardware a month early (in theory, of course), in which case the critical path is shorter and the system can go live earlier (the resources are available).

Of course, you need to check that your client is prepared to receive the system earlier and that management approves it.

As soon as the steering committee approves the baseline change (according to the project management plan), the schedule must be rebaselined.

1.  Add the **Baseline Start1** column and name it "Original Baseline Start".

2.  Add the **Baseline Finish1** column and name it "Original Baseline Finish". These columns will stay unchanged for the rest of the program/project.

3.  Copy the baseline start to **Baseline Start1**.

4.  Copy the baseline finish to **Baseline Finish1**. These columns will be updated for each new baseline.

5.  Save and publish the new plan.

## Prerequisites

Prerequisites for the above procedures include:

- ◆ Defining the reporting format

- ◆ Creating the schedule indicator enterprise field

- ◆ Creating the critical path candidate indicator

- ◆ Creating the schedule tracking view

- ◆ Defining the task reporting time frame

- ◆ Creating the "previous report" macro

- ◆ Creating the project schedules document library

### To define the reporting format:

1.  From the Project Web Access (development environment) quick launch menu, select **Server Settings**:

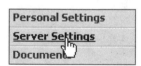

2.  On the page that opens, under **Time and Task Management**, select **Task Settings and Display**:

**Time and Task Management**

- Financial Periods
- Timesheet Periods
- Timesheet Classifications
- Timesheet Settings and Defaults
- Administrative Time
- Task Settings and Display
- Close Tasks to Update

3.  On the next page, select the method you want to use for the reports:
    ◆  **Percent of work complete**
    ◆  **Actual work done and work remaining**
    ◆  **Hours of work done per period**

## Task Settings and Display

**Tracking Method**

Specify the default method for reporting progress or tasks, and whether the tracking mode should be enforced on all projects.

⦿ **Percent of work complete.** Resources report the percent of work they have completed, from 0 through 100 percent.

○ **Actual work done and work remaining.** Resources report the actual work done and the work remaining to be done on each task.

○ **Hours of work done per period.** Resources report their hours worked on each task per period.

☐ Force project managers to use the progress reporting method specified above for all projects.

**Reporting Display**

Specify how you want resources to report their hours.

⦿ Resources should report their hours worked every day.

○ Resources should report their total hours worked for a week.

Week starts on: Monday ▼

4. Select the relevant settings and restrictions.

5. Click **Save**.

---

 If you click **Force project managers to use the progress reporting method specified above for all projects,** a project manager will not be able to decide how the reporting is done for his or her specific project.

---

### To create the schedule indicator enterprise field:

1. From Project Web Access (development environment), select **Server Settings**:

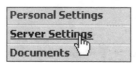

Personal Settings

**Server Settings**

Documents

2. In the **Enterprise Data** section, select **Enterprise Custom Field Definition**:

**Enterprise Data**

▫ Enterprise Custom Field Definition

▫ Enterprise Global

▫ Enterprise Calendars

▫ Resource Center

▫ About Project Server

3. On the toolbar, click **New Field**:

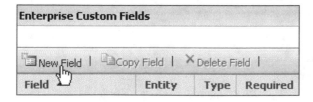

**Enterprise Custom Fields**

New Field  |  Copy Field  |  × Delete Field  |

| Field | Entity | Type | Required |
| --- | --- | --- | --- |

4. The following is an example of a formula for the **Schedule indicator**. Because the formula is in the task level, under **Entity** select **Task**. As we want the formula in this example to return a text value, in the **Type** field select **Text**. In the **Custom Attributes** section, check the **Formula** box and enter the formula:

| Name | | |
|---|---|---|
| Type a unique name for the custom field. | Name | |
| | Schedule indicator | |
| **Entity and Type** | Entity | |
| The entity and type for this custom field. | Task | ▾ |
| | Type | |
| | Text | ▾ |
| **Custom Attributes** | ○ None | |
| Choose whether the field has a lookup table, a calculated formula, or neither. | ○ Lookup Table | |
| | ● Formula | |

'Schedule indicator' =

```
Switch([Duration]>-1,IIf([% Complete]=100,"Complete",IIf
([Baseline Finish]=4294967295,"Not Baselined",IIf(([Finish]-
[Baseline Finish])>7,">1 week late",IIf(([Finish]-[Baseline
Finish])<=7 And ([Finish]-[Baseline Finish])>0,"0 to 1
weeks late","On schedule"))))),[Duration]<>0,"N/A")
```

| Insert Function: | Pick Function |
|---|---|
| Insert Operator: | Pick Operator |

Insert field names enclosed by brackets. For example, [Work].

If you want graphical indicators to appear, on the same page, in the **Values to Display** section, check the **Graphical indicators** box.

Select the **Image** for each graphical indicator.

◆ For non-summary rows:

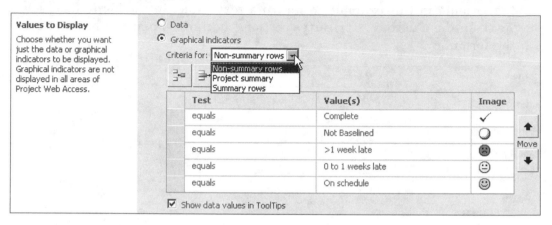

◆ For summary rows—On the same page (in the current example, **Schedule indicator**), under **Values to Display**, from the **Criteria for** drop-down list select **Summary rows** (and check the **Inherit criteria from non-summary rows** box to inherit the indicators):

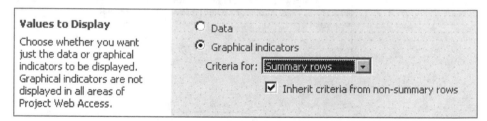

◆ For a project—On the same page (in the current example, **Schedule indicator**), under **Values to Display**, from the **Criteria for** drop-down list select **Project summary** (and check the **Inherit criteria from summary rows** box to inherit the indicators):

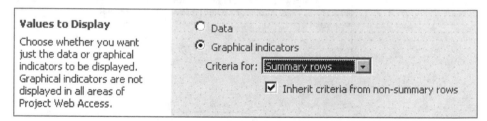

5. Click **Save**.

## To create the critical path candidate indicator:

1. From Project Web Access (development environment), select **Server Settings**.

2. In the **Enterprise Data** section, select **Enterprise Custom Field Definition**:

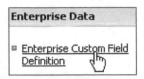

3. On the toolbar, click **New Field**.

4. On the **New Field** page, enter the required data:

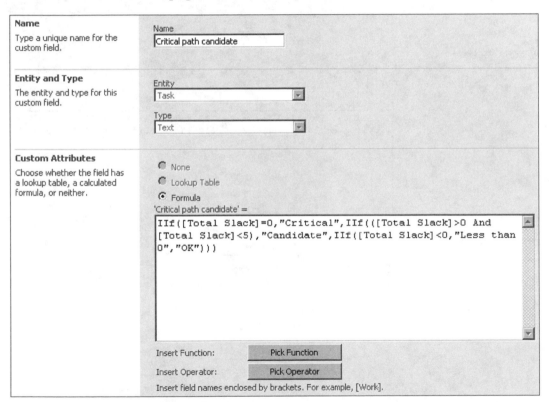

In the example above, a critical path candidate is defined as an activity with total slack less than 5 days. Defining critical path candidates depends on the length of a project. For example, if the duration of a typical project in your organization is usually a year or more, 5 days of slack is not enough to be a critical path candidate and you might use a month. On the other hand, if the typical project in your organization is around 6 months, you would probably use 2 weeks.

5. Create the graphical indicators:

6. Click **Save**.

## To create the schedule tracking view in Project Professional:

1. In Project Professional, from the **Tools** menu, select **Open Enterprise Global**:

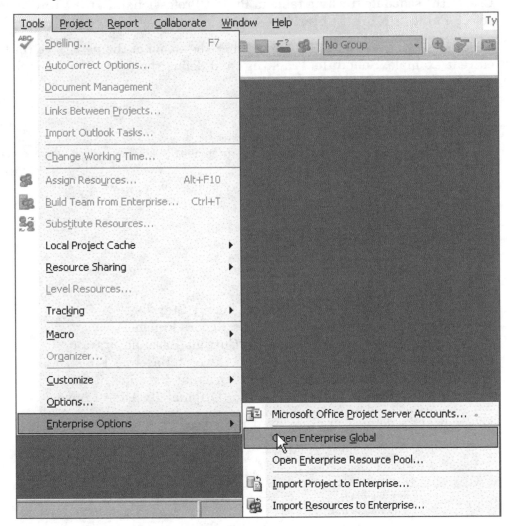

The **Enterprise Global** file opens.

2. In this file, define the views for tracking purposes (in the following example, **Tracking view**).

3. Create the schedule tracking table in Project Professional. In the **View** menu, select **Table > More Tables**.

4. On the following screen, select **New**. Enter the name of the new table (in the current example, **Schedule Tracking**) and define the fields. For example:
   - ◆ **ID**
   - ◆ **Indicators**
   - ◆ **Task Name**
   - ◆ **Schedule indicator** (from Enterprise)
   - ◆ **Critical path candidate** (from Enterprise)
   - ◆ **Duration**
   - ◆ **Start**
   - ◆ **Finish**
   - ◆ **% Complete**
   - ◆ **Physical % Complete**
   - ◆ **Work**
   - ◆ **Baseline Work**
   - ◆ **Actual Work**
   - ◆ **Start1** (change name to "Previous Report Start")
   - ◆ **Finish1** (change name to "Previous Report Finish")
   - ◆ **Baseline Start** (change name to "Current Baseline Start")
   - ◆ **Baseline Finish** (change name to "Current Baseline Finish")
   - ◆ **Baseline1 Start** (change name to "Original Baseline Start")
   - ◆ **Baseline1 Finish** (change name to "Original Baseline Finish")

The indicators defined are displayed in Project Professional:

| | ⓘ | Task Name | Schedule indicator | Critical path candidate | Duration | Start | Finish |
|---|---|---|---|---|---|---|---|
| 9 | | ⊟ **Development** | ☺ | ♥ | 28 days | Thu 11/23/06 | Tue 1/2/07 |
| 10 | | ⊟ **Sub System A** | ☺ | ☹ | 28 days | Thu 11/23/06 | Tue 1/2/07 |
| 11 | | ⊟ **Sub System A** | ☺ | ☹ | 23 days | Thu 11/23/06 | Tue 12/26/06 |
| 12 | | Sub System A | ☺ | ☹ | 0 days | Thu 11/23/06 | Thu 11/23/06 |
| 13 | | Sub System A | ☺ | ☹ | 20 days | Fri 11/24/06 | Thu 12/21/06 |

5. Create a view (in the following example, **Project Tracking Gantt**):

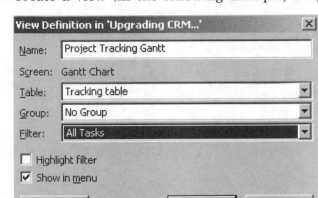

6. Select a filter to use in the view (in the example above, **All Tasks** are displayed).

7. Select the grouping to be used (in the example above, **No Group** is selected).

8. Click **OK** and save the file.

9. Close the file and close and reopen Project Professional in order to see the changes.

From now on, when you open a project from the server, you can select the view you have defined.

---

 Be sure to design the graphical indicators in such a way that even when the indicators do not appear in color (black-and-white printer, color-blind reader), the reader will be able to distinguish between them.

---

### To define the task reporting time frame:

Define the period of time for the activities to be reported. In the following example, the time frame is activities that were supposed to be finished within the last two weeks and activities to be finished in the next two weeks.

1. In Project Web Access (development environment), select **Server Settings**:

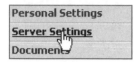

2. In the **Time and Task Management** section, select **Task Settings and Display**:

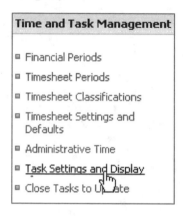

3. On the following page, select the time frame (in the example below, ±14 days):

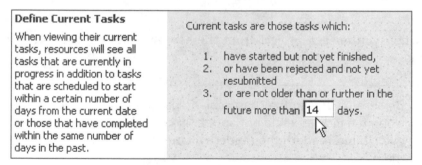

## To create the "previous report" macro:

1. In Project Professional, open **Enterprise Global**. From the **Tools** menu, select **Macro > Record New Macro...**:

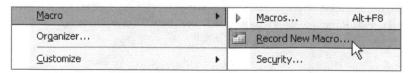

2. Enter the required data in the **Record Macro** dialog:

Perform the following actions:
- ◆ Copy the **Start** column to the **Previous Report Start** (Start1) column.
- ◆ Copy the **Finish** column to the **Previous Report Finish** (Finish1) column.

3. From the **Tools** menu, select **Macro > Stop Recorder**:

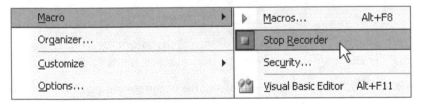

## To create the project schedules document library:

Create a project schedules document library. For the procedure to create a document library, see Appendix A.3.

# Cost Management

## Objectives

◆ To verify that funds and working hours budgeted for the project are spent on executing the project and delivering the program/project deliverables

◆ To collect all relevant costs and validate cost reports as raw data for monitoring the current budget consumption status and budget analysis, for invoicing, and for improved future estimates

## Procedure

### To collect project costs and expenses:

1. Verify that all costs are reported at all levels as soon as possible after they are incurred.

2. Verify that the costs reported are correct and, for example, do not belong to another program, to verify that team members charge the program/project budget codes report correctly and validate the costs against the reporting codes. Make adjustments to time sheets according to the program manager's instructions.

3. Escalate cost reporting delays after the grace period has expired, as defined in the system and the program work instructions.

---

◆ A cost is either fixed for an assignment or depends on the resource rate. It gets its parameters from the assignment.

◆ A cost is updated only after the project manager has accepted the reported tasks (see the "Time Management" section in this chapter).

---

## Prerequisites

### To create the cost indicator enterprise field:

1. In Project Web Access, select **Server Settings**.

2. Under **Enterprise Data** on the **Server Settings** page, select **Enterprise Custom Field Definition**:

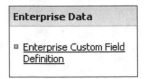

3. On the **Custom Fields and Lookup Tables** page, click **New Field**.

4. On the page that opens, fill in the required fields:

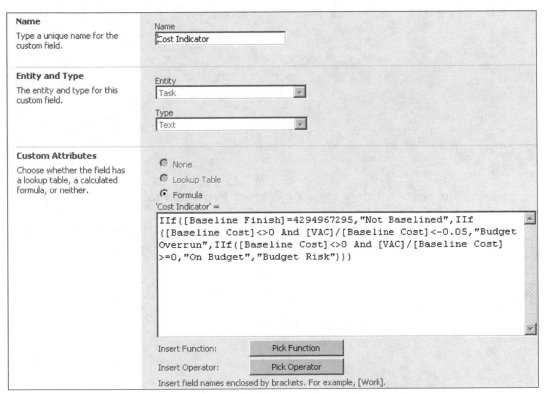

In the example above, **VAC** (variance at completion) is defined to be checked against **Baseline Cost**.

5. Check the **Graphical indicators** box in order to create the indicators. Since we want the indicators to appear near the tasks, select **Non-summary rows** from the **Criteria for** drop-down list. Select the **Image** for each indicator according to the value returned from the formula defined.

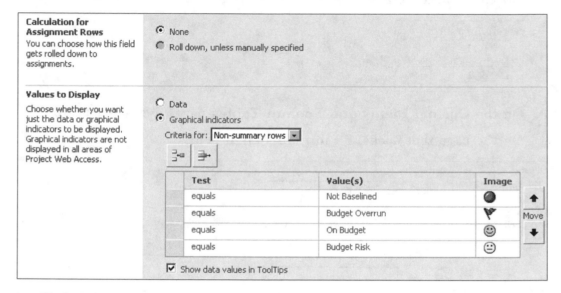

6. Click **Save**.

## To create the cost tracking view in Project Professional:

1. In Project Professional, from the **Tools** menu, select **Enterprise Options > Open Enterprise Global**:

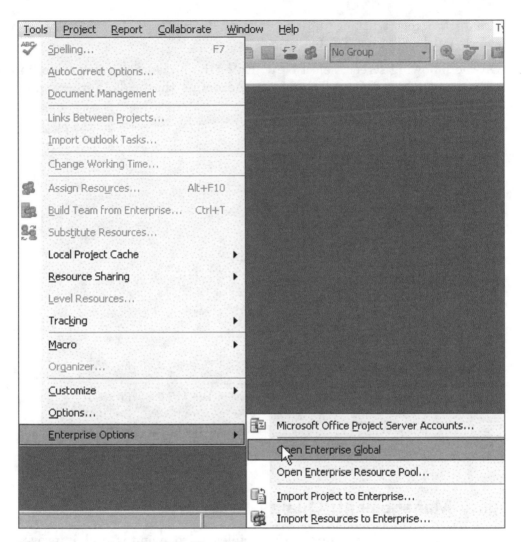

The **Enterprise Global** file opens.

2. In this file, define the views applicable for tracking purposes (in the following example, the **3 Cost Tracking** view).

3. Create the cost tracking table in Project Professional. In the **View** menu, select **Table > More Tables**.

4. On the following screen, select **New**. Enter the name of the new table (in the current example, **3 Cost Tracking**) and define the fields. For example:

- ◆ **ID**
- ◆ **Indicators**
- ◆ **Task Name**
- ◆ **Cost indicator** (from Enterprise)
- ◆ **Duration**
- ◆ **Start**
- ◆ **Finish**
- ◆ **% Complete**
- ◆ **VAC**
- ◆ **Work**
- ◆ **Actual Work**
- ◆ **Cost**
- ◆ **Baseline Cost**

The resulting view looks as follows:

| | ❶ | Task Name | APCost Indicator | Duration | Start | Finish |
|---|---|---|---|---|---|---|
| 0 | | ⊟ **Upgrading CRM Syst** | ☺ | **64 days?** | **Tue 11/7/06** | **Fri 2/2/07** |
| 1 | ✓ | Kickoff Meeting | ☺ | 0 days | Tue 11/7/06 | Tue 11/7/06 |
| 2 | | ⊟ **Design** | ☺ | **13 days** | **Tue 11/7/06** | **Thu 11/23/06** |
| 3 | | High Level Design | ☺ | 2 days | Tue 11/7/06 | Wed 11/8/06 |

# Quality Management: Quality Assurance

One of the basic quality assurance principles is to monitor and improve the quality of all intermediate process deliverables, through extensive design reviews, code and document inspections, and other techniques.

All documents and source code generated during the development process are subject to one or more of the following:

- ◆ Design review
- ◆ Document inspection
- ◆ Code inspection
- ◆ Document approval

More specifically, the following rules are applied:

- ◆ All major documents (specifications, design, test plan, etc.) are subject to a design review.

- ◆ Lower-level documents (module design, unit test design, etc.) are subject to document inspection.

- ◆ All source code is subject to extensive code inspection.

- ◆ Documents circulated out of the project (to clients, corporate, or other projects) are subject to document approval, usually in addition to a design review or inspection.

Inspection is performed on a sample basis. The purpose of this independent audit is to check in depth the quality of the development process and to assure the continuous improvement of the development process quality.

## Objective

- ◆ To monitor and improve the quality of all intermediate process deliverables and final deliverables

## Procedures

### To implement the quality assurance process:

Implement the quality assurance process according to the quality standards defined in the project management plan.

### To perform quality audits and report quality progress:

Perform quality audits, including the following activities:

1. Meetings with the program manager and team leaders

2. Meetings with other project personnel (testers, developers, and others)

3. Document audits

4. Source code audits

5. Intermediate reports, including major conclusions, suggested action items, and minutes of meetings (Save these reports in the quality reports folder of the quality management document library.)

6. Audit summary meetings with the program/project manager and senior team leaders, including conclusions, action items, and priorities (Upload the minutes of meeting document to the quality management document library.)

7. Audit summary reports

Quality audits are performed according to the quality audit checklists, which are part of the quality management plan.

## Prerequisite

**To create the supporting document folders:**

1. Create the quality management document library:

For the procedure to create a document library, see Appendix A.3.

2. Under the quality management document library, create the quality reports folder.

# Human Resource Management

## Objectives

◆ To manage the resources acquired to execute the program/project

◆ To develop the team members as individuals and as a team

## Procedures

**To assign resources to activities:**

After the project schedule is built, all the resources are allocated to the activities in the project plan. Resource assignments can be viewed in Project Professional.

1.  Open the project plan in Project Professional.

2.  From the **View** menu, select **Resource Usage**:

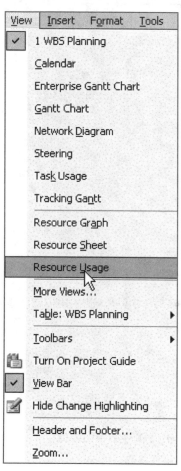

Resource assignments are displayed:

| Resource Name |
| --- |
| ⊟ **VB Team** |
|     *Design Review* |
|     *Sub System A Infrastructure r* |
|     *Sub System A S/W Developm* |
|     *Sub System A S/W Installatio* |
|     *Sub System A Unit Test* |
|     *Sub System Test* |
|     *System Test Design* |
|     *Testing Environment Ready* |
|     *System Test* |
|     *Go/NoGo Decision* |
| ⊟ farmadmin |
|     ⊞ *Other projects and commitme* |
| ⊟ Hagit Landman |
|     *Kickoff Meeting* |
|     *Design Review* |
|     *Sub System A Unit Test* |
|     *Sub System B Development* |
|     *Sub System B Unit Test* |
|     *Go/NoGo Decision* |
|     *System Go Live* |

3. Modify the resource assignments. Make sure that the resources are not overallocated.

4. In the sample screen shot above, you can see that **farmadmin** is assigned to other projects.

5. Save and publish the project plan.

As soon as the project plan is published to the project server, the assignments are sent to the resources, and the resources can see that they have new tasks assigned to them in Project Web Access, either in the **Reminders** section or by clicking the **My Tasks** link in the **My Work** menu:

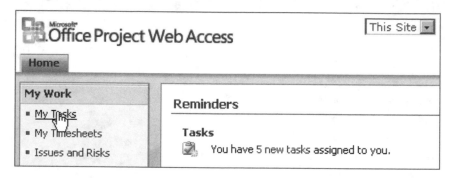

## To orient and coach new team members:

Conduct an orientation meeting for new project team members. Show them the orientation materials for team members and explain to them how to access these materials on the project home page.

1. On the project home page, from the quick launch menu, select **Documents > Project Management Plan**:

2. On the **Project Management Plan** page, click **Communication Management Plan**:

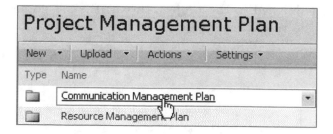

3. On the screen that opens, select **Orientation Kit**:

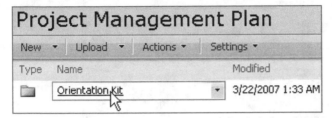

## To communicate new and/or changed assignments:

◆ Immediately communicate to the task owner all new assignments and changes in the scope of an assignment. Be as explicit as possible to ensure that the scope is clear.

◆ Communication must be both verbal and written to avoid confusion.

## To develop the project team:

◆ Perform the activities required to develop the team.

◆ Offer training for team members to enhance their knowledge in the project area.

◆ To communicate such activities, use the **Announcements** section on the project home page.

◆ Add the training sessions to the project calendar or use e-mail to notify the team members.

## To manage human resources:

◆ Make sure the team leaders hold weekly team meetings in which all team members report their status, problems, etc.

◆ Hold a weekly meeting with the team leaders and a working meeting with each of the team leaders.

◆ Make sure the team members and their team leaders know their roles and responsibilities. For example, refer the quality assurance team leader to the document that defines his or her roles and responsibilities in the roles and responsibilities document library:

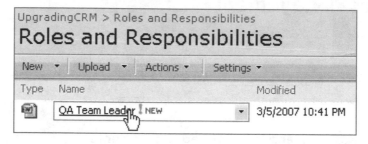

## To build the project team:

◆ Hold team-building activities, where the team members can socialize in order to get to know each other and discuss topics that are not necessarily connected to their work.

◆ If possible, organize an event for a day or half a day as a team-building activity, such as sports contests, scavenger hunts, and so on.

## Prerequisites

There are no prerequisites for these procedures.

# Communication Management

## Objectives

◆ To manage and execute the communication plan

◆ To distribute information to the relevant stakeholders according to their needs

## Procedures

### Managing and Implementing the Communication Plan

**To add announcements to the project home page:**

1. On the project home page, in the **Announcements** section, click **Add new announcement**:

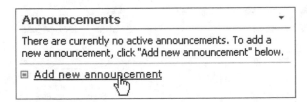

2. On the page that opens, enter the announcement text:

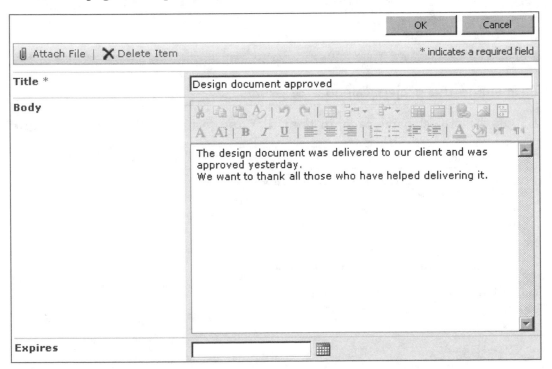

3. Click **OK**. The announcement will appear on the project home page:

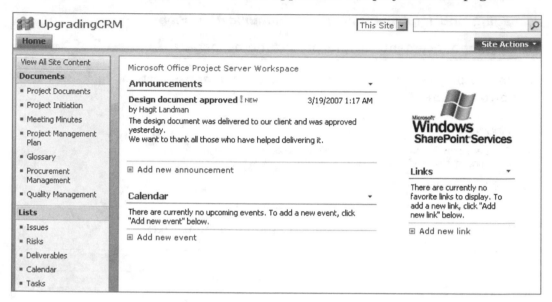

## To manage the project calendar of events:

1. On the project home page, in the **Calendar** section, click **Add new event**:

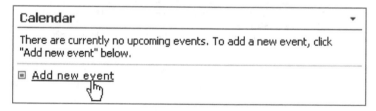

The **Calendar: New Item** page opens.

2. Fill in the details for the event:

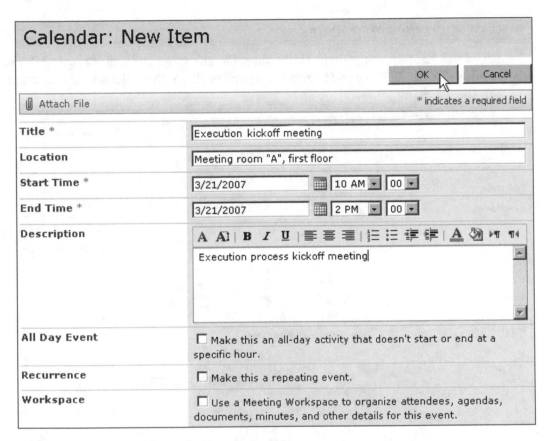

3.  Click **OK**. The event will appear in the calendar on the project home page:

## To create a meeting workspace:

1. From the **Lists** menu, select **Calendar**. On the page that opens, select **New > New Item**. The **New Item** page opens. Fill in the relevant information for the meeting.

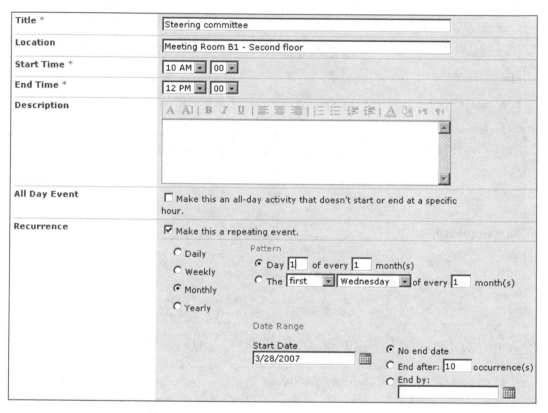

2. Check the **Use a Meeting Workspace to organize attendees, agendas, documents, minutes, and other details for this event** box:

| Workspace | ☑ Use a Meeting Workspace to organize attendees, agendas, documents, minutes, and other details for this event. |
|---|---|

3.  Click **OK**. The **New Meeting Workspace** page opens:

## New Meeting Workspace

Use this page to create a new Meeting Workspace site for the event. There are no existing Meeting Workspaces that you can link the event to.

**Title and Description**

Type a title and description for your new site. The title will be displayed on each page in the site.

Title:

[Steering committee]

Description:

[                    ]

**Web Site Address**

Users can navigate to your site by typing the Web site address (URL) into their browser. You can enter the last part of the address. You should keep it short and easy to remember.

For example, http://ps2007 demo/DEV/UpgradingCRM/*sitename*

URL name:

http://ps2007demo/DEV/UpgradingCRM/ [Steering committee]

**Permissions**

You can give permission to access your new site to the same users who have access to this parent site, or you can give permission to a unique set of users.

User Permissions:

◉ Use same permissions as parent site

○ Use unique permissions

4.  Fill in the required information.

5. Select a template for the workspace:

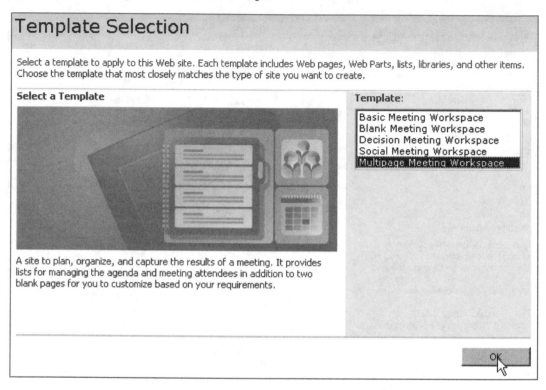

The system creates the workspace:

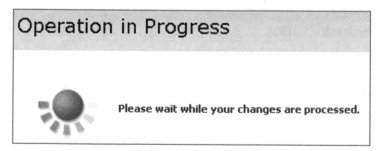

Now you can see the meeting workspace:

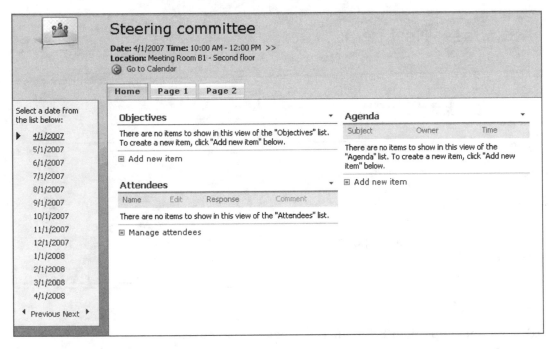

6. Add the list of attendees by selecting **Attendees** from the meeting workspace. The **Attendees** page opens.

7. On the **Attendees** page, select **New Item**:

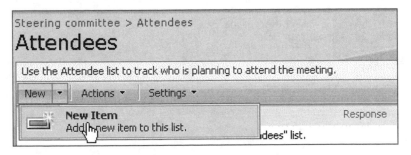

8. Fill in the required information:

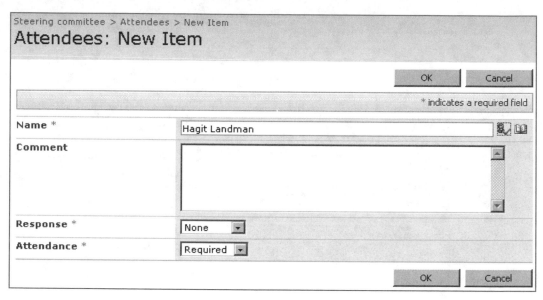

9. Click **OK**.

10. Repeat steps 6 to 8 for all the meeting attendees.

11. From the meeting workspace, select **Agenda > Add new item**:

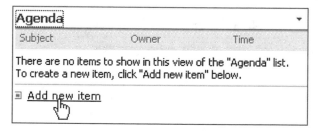

12. On the **Agenda: New Item** page, fill in the agenda for the meeting:

13. Click **OK**. Now you can see on the meeting workspace the details of the meeting (objectives, agenda, and attendees):

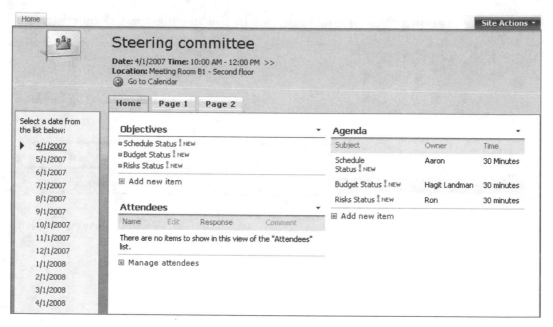

On the project home page, under **Calendar**, you can see all the meetings:

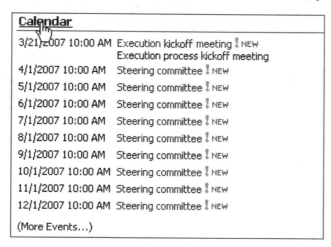

14. To see the calendar of all the major project events, on the project home page click **Calendar**:

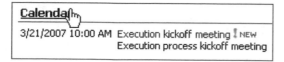

The planned activities are displayed in a calendar:

| | | | | | | |
|---|---|---|---|---|---|---|
| ← → **March, 2007** | | | Expand All  Collapse All | ⊞ Day  🗓 Week  🗓 **Month** | | |
| Sunday | Monday | Tuesday | Wednesday | Thursday | Friday | Saturday |
| 25 | 26 | 27 | 28 | 1 | 2 | 3 |
| 4 | 5 | 6 | 7 | 8 | 9 | 10 |
| 11 | 12 | 13 | 14 | 15 | 16 | 17 |
| 18 | 19 | 20 | 21<br>10:00 AM<br>**Execution kickoff meeting** | 22<br>4:00 PM<br>**QA Happy hour** | 23 | 24 |
| 25 | 26 | 27 | 28 | 29<br>4:00 PM<br>**QA Happy hour** | 30 | 31 |

15. When a meeting is over and the minutes of meeting document is completed, save this document either to the minutes of meetings document library or in the meeting workspace (if one was created).

16. In the project workspace, select the relevant meeting:

> **Calendar**
>
> 3/21/2007 10:00 AM Execution kickoff meeting ⚡ NEW
> Execution 🖱 cess kickoff meeting

The page with the details of that meeting opens.

17. Click on the link of the workspace:

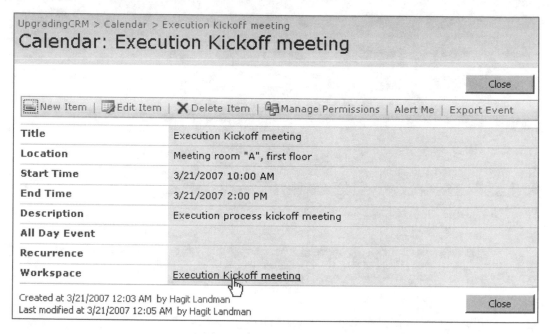

The meeting workspace opens.

18. Select **Add new document** and upload the minutes of meeting document:

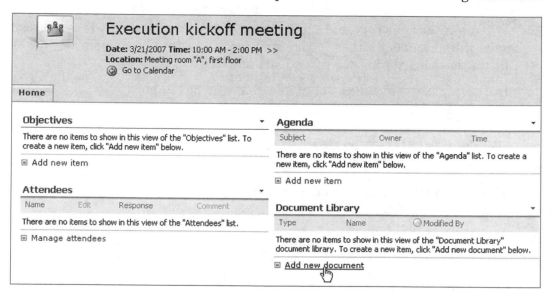

### *Managing Action Items*

The execution process ensures that the status of action items is tracked, actions are assigned and monitored, and any action item that is not satisfactorily resolved is escalated.

Action items can be managed in three ways:

◆ In the minutes of meeting document, while reviewing the status of action items in each meeting

◆ In the meeting workspace

◆ In a specialized list

The following are suggestions for procedures to manage action items.

## To log action items:

Record action items taken in a meeting in the relevant log.

## To execute action items:

The action item owner carries out the activities necessary to execute the action item and provides the expected deliverable to the action item owner.

## To update, log, and communicate progress to stakeholders:

Progress in the execution of an action item is tracked by the PMO on a regular basis.

Any status change is communicated to stakeholders and other parties as necessary.

## To verify if an action item is executed satisfactorily:

Once an action item is completed, the owner validates whether the outcome meets the original expectations.

As necessary, the action item owner indicates any required modifications/enhancements.

## To reopen an action item and escalate if necessary:

If the execution of an action item requires modifications/enhancements, the action item is reopened.

An action item may be escalated to the program manager and PMO if the owner believes that the action item requires review due to the possible consequences of its outcome.

## To report action item status:

To enable review, the PMO ensures that the minutes of meetings, including any action items raised during a meeting, are distributed to the participants and to other distribution lists as required. Ad hoc action item reports are also distributed.

## Prerequisites

There are no prerequisites for these procedures.

# Risk Management

## Managing Risks

### *Objectives*

◆ To manage the risks anticipated during the project life cycle

◆ To anticipate risks in advance and apply contingency plans to prevent risks from occurring

◆ In order to meet risk effectively, to identify all foreseeable project risks and rate them in terms of their probability of occurrence and potential impact on the project

◆ To implement mitigation plans as soon as a risk occurs in order to minimize the impact

◆ To escalate risks according to the risk management plan and communication management plan

◆ If project risks impact the program, to manage these risks at the program level

◆ To provide status reports to the different forums

Some risks were identified during the planning process, but new risks may be identified during the execution process.

### *Procedures*

### To log a new risk:

When a new risk is identified, it is added to the risks list. To log a new risk, refer to the procedure "To update the risks log" in the section on "Defining the Risk Management Plan" in Chapter 5.

### To assess risks:

1. As soon as a risk is entered in the risks log, the risk owner should verify that it is properly classified.

2. To modify the risk information or add more details, such as contingency plans, reassign the risk or link it to a task in the project plan. In the risks log, select the risk to be edited:

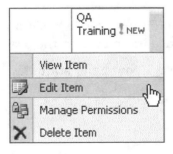

3. The selected risk's page opens:

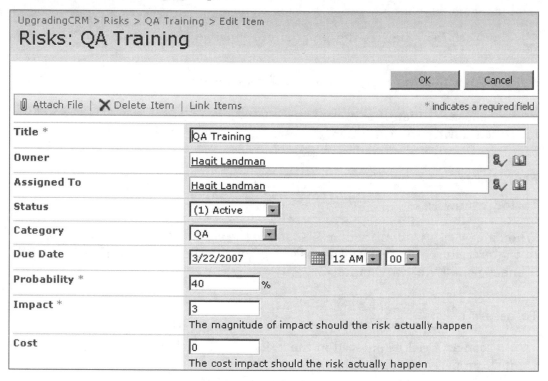

4. Modify the risk information as required, and then save the modifications.

## To perform risk assessment throughout the execution phase:

1. Evaluate each risk. Evaluate the actions to be taken in order to avoid a risk or, if a risk occurs, the actions to be taken to reduce its impact on the project.

2. Change the risk status as the project progresses. Update the status in the risks log.

 Identify risks clearly and specifically. Vague identification of risks results in responses/actions that are ambiguous, intangible, not clearly defined, and difficult to implement adequately. **Do not** attempt to document **all** possible risks and outcomes. This can often introduce improbable scenarios.

## To define risk mitigation and contingency plans:

1. Develop appropriate responses to minimize the possibility of a risk occurring, and document the responses according to characteristic actions (e.g., avoidance, acceptance, transfer, etc.).

2. Develop an overall response to each risk. The response may be an obvious set of actions that annul a risk or limit the possibility that it will occur. Alternatively, the response may be an intuitive "best guess" of actions that are likely to be effective.

3. Analyze the development of the responses to each risk. The initial reactions to a risk must allow quantification of the risk.

4. Link the relevant risks to the project work plan.

## To manage risks:

Manage the risks on the risks list according to the risk management plan. Check them periodically (at least once a week). Identify those risks for which the mitigation plans should be implemented, those risks that do not need to be addressed, and those risks that have occurred and for which the contingency plans must be implemented.

Assign resources to handle the risks and implement the mitigation or contingency plans. Allocate a budget to carry out these plans.

If the risk status needs to be updated, perform the following procedure.

1. In the **Lists** section, select **Risks**:

2. Select the risk that you want to update (in the example below, **Lack of QA resources**):

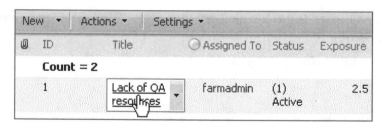

3. On the toolbar, click **Edit Item**:

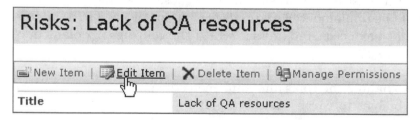

4. Make the required changes (in the example below, change the risk status from **Active** to **Postponed**):

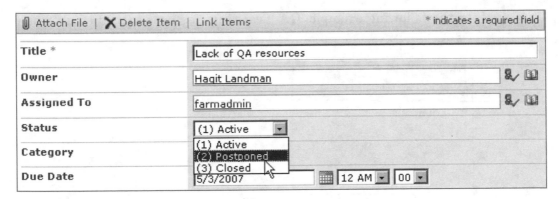

5. Click **OK**.

## To manage mitigation plans:

1. For the risks in the risks log, identify and record actions that could be taken to avoid or mitigate each risk based on its level of impact.

2. For any given risk, identify activities that should be incorporated into the project schedule. These activities can be mitigation plans or, when a risk becomes an issue, contingency plans.

3. If multiple alternative responses have been identified for a risk, evaluate the responses and select the preferred one. For risks with lower impact, mitigation and corrective plans may be optional. However, once the risk rank changes to "major", the plans must be defined. Both mitigation and contingency plans must be defined to ensure that the project is well prepared to deal with the risks identified.

4. Perform the following decomposition, estimating, and scheduling steps for each of the risk responses identified:
   ◆ Decompose the selected risk responses into their constituent work activities. The level of detail must be consistent with the level used to plan the work in the master or detail work plan.
   ◆ Estimate the resources required to implement the risk responses and schedule the detailed work activities. Note that:
   a. This involves modifying the program/master/detail work plan for any actions to be incorporated immediately.

In the following example, **QA Training** has been identified as a new risk:

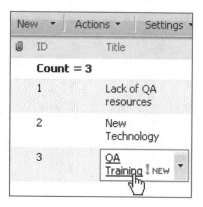

The mitigation plan is to add more training to the quality assurance team, and the corresponding activity is added to the project schedule:

| 5 | ⊟ **System Test** |
|---|---|
| 5.1 | System Test Design |
| 5.2 | Testing Environment Ready |
| 5.3 | QA Team Training |
| 5.4 | System Test |

Add the activity work hours and costs related to it.

Link the risk to the project plan. Select the risk you want to link to the project plan (in the example above, **QA Team Training**). From the menu, select **Edit Item**:

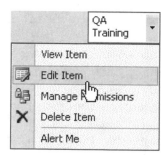

In the following screen, select **Link Items**:

The following dialog is displayed:

| Link | ID ▲ | Title | Relation |
|------|------|-------|----------|
| ☐ | 1 | Kickoff Meeting | Risk affects task |
| ☐ | 2 | Design | Risk affects task |
| ☐ | 3 | High Level Design | Risk affects task |
| ☐ | 4 | Detailed Design | Risk affects task |
| ☐ | 5 | Sub System A Design | Risk affects task |
| ☐ | 6 | Sub System B Design | Risk affects task |
| ☐ | 7 | Detailed Design Document | Risk affects task |
| ☐ | 8 | Design Review | Risk affects task |
| ☐ | 9 | Development | Risk affects task |
| ☐ | 10 | Sub System A | Risk affects task |
| ☐ | 11 | Sub System A Development | Risk affects task |

**Project Web Access -- Web Page Dialog**

Project Tasks ▾   All Tasks ▾

[ OK ]   [ Cancel ]

Specify whether you want to connect the risk to the project tasks (from the project schedule) or to a document library, project issues, or project risks by selecting the corresponding option from the drop-down list:

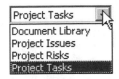

In the example below, the risk is linked to the project tasks:

| | | | |
|------|------|-------|----------|
| ☑ | 28 | QA Team Training | Risk affects task |
| ☐ | 29 | System Test | Risk affects task |
| ☐ | 30 | User Acceptance Test | Risk affects task |

Click **OK**. The link icon appears next to the activity linked to the risk:

This means:

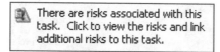

b. Only activity duration, not specific schedule dates, can be defined for corrective risk actions.

c. Incorporating these actions into the plan may affect the program/project baseline.

5. Update the risk mitigation plan to reflect the results of the risk status monitoring.

6. Document the effects of any program/project replanning changes. This involves:

a. Adding newly identified risks and associated risk reduction actions to the risk mitigation plan

b. Modifying ineffective risk reduction actions and updating the risk mitigation plan and risk watch list accordingly

At the program level, this step also involves updating the program risk mitigation plan and risk watch list to reflect any risks identified at the project level that are not properly reflected and are significant to the overall program.

A mitigation plan may or may not be developed if the strategy to be employed to mitigate the risk is one of the following:

◆ **Risk acceptance**—The manager will actively choose not to prepare any mitigation work plan. This is done when the manager can "live" with the loss if it materializes.

◆ **Risk avoidance**—The manager will attempt to avoid the risk. For example, if the cost of executing a project is very high, then the manager will avoid the project.

◆ **Risk protection**—The manager will execute several mitigation plans that create redundancy, so if one plan fails, another may succeed.

◆ **Risk reduction**—The manager will execute mitigation plans to decrease the probability of the risk occurring.

◆ **Risk research**—The manager needs more information (e.g., employ prototyping techniques, client questionnaire, etc.).

◆ **Risk transfer**—The manager will shift responsibility for the risk to another person, group, or organization (e.g., the high cost of software development can be deflected by using contractors instead of in-house staff).

## To escalate risks:

Risks are escalated according to the risk management plan. Some examples of risk escalation situations are:

◆ **Risk factor has increased significantly**—A change in the risk factor value may be caused by many factors, such as change in the initial assessment of the probability or impact of the risk, added information in subsequent analysis of the risk, administrative decision based on status reports, etc.

◆ **Nearing major milestones**—All open risks must be reviewed at least two weeks prior to a major milestone. The risks are reassessed, and mitigation and contingency plans are defined and executed as required.

1. To escalate a risk, open the **Risks** page:

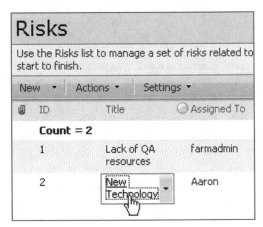

2. Click the risk that you want to escalate (in the example below, **New Technology**).

3. From the drop-down menu, select **Edit Item**:

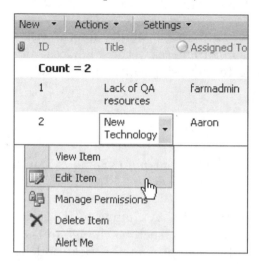

4. On the following screen, in the **Reporting level** section, select the escalation for the risk (in the example below, **Program** level):

5. Click **OK**.

## To report risk status:

Risk status is reported according to the risk management plan. The project risk status and the risk changes are reported and reviewed in the project status meetings.

To ensure visibility of risks and progress in mitigating them, reports are distributed to management on a regular basis.

One way to report the status is to export the risk information to an Excel file and analyze it in Excel. Use the following procedure to export the list to Excel.

1. On the **Risks** page, from the **Actions** menu, select **Export to Spreadsheet**:

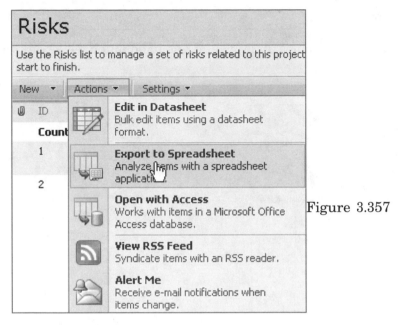

Figure 3.357

An Excel file opens with the risks data.

2. Build a PivotTable according to the reporting instructions in the risk management plan:

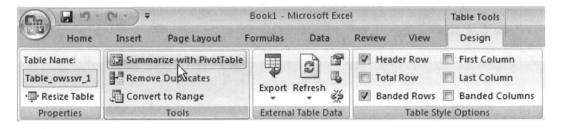

## Managing Issues

### *Objective*

◆ To manage risks that have occurred

### *Procedures*

## To upgrade a risk to an issue:

Once a risk has occurred, it becomes an issue and has to be managed as an issue.

1. Open the **Risks** page:

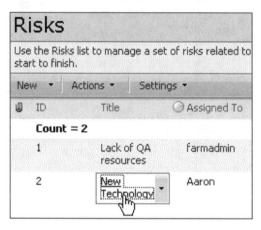

2. Click on the risk that you want to escalate (in the example above, **New Technology**).

3. From the drop-down menu, select **Edit Item**:

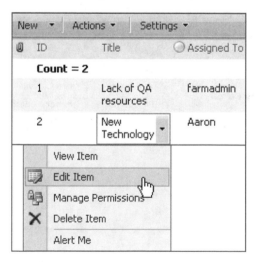

4. On the following screen, change the risk status to **Issue**:

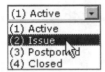

5. Open a new issue. Issues are managed in the issues log.

## To open a new issue:

1. Enter the risk that has become an issue in the issues log.

2. In the **Lists** section, select **Issues**:

3. From the **New** menu, select **New Item**:

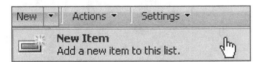

4. On the page that opens, enter the issue details. Copy the following field values for the risk:
   - ◆ **Description**
   - ◆ **Risk Owner** (becomes **Issue Owner**)
   - ◆ **Contingency Plan** (becomes **Resolution Plan**)

5. To connect the issue to the relevant risk, click **Link Items**:

The following dialog is displayed:

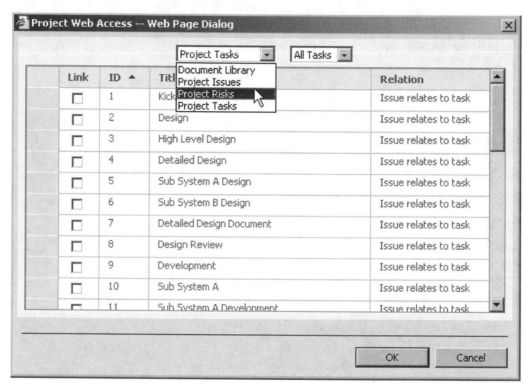

6. From the drop-down list at the top of the page, select **Project Risks**.

7. On the page that opens, select the risk related to the issue (in the example below, **Java developer resigned**):

| | Link | ID ▲ | Title | Status | Assigned To |
|---|---|---|---|---|---|
| | ☐ | 1 | Lack of QA resources | (2) Postponed | farmadmin |
| | ☐ | 2 | New Technology | (1) Active | Aaron |
| | ☐ | 3 | QA Training | (1) Active | Hagit Landman |
| | ☑ | 4 | Java developer resigned | (2) Issue | Hagit Landman |

8. Click **OK**. The issue is now linked to the risk:

| Links | Issues |
|-------|--------|
|       | 2   Java developer resigned |

### To view the issues log:

In the project workspace, select **Issues** in the left pane:

The issues log opens.

## Prerequisites

### To add the issue status to the risk status drop-down list:

For the procedure to add the issue status to the risk status choice menu, see Appendix A.9 on adding a choice column to a list. The following screen shot shows an example of status choice for issues:

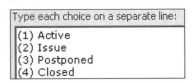

### To create the reports view:

Create views for reporting risks based on their escalation level (according to the risk management plan).

For the procedure to create a list view, see Appendix A.21.

### To change issue categories:

Change the choice values in the issue categories list as follows (for example):

◆ Time

◆ Budget

◆ Technology

◆ QA

◆ Human Resources

◆ Other

For the procedure to modify an existing column, see Appendix A.22.

## Procurement Management

### Objectives

◆ To collect the sellers' responses to the request for proposals

◆ After the sellers are selected, to manage them in order to ensure that they deliver and provide what was agreed to, according to the statement of work

### Procedures

### To receive suppliers' responses:

Receive the suppliers' responses and upload them to the sellers responses folder in the procurement management document library:

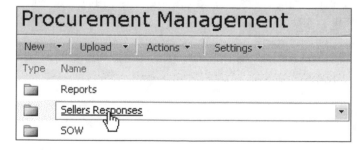

For the procedure to upload a document to a document library, see Appendix A.6.

## To select sellers using the supplier evaluation table:

One of the tools that can help in selecting the right suppliers for a program/project is the supplier evaluation table.

1. In the project workspace under **Lists**, select **Supplier Evaluation**:

The supplier evaluation table opens.

2. Fill in the grades and scores for each supplier for each of the subjects:

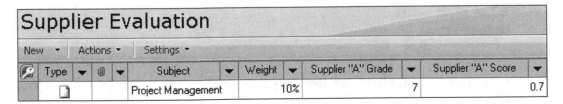

| Type | | 📎 | | Subject | | Weight | | Supplier "A" Grade | | Supplier "A" Score | |
|---|---|---|---|---|---|---|---|---|---|---|---|
| 🗋 | | | | Project Management | | 10% | | 7 | | 0.7 | |

When the table is completed, it will help in selecting the right supplier.

## To issue a purchase order:

Once a supplier has been selected, a statement of work (SOW) is prepared to define the scope of work for the supplier.

1. Save the SOW to the SOW folder in the procurement management document library:

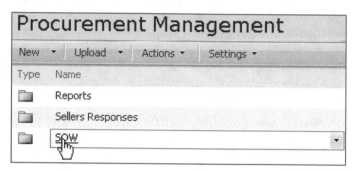

The purchasing department will issue a purchase order to the supplier, which will include the SOW.

2. Save all contracts to the SOW folder.

## To manage suppliers:

1. Receive periodic reports from the sellers and upload them to the reports folder in the procurement management document library:

2. Check suppliers' progress.

3. Verify that the suppliers are working according to the defined schedule and timeline.

4. Verify that the deliverables are delivered according to the contract (per the specifications, on time, and on budget).

5. Approve/disapprove change requests.

6. Issue change requests.

## Prerequisites

### To create the supplier evaluation table:

1. Create a table with the fields shown in Table 6.2. For the procedure to create a new list, see Appendix A.7.

2. Create grade and score columns for each supplier.

### To create the procurement management document library:

1. Create the procurement management document library. For the procedure to create a document library, see Appendix A.3.

2. Create the sellers' responses document folder under the procurement management document library.

3. Create the SOW document folder under the procurement management document library.

### Table 6.2. Supplier Evaluation

| Column | Description | Type |
|---|---|---|
| Subject | The evaluated subject | Single line of text |
| Weight | The weight of the subject (percent) | Number |
| Supplier A grade | The grade given to supplier A in the subject evaluated | Number |
| Supplier A score | The score given to supplier A in the subject evaluated | Calculated (calculation based on other columns) |
| Supplier B grade | The grade given to supplier B in the subject evaluated | Number |
| Supplier B score | The score given to supplier B in the subject evaluated | Calculated (calculation based on other columns) |

# Monitoring and Control Process

## Overview

This process monitors and controls all other management processes. The monitoring and control process compares planned vs. actual activities in the various areas of project management in terms of their schedule, deliverables, scope, and cost.

In the monitoring and control process, deviations from planning are identified, these deviations are analyzed, and corrective actions suggested.

In the course of this process, program/project status reports are gathered, analyzed, and submitted to the various stakeholders. This enables the stakeholders to understand the status of the program/project and actions at the corresponding level: initiate corrective action, escalation, or, at a higher level, make decisions.

The main goals of this process are to provide information regarding the program/project status, to analyze this information, and to ensure that the right action is taken.

The monitoring and control process ensures that the information pertaining to the program/project is up-to-date and is available to the various stakeholders in the format and with the frequency agreed upon in the project management plan.

The process must provide an early warning of serious issues or risks that might result in cost, quality, and/or timing deviations from the baseline.

## Workflow

To provide a solution that meets the requirements that are defined for the monitoring and control process, the features/functions listed in Table 7.1 must be implemented.

### Table 7.1. Monitoring and Control Feature/Function Processes

| Requirement | Solution Feature/ Function Guidelines | Relevant Procedure |
|---|---|---|
| **Scope Management** | | |
| Administer contracts | | "To administer contracts" |
| Monitor change requests | Use the Windows Share-Point Services list to view the change request reports | "To monitor change request status" |
| **Time Management** | | |
| Collect reports | Use Project Professional to collect status reports | "To collect reports from the different projects/teams" |
| View actual finish dates vs. planned finish dates for primary tasks and milestones | Use Project Professional to collect status reports | "To view primary task/milestone actual finish dates vs. planned finish dates" |
| View achieved milestones vs. planned milestones | Use Project Professional to collect status reports | "To view actual milestones achieved vs. planned milestones achieved" |
| View actual schedule progress vs. planned schedule progress | Use Project Professional to collect status reports | "To view actual project schedule progress vs. planned project schedule progress" |

## Table 7.1. Monitoring and Control Feature/Function Processes (continued)

| Requirement | Solution Feature/ Function Guidelines | Relevant Procedure |
|---|---|---|
| Identify tasks that cause slippage | Use Project Professional to collect status reports | "To identify tasks that cause slippage" |
| Identify inter-dependencies | Use Project Professional to collect status reports | "To view the impact of current project deliverables and project dependencies on the status of other projects" |
| Perform critical path analysis | Use Project Professional to analyze the critical path | "To analyze the critical path" |

**Cost Management**

| | | |
|---|---|---|
| Collect the cost reports | Use Project Professional to collect cost reports | "To collect and validate cost reports" |
| View actual costs vs. scheduled costs | Use Project Professional to view costs | "To collect and validate cost reports" |
| Control costs and budget | Use Project Professional and Project Web Access to control costs and budget | ◆ "To re-estimate activities"<br>◆ "To approve budget changes"<br>◆ "To take corrective action"<br>◆ "To update the budget and save the baseline"<br>◆ "To communicate changes" |

**Quality Management**

| | | |
|---|---|---|
| Perform quality control | | ◆ "To perform quality audits"<br>◆ "To conduct quality reviews"<br>◆ "To ensure that the defined standards are maintained"<br>◆ "To analyze quality reports and checklists"<br>◆ "To decide whether to accept or reject a deliverable" |

**Table 7.1. Monitoring and Control Feature/Function Processes (continued)**

| Requirement | Solution Feature/ Function Guidelines | Relevant Procedure |
|---|---|---|
| **Human Resource Management** | | |
| View actual resource assignment load vs. planned resource assignment load | Use Project Web Access to see reports | "To view resource availability" |
| **Communication Management** | | |
| Manage performance and status reports | Use Windows SharePoint Services to save reports and use Project Professional and Project Web Access to produce reports and prepare for meetings | ◆ "To hold status meetings" ◆ "To monitor action items" |
| Manage stakeholders | Use Windows SharePoint Services to save relevant documentation | "To verify that stakeholders receive the relevant information" |
| **Risk Management** | | |
| Monitor and control risks | Use the Windows SharePoint Services risks list to monitor and control risks | ◆ "To track and monitor risks" ◆ "To report risk status" ◆ "To escalate risks" |
| **Procurement Management** | | |
| Contract administration | Use Windows SharePoint Services to document relevant materials | ◆ "To hold status meetings" ◆ "To check supplier quality" ◆ "To verify invoices" ◆ "To monitor contracts" ◆ "To monitor change control" |

# Scope Control

## Objectives

◆ To assess the impact of, prioritize, and approve scope changes and communicate them to the appropriate parties

◆ To monitor progress and the impact of change requests

## Procedures

### To administer contracts:

1. Check the contract regularly to ensure that there are no deviations from the requirements.

2. Manage the relationship with the client.

### To monitor change request status:

1. Open the requirements matrix.

2. Select the **Change Requests Report** view:

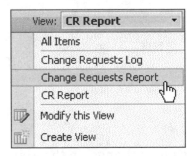

3. Check the status of the change requests. For example: How many change requests were supposed to be finished? What is their status?

4. Check the status of those change requests with high priority (**Priority : High**). The following example has one change request with high priority and the status is the high-level estimate was received (**HLE received**):

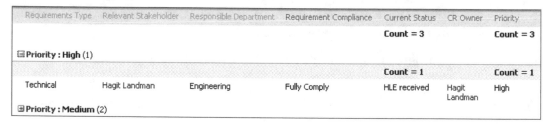

| Requirements Type | Relevant Stakeholder | Responsible Department | Requirement Compliance | Current Status | CR Owner | Priority |
|---|---|---|---|---|---|---|
| | | | | Count = 3 | | Count = 3 |
| ⊟ Priority : High (1) | | | | | | |
| | | | | Count = 1 | | Count = 1 |
| Technical | Hagit Landman | Engineering | Fully Comply | HLE received | Hagit Landman | High |
| ⊞ Priority : Medium (2) | | | | | | |

## Prerequisite

An optional prerequisite for the above procedures is report grouping(s).

## To define the group view in a report:

1. In the requirements matrix, from the **Settings** drop-down list, select **List Settings**:

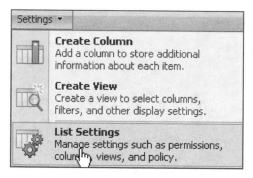

2. In the **Views** section, select the view that you want to change (in the example below, **Change Requests Report**):

3. The **Edit View: Requirement Matrix** opens. In the **Group By** section, select **Priority**:

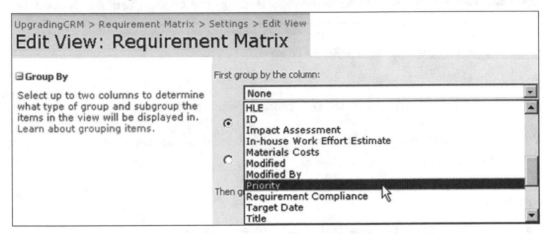

Using the grouping you defined, it will be easier to see how many change requests have a specific priority (e.g., **High**):

| Requirements Type | Relevant Stakeholder | Responsible Department | Requirement Compliance | Current Status | CR Owner | Priority |
|---|---|---|---|---|---|---|
| | | | | Count = 3 | | Count = 3 |
| **Priority : High** (1) | | | | | | |
| | | | | Count = 1 | | Count = 1 |
| Technical | Hagit Landman | Engineering | Fully Comply | HLE received | Hagit Landman | High |
| **Priority : Medium** (2) | | | | | | |

# Time and Schedule Control

## Objectives

◆ To monitor and manage schedules according to the standards and procedures defined in the project management plan

◆ To ensure that changes made to the project schedule are justified and to analyze those changes and their effect

◆ To escalate items according to the escalation procedure defined in the communication management plan

 Major schedule changes that result in changing the contractual delivery dates usually go through the change request procedure.

◆ To monitor the use of the time reserves

◆ To check the total slack

◆ To analyze the critical path and critical path candidates

You can use the earned value method implemented as an option in Project Professional.

## Procedures

### To collect reports from the different projects/teams:

1. Collect schedule reports from the various projects/teams.

2. If required, integrate the information received into one summary project plan and check the impact on the master milestones.

### To view primary task/milestone actual finish dates vs. planned finish dates:

The tracking Gantt chart uses graphical indicators to represent:

◆ Slippage against the baseline

◆ Task total slack (how close the task is to being on the critical path)

Use the graphical indicators to check the actual finish dates vs. planned finish dates.

1. In Project Web Access, select **Project Center** and check the activity status. It is recommended that you first check the red-flagged indicators and then the yellow ones.

2. Check the high-level milestones and their status.

3.  Note indication of primary tasks and milestones that slip by more than 15% of the planned schedule.

| ▲ ID | 🛈 | Task Name | Sched | Duratio | Start | Finish |
|------|---|-----------|-------|---------|-------|--------|
| 0 | 📰 | ⊟ **Upgrading CRM System** | ☺ | 64d | 11/7/2006 | 2/2/2007 |
| 1 | | Kickoff Meeting | ✓ | 0d | 11/7/2006 | 11/7/2006 |
| 2 | | ⊟ **Design** | ☺ | 13d | 11/7/2006 | ./23/2006 |
| 3 | | High Level Design | ☺ | 2d | 11/7/2006 | 11/8/2006 |

## To view actual milestones achieved vs. planned milestones achieved:

1.  Select the view that was defined to check the planned milestones vs. actual milestones. For example, select the **4 Milestone Control** view that shows the milestones that are supposed to be achieved by now:

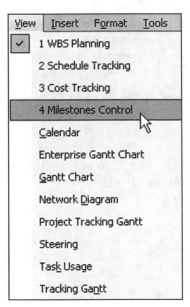

2.  In the selected view, count how many milestones are supposed to be achieved by now and how many have been achieved. The milestones that have been achieved are marked with ✓.

3.  Add the above information to the status report.

## To view actual project schedule progress vs. planned project schedule progress:

In Project Professional, in the tracking view, check the status of the activities.

In the example below, the solid line (which will appear in red) in the Gantt chart indicates the **Current Date**. You can see that activities 5 and 6 are supposed to have been completed, and they are not. You can also see that activity 7 is 11% complete, whereas it was supposed to have been finished, and it will be late.

| | ❶ | Task Name | Schedule indicator | Critical path candidate | Duration | | |
|---|---|---|---|---|---|---|---|
| | | | | | | ember | December |
| | | | | | | 11/5 11/12 11/19 11/26 | 12/3 12/10 |
| 0 | | ⊟ **Upgrading CRM S** | ☹ | ⬤ | **80 days** | #; | |
| 1 | ✓ | Kickoff Meeting | ✓ | ⬤ | 0 days | ◆ 11/7 | |
| 2 | | ⊟ **Design** | ☹ | ☺ | **22.5 days** | | 21% |
| 3 | | High Level Desigr | ☺ | ☺ | 2 days | 20% | |
| 4 | | ⊟ **Detailed Desigr** | ☹ | ☺ | **20.5 days** | | 21% |
| 5 | | Sub System A | 😐 | ☺ | 7 days | 15% | |
| 6 | | Sub System B | 😐 | ☺ | 8 days | 45% | |
| 7 | | Detailed Desig | ☹ | ☺ | 14 days | | 11% |
| 8 | | Design Review | ☺ | ⬤ | 0 days | 11/23 | |

## To identify tasks that cause slippage:

1. In order to check which activities (tasks) cause the slippage of a certain task, in Project Professional select the task you want to check.

2. Select **Project > Task Drivers**:

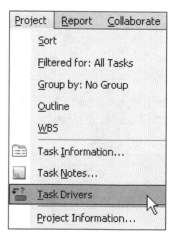

3. The **Task Drivers** section opens, where you can check the tasks that are the cause of the slippage:

| Task Drivers | | | ✕ |
|---|---|---|---|
| The following factors are affecting the start date of: | | | |
| Task: **29 - System Test** | | | |
| Start: **Wed 1/3/07** | | | |
| ● Predecessor Tasks: | | | |
| Name | Type | | Lag |
| 24 - Sub System Test | Finish To Start | | 0d |
| ● Calendars: | | | |
| Resource: VB Team | | | |
| Hagit Landman | | | |

|  | WBS | Name | redecessor: |
|---|---|---|---|
| 16 | 3.1.3 | Sub System A Ready for Sub Sys | 15 |
| 17 | **3.2** | ⊟ **Sub System B** | |
| 18 | **3.2.1** | ⊟ **Sub System B Development** | |
| 19 | 3.2.1.1 | Sub System B Infrastructure Re | 8 |
| 20 | 3.2.1.2 | Sub System B S/W Developmer | 19 |
| 21 | 3.2.1.3 | Sub System B S/W Installation | 20 |
| 22 | 3.2.2 | Sub System B Unit Test | 21 |
| 23 | 3.2.3 | Sub System B Ready for Sub Syst | 22 |
| 24 | 4 | Sub System Test | 23 |
| 25 | 5 | ⊟ **System Test** | |
| 26 | 5.1 | System Test Design | 8 |
| 27 | 5.2 | Testing Environment Ready | 26FF |
| 28 | 5.3 | QA Team Training | 29SF |
| 29 | 5.4 | System Test | 24,26 |

In the example above, activity 29 has two predecessors: activities 24 and 26. However, only activity 24 caused activity 29 to start late. In the left-hand section, you can see those activities that affect activity 29. Activity 26 does not appear there because it is not affecting activity 29 yet.

### To view the impact of the current project deliverables and project dependencies on the status of other projects:

Many of the project elements cannot be started until other elements in other projects, for example, are completed. This creates a large number of interdependencies. Handover dates agreed upon for the dependent deliverables are tracked using the Deliverables option of Project Professional.

If there is a possibility of deviation from the handover dates, the projects/teams involved must negotiate an alternative approach to avoid potential impact on the overall delivery. If necessary, the PMO must facilitate or replan dependent activities throughout the program.

1. In Project Professional, from the **Collaborate** menu, select **Manage Dependencies on Deliverables**:

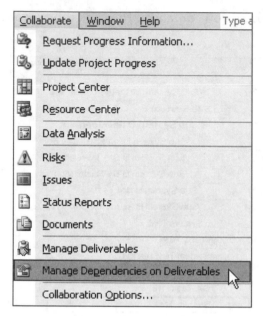

Activities that are connected to other projects are denoted by .

2. Select the activity for which you want to check the status of its dependencies on other projects or teams (in the following example, activity **13 Sub System A Infrastructure Ready**).

3. The following screen will open:

| Dependency | | Sort By | |
|---|---|---|---|
| Title | Finish | | |
| Document A | 12/1/2006 | **Title** | Document A |
| | | **Start** | |
| | | **Finish** | 12/1/2006 |
| | | **Task ID** | 13 |
| | | **Task Name** | Sub System A Infrastructure Ready |
| | | **Source Project** | DEV/Test |

4. Check the status of the deliverable from the dependent project (in the example above, **Document A** from project **DEV/Test**).

## To analyze the critical path:

The critical path activities must be monitored closely, so that their total slack does not become negative and delay the entire schedule.

1. In Project Professional, from the **Project** menu, select **Filtered for: Critical > Critical**:

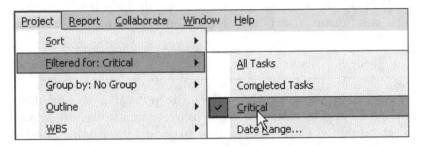

The critical path activities are displayed:

| | | Task Name | Schedul Indicato | Critical path candidate | Duration | Start | Finish | Total Slack |
|---|---|---|---|---|---|---|---|---|
| 1 | | ⊟ **Upgrading CRM System** | ☹ | ● | **87 days** | **Wed 2/28/07** | **Thu 6/28/07** | **0 days** |
| 2 | ▦ | Kickoff Meeting | ☺ | ● | 0 days | Wed 2/28/07 | Wed 2/28/07 | 0 days |
| 3 | | ⊟ **Design** | ☺ | ● | **10 days** | **Wed 2/28/07** | **Tue 3/13/07** | **0 days** |
| 4 | | High Level Design | ☺ | ● | 2 days | Wed 2/28/07 | Thu 3/1/07 | 0 days |
| 5 | | ⊟ **Detailed Design** | ☺ | ● | **8 days** | **Fri 3/2/07** | **Tue 3/13/07** | **0 days** |
| 6 | | Sub System A Design | ☺ | ● | 5 days | Fri 3/2/07 | Thu 3/8/07 | 0 days |
| 7 | | Sub System B Design | ☺ | ● | 5 days | Fri 3/2/07 | Thu 3/8/07 | 0 days |
| 8 | | Detailed Design Docum | ☺ | ● | 3 days | Fri 3/9/07 | Tue 3/13/07 | 0 days |
| 10 | | ⊟ **Development** | ☺ | ☺ | **31 days** | **Tue 3/13/07** | **Wed 4/25/07** | **46 days** |
| 11 | | ⊟ **Sub System A** | ☺ | ● | **31 days** | **Tue 3/13/07** | **Wed 4/25/07** | **0 days** |
| 12 | | ⊟ **Sub System A Devel** | ☺ | ● | **23 days** | **Tue 3/13/07** | **Fri 4/13/07** | **0 days** |
| 14 | | Sub System A S/W | ☺ | ● | 20 days | Wed 3/14/07 | Tue 4/10/07 | 0 days |
| 15 | | Sub System A S/W | ☺ | ● | 3 days | Wed 4/11/07 | Fri 4/13/07 | 0 days |
| 16 | | Sub System A Unit Tes | ☺ | ● | 8 days | Mon 4/16/07 | Wed 4/25/07 | 0 days |
| 17 | | Sub System A Ready f | ☺ | ● | 0 days | Wed 4/25/07 | Wed 4/25/07 | 0 days |
| 25 | | Sub System Test | ☺ | ● | 10 days | Thu 4/26/07 | Wed 5/9/07 | 0 days |
| 26 | | ⊟ **System Test** | ☺ | ● | **51 days** | **Wed 3/14/07** | **Wed 5/23/07** | **0 days** |
| 29 | | System Test | ☺ | ● | 10 days | Thu 5/10/07 | Wed 5/23/07 | 0 days |
| 30 | | ⊟ **User Acceptance Test** | ☺ | ● | **73 days** | **Wed 3/14/07** | **Fri 6/22/07** | **0 days** |
| 32 | | User Acceptance Tests | ☺ | ● | 11 days | Thu 5/24/07 | Thu 6/7/07 | 0 days |
| 33 | | System Bug Fixes | ☺ | ● | 10 days | Fri 6/8/07 | Thu 6/21/07 | 0 days |
| 34 | | Go/NoGo Decision | ☹ | ● | 1 day | Fri 6/22/07 | Fri 6/22/07 | 0 days |
| 35 | ▦ | System Go Live | ☹ | ● | 2 days | Wed 6/27/07 | Thu 6/28/07 | 0 days |

2. Check the activities that are close to being on the critical path. Which activities fall within this category depends on the project type, duration, etc. However, you can decide that all the activities that have total slack less than 2 days are critical path candidates and must be tracked closely.

## To take corrective action:

If there are slippages in the schedule that affect the critical path and delivery dates, corrective action should be taken in order to overcome these slippages and not delay the project schedule. Corrective action may include adding resources, delaying activities that are not on the critical path, etc.

## To update the schedule and save the baseline:

1. If the corrective action involves changing the schedule and deliverable due dates, approval for these changes must be obtained.

2. If the changes are approved, update the schedule and save the updated baseline.

## To communicate changes:

All major changes must be approved and communicated.

## Prerequisites

### To create the milestones filter:

1. In Project Professional, from the **Tools** menu, select **Enterprise Options > Open Enterprise Global**:

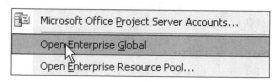

2. On the **Enterprise Global** page, from the **Project** menu, select **Filtered for: All Tasks > More Filters...**:

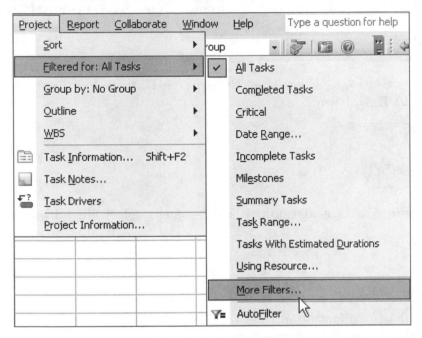

3. Create a filter to use for displaying milestones. The following example shows a filter that selects those activities marked as milestones and prompts you for the date by which the milestones to display should have been achieved:

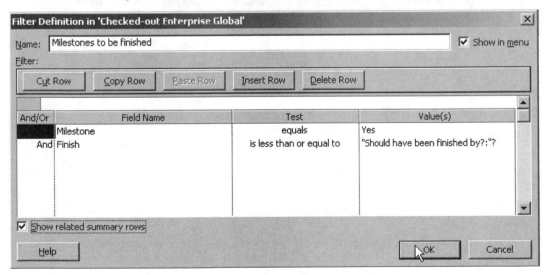

## To define the milestone indicators (enterprise custom fields):

1. In Project Web Access (development environment), select **Server Settings**:

2. In the **Server Settings** view, under **Enterprise Data**, select **Enterprise Custom Field Definition**:

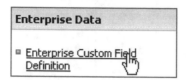

3. On the **Custom Fields and Lookup Tables** page, select **New Field**:

4. The **New Custom Field** page will open.

5. Fill in the following information:
   - ◆ **Name**—Enter "Number of milestones in project"
   - ◆ **Entity**—Select **Task**
   - ◆ **Type**—Select **Number**
   - ◆ **Custom Attributes**—Select **Formula** and write the formula
   - ◆ **Calculation for Summary Rows**—Check **Rollup** and select **Sum**

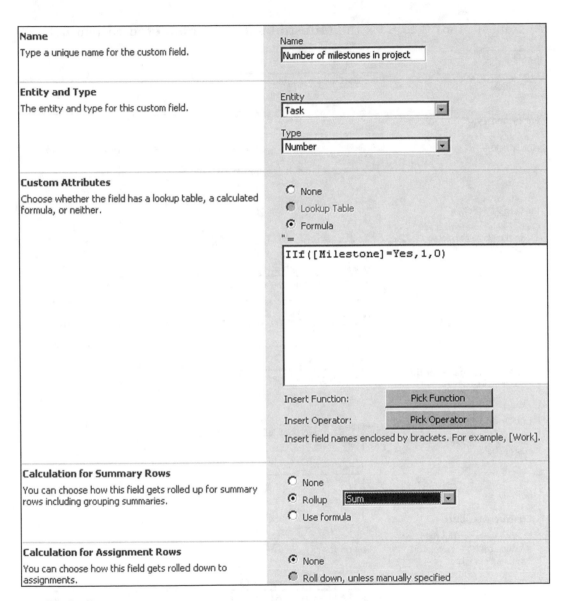

6. Click **Save**.

7. Repeat steps 3 to 6 for the **Milestones to be completed** custom field:

| Name | |
|---|---|
| Type a unique name for the custom field. | Name<br>Milestones to be completed |
| **Entity and Type** | |
| The entity and type for this custom field. | Entity<br>Task<br><br>Type<br>Number |
| **Custom Attributes** | |
| Choose whether the field has a lookup table, a calculated formula, or neither. | ○ None<br>○ Lookup Table<br>◉ Formula<br>'Milestones to be completed' =<br>`IIf([Milestone]=Yes And [Finish]<=[Status Date],1,0)` |

8. Repeat steps 3 to 6 for the **Number of milestones completed** custom field:

| Name | |
|---|---|
| Type a unique name for the custom field. | Name<br>Number of milestones completed |
| **Entity and Type** | |
| The entity and type for this custom field. | Entity<br>Task<br><br>Type<br>Number |
| **Custom Attributes** | |
| Choose whether the field has a lookup table, a calculated formula, or neither. | ○ None<br>○ Lookup Table<br>◉ Formula<br>'Number of milestones completed' =<br>`IIf([Milestone]=Yes And [% Complete]=100,1,0)` |

## To create the milestone tracking table:

1. In Project Professional, from the **Tools** menu, select **Enterprise Options > Open Enterprise Global**:

On the **Enterprise Global** page, from the **View** menu, select **Table <table name> > More Tables...**:

2. In the **More Tables** dialog, click **New**:

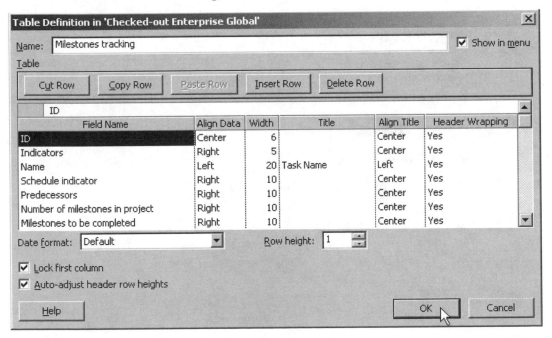

3. The table should include the following fields:
   ◆ **ID**
   ◆ **Indicators**
   ◆ **Name**

   ◆ **Schedule indicator**
   ◆ **Number of milestones in project** (enterprise field)
   ◆ **Milestones to be completed** (enterprise field)—The number of milestones that should have been completed by the status date
   ◆ **Number of milestones completed** (enterprise field)—The number of milestones that were completed by the status date
   ◆ **Start**
   ◆ **Finish**

4. Click **OK**.

## To create the milestones control view in Project Professional:

1. In Project Professional, from the **Tools** menu, select **Enterprise Options > Open Enterprise Global**:

   On the **Enterprise Global** page, from the **View** menu, select **More Views...**:

2. In the **More Views** dialog, click **New**:

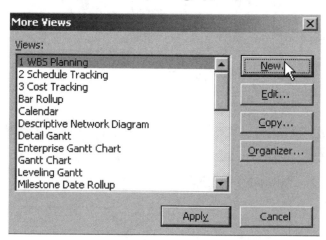

3. In the **View Definition** dialog, define a new view. The following example shows a view that uses the filter created in the previous section:

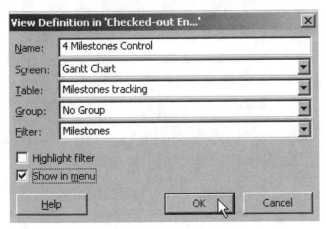

**To create the milestones control view in Project Web Access:**

1. In Project Web Access (development environment), select **Server Settings**:

2. On the **Server Settings** page, under **Look and Feel**, select **Manage Views**:

3. On the **Manage Views** page, select **New View**:

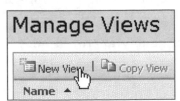

4. On the **New View** screen, fill in the information for the **Milestone Control** view.

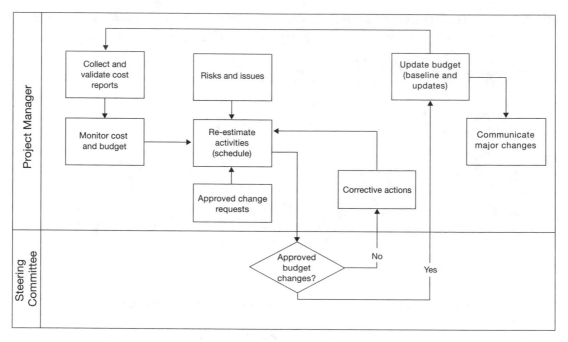

**Figure 7.1. Cost Control Workflow**

# Cost Control

The cost control process (Figure 7.1) tries to minimize changes to the budget and verifies that the changes made to the budget are justified. This process checks and analyzes costs variances. It also warns in advance of budget variances.

## Objectives

◆ To ensure that deviations from the original budget will be as minimal as possible (preferably none)

◆ To escalate and approve deviations from the originally approved budget

◆ To recalculate the estimate at completion

◆ To obtain additional funding if required

◆ To manage budget reserve

◆ To check cost variances and analyze them

## Procedures

### To collect and validate cost reports:

Collect and validate cost reports as raw data for invoicing, for monitoring the up-to-date budget consumption status and budget analysis, and for future estimations. The information required can be found in Project Professional.

1. Select the predefined cost view (for the example below, **3 Cost Tracking**). The planned vs. actual costs are displayed:

| Task Name | APCost Indicator | Duration | Start | Finish | % Complet | VAC | Work | Actual Work | Cost | Baseline Cost |
|---|---|---|---|---|---|---|---|---|---|---|
| High Level Design | ☺ | 2 d | 11/7/06 | 11/8/06 | 20% | $0.00 | 16 h | 3.2 h | $3,200.00 | $3,200.00 |
| ⊟ **Detailed Design** | ☺ | **11 d** | **11/9/06** | **11/23/06** | **13%** | **$0.00** | **112 h** | **14.4 h** | **$0.00** | **$0.00** |
| Sub System A De | ☺ | 3 d | 11/9/06 | 11/13/06 | 10% | $0.00 | 24 h | 2.4 h | $0.00 | $0.00 |
| Sub System B De: | ☺ | 6 d | 11/9/06 | 11/16/06 | 25% | $0.00 | 48 h | 12 h | $0.00 | $0.00 |
| Detailed Design Dc | ☺ | 5 d | 11/17/06 | 11/23/06 | 0% | $0.00 | 40 h | 0 h | $0.00 | $0.00 |
| Design Review | ☺ | 0 d | 11/23/06 | 11/23/06 | 0% | $0.00 | 0 h | 0 h | $0.00 | $0.00 |

2. Estimate effort to complete for the work plan tasks.

3. Use the **Earned Value Cost Indicators** table to check the cost variances. Any variance must be tracked at the estimation unit level. For example, for each change request issue that was estimated, there must be a separate line in the project schedule.

4. Analyze variance at completion and mark items for escalation/investigation.

5. Check the actual figures vs. planned figures. Compare the planned and actual income and costs per actual plan and the current version plan. Compare the planned measurements vs. actual measurements (as defined earlier), both current and estimated at completion, and analyze the reasons for differences, if any.

6. Escalate problems and concerns according to the escalation procedure defined in the project management plan.

7. Add the information to the cost status report.

### To re-estimate activities:

1. Receive cost and budget information for approved change requests.

2. Receive cost and budget information for issues and risks.

3. Re-estimate the cost and budget.

You can save the project schedule locally on your hard drive and check the impact of the changes.

### To approve budget changes:

Changes to the budget and costs above a certain level, which was defined in the project management plan, must be approved by the project sponsor and/or the steering committee.

### To take corrective action:

To reduce the effect of deviations from the approved budget on the program/project budget and costs, corrective action must be taken.

### To update the budget and save the baseline:

If the changes are approved, update the budget and save the baseline.

### To communicate changes:

Approve and communicate major changes.

## Prerequisites

There are no prerequisites for these procedures.

# Quality Control

## Objectives

◆ To verify that the deliverables meet the quality requirements and standards defined in the project management plan

◆ To measure the system performance, compare product quality vs. quality requirements, accept or reject the product, and redesign the product if it does not meet the requirements

◆ To ensure that quality assurance reviews and audits occur at appropriate times and are properly documented

## Procedures

### To perform quality audits:

1. Perform quality audits.

2. Verify the product quality against the quality requirements.

### To conduct quality reviews:

Conduct quality reviews and follow the quality management plan.

### To ensure that the defined standards are maintained:

Verify that the standards defined for the program/project are maintained.

### To analyze quality reports and checklists:

1. Collect and analyze the quality measurement results.

2. Produce quality reports.

3. Save the reports to the quality reports document library in the quality management document library:

### To decide whether to accept or reject a deliverable:

1. Verify that the deliverable meets the performance requirements.

2. Check the deliverable and decide whether to accept or reject it based on the quality standards defined.

3. Identify the need for corrective action.

## Prerequisites

There are no prerequisites for these procedures.

# Human Resource Management

## Objectives

◆ To check resource availability vs. allocation

◆ To identify shortages or overallocation

## Procedures

### To monitor and control resources:

Collect and validate assignment reports and staffing plans, as defined in the project management plan.

Check planned resource usage vs. actual allocations. Check that resources are not overloaded.

The assignments or availability reports are in Project Web Access.

**To view resource availability:**

1. In Project Web Access, select **Resource Center**:

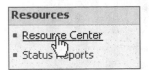

2. On the **Resource Center** page, select the view (in the example below, **All Resources**):

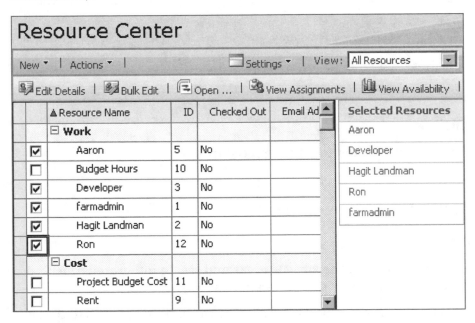

3. Select the resources whose availability you want to check.

4. Select **View Availability**:

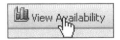

You will be able to see the availability of resources according to your selection. The following example shows **Aaron**'s availability:

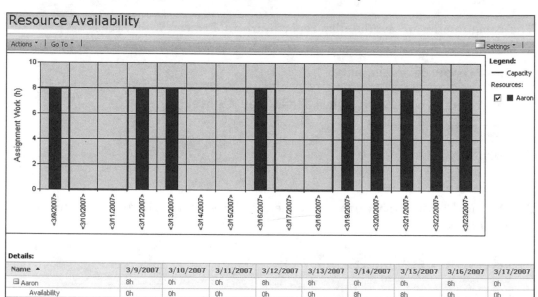

Resource Availability

| Name ▲ | 3/9/2007 | 3/10/2007 | 3/11/2007 | 3/12/2007 | 3/13/2007 | 3/14/2007 | 3/15/2007 | 3/16/2007 | 3/17/2007 |
|---|---|---|---|---|---|---|---|---|---|
| ⊟ Aaron | 8h | 0h | 0h | 8h | 8h | 0h | 0h | 8h | 0h |
| Availability | 0h | 0h | 0h | 0h | 0h | 8h | 8h | 0h | 0h |
| Capacity | 8h | 0h | 0h | 8h | 8h | 8h | 8h | 8h | 0h |
| Upgrading CRM System | 8h | 0h | 0h | 8h | 8h | 0h | 0h | 8h | 0h |

## Prerequisites

There are no prerequisites for these procedures.

# Communication Management

## Objectives

◆ To collect reports from the various areas and create integrated reports according to the definitions in the project management plan

◆ To analyze the various reports and present the analysis results to the relevant forums

◆ To collect and present the information as defined in the communication management plan

◆ To hold status meetings and performance reviews

◆ To take corrective action

## Procedures

### To hold status meetings:

1. Update status reports at the various reporting levels, with the required frequency (weekly, daily, quarterly, etc.), according to the project management plan. These reports summarize the status of the various aspects of the program/project (e.g., schedule status, budget status, risk status, etc.).

2. Measure the project progress vs. the baseline plan using the various measuring methods, such as earned value analysis, trend analysis, etc.

3. Analyze variances and deviations, and analyze trends. The resulting reports provide information about the progress made since the previous report, planned activities for the next period, corrective actions required, and change requests. The content of the reports depends on the reporting level and forum.

4. Hold status meetings according to the communication management plan. For example, the goals defined for the program steering committee meeting are:
   ◆ Monitor overall progress against business objectives specified in the contractual arrangements
   ◆ Resolve escalated issues, risks, and changes that cannot be resolved at the operating program level
   ◆ Handle public announcements related to program progress and delivery
   ◆ Approve and sign off on major milestones and payment points

### To issue the agenda prior to each meeting:

Issue the meeting agenda prior to each meeting. The agenda will vary according to the needs of the program. For example, the agenda for the steering committee meeting would include:

   ◆ Review of progress against the plan (timeline, scope, and cost)

   ◆ Escalated risks, issues, and changes

   ◆ External dependencies (e.g., legislation or external program dependencies/risks)

   ◆ Approval and formal sign-off on major milestone completion points

   ◆ Confirmation/commitment to plan/actions for next month

## To verify the output of meetings:

Make sure that meetings result in the relevant output. For example, for the steering committee meeting, the output must include:

◆ Recommendations/agreement to resolve specific risks and issues

◆ Approval of key milestones and change requests

◆ Request for specific actions to be carried through by the program management team

◆ Confirmation of plans/commitments for the next month

◆ Escalation to the executive level of any issues that cannot be resolved by the steering committee

◆ Corrective actions

## To verify that stakeholders receive the relevant information:

1. Verify periodically that the stakeholders are satisfied with the information they receive. For example:
   ◆ **Management**—Receives enough information to make decisions
   ◆ **Team members**—Receive enough information to perform their tasks correctly and efficiently

2. If the information and communication require improvement, update the communication management plan and the reporting formats.

3. Verify that meetings are necessary, productive, and documented.

## To monitor action items:

After status meetings, record all action items, and monitor their progress and closure.

Report the status of action items from the previous meeting in the meeting that follows.

## Prerequisites

### To change the project home page to reflect the project status:

1. On the project home page, from the **Site Actions** menu, select **Edit Page**:

2. Select the area (left or right) where you want to add or delete a web part.

3. Click **Add a Web Part**:

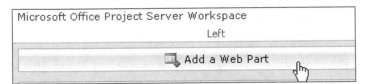

   The **Add Web Parts – Web Page Dialog** opens. In the following example, the web part of the project schedule will be inserted.

4. Check the **Project Details** box:

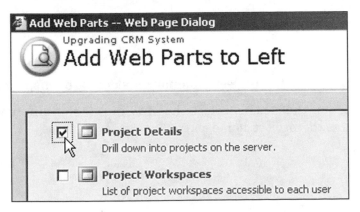

5. Click **Add**. The web part now appears on the project home page.

6. On the right-hand side, select **Exit Edit Mode**:

7. In the project workspace, on the web part that was added, from the **View** drop-down list select the required view (in the example below, **Project Tracking w. Indicators**):

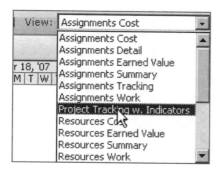

8. To change the level of the view, from the **Settings** menu select **View Options**:

In the following example, only the project summary tasks will be displayed.

9. In the view options section that opens, select the view and the outline level that you want to see on the project home page:

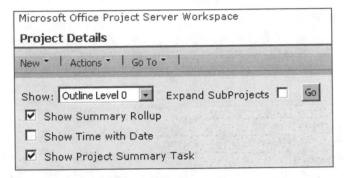

The following view is displayed:

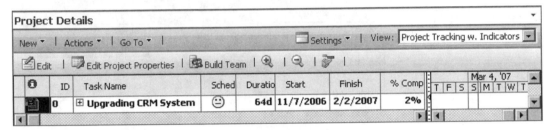

## To create the project-level home page status view:

1. In Project Web Access (development environment), select **Server Settings**.

2. In the **Look and Feel** section, select **Manage Views**:

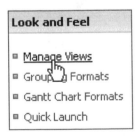

The **New View** page opens:

3. Select the level of the view (in the example above, project-level view).

4. Select the fields to add to the view and the order of those fields. For example, select the following:
   ◆ **Task Name**
   ◆ **Schedule indicator**
   ◆ **Duration**
   ◆ **% Complete**
   ◆ **Start**
   ◆ **Finish**

5. Select the **Format View** (in the following example, **Tracking Gantt**, with no filters):

6. Select **Security Categories** for the view:

7. Click **Save**. The view is added to the project home page.

## To create the executive-management-level view (Project Center):

1. On the **Server Settings** page, in the **Look and Feel** section, select **Manage Views**:

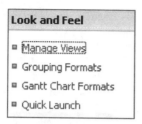

2. On the page that opens, click **New View**:

3. On the next page, in the **Name and Type** section, from the **View Type** drop-down list, select **Project Center**:

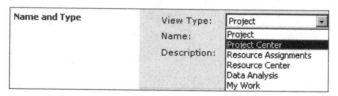

Type the name of the view.

4. On the same page, select the relevant tables for that view and format the view.

5. Optionally, create a filter that, for example, will display only a specific division's projects:

6. Click **Save**.

7. Open the **Project Center** page. The **Monitoring View** appears in the list of views:

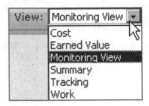

# Risk Control

Risks change during the life cycle of a program/project in terms of probability and severity. That is why risks must be monitored and controlled. Risks are monitored and controlled based on the standards and procedures defined in the project management plan.

## Objectives

◆ To ensure that the status of risks is tracked, that the risks are managed, and that the risk management strategy is executed

◆ To ensure that risks are escalated if they cannot be dealt with as planned

◆ To regularly compare actual risks vs. planned risks

◆ To escalate risks according to the escalation procedures defined in the risk management plan

◆ To monitor and assess progress of risk reduction

◆ To monitor the occurrence of those risks that require the initiation of contingent risk responses

◆ To evaluate the effectiveness of the risk reduction actions implemented and to identify the need for modifying these actions

◆ To implement the risk mitigation plan

The monitoring and control process ensures that risk status is tracked, appropriate action is taken, and a risk is escalated if it cannot be dealt with as planned.

## Procedures

### To track and monitor risks:

Monitor risk data changes. Perform ongoing risk identification, analysis, and planning. Immediately incorporate all changes in the data into the risks log.

1. Open the **Risks** list:

2. Select the **Risks monitoring** view:

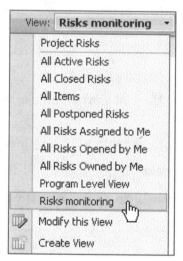

3. Check the status of all the risks whose due dates have passed.

4. Check the status of all the risks whose due dates are approaching.

5. Monitor warning signals.

6. Execute the risk mitigation plan.

7. If a risk has occurred, implement the contingency plan and deal with it as an issue. Add the risk to the issues log.

8. Check the risk status to verify that the risk was dealt with.

9. If a new risk is identified, process it starting from the "To log a new risk" and "To assess risks" procedures in the "Risk Management" section in Chapter 6.

### To report risk status:

Report the risk status periodically in the account/project status report.

### To escalate risks:

Escalate risks as defined in the project management plan.

## Prerequisites

### To create the risks monitoring view:

1. Open the risks log.

2. Define the following fields for the new risks monitoring view:

| ⊟ Columns | Display | Column Name | Position from Left |
|---|---|---|---|
| Select or clear the check box next to each column you want to show or hide in this view. To specify the order of the columns, select a number in the **Position from left** box. | ☑ | Attachments | 1 ▾ |
| | ☑ | ID | 2 ▾ |
| | ☑ | Title (linked to item with edit menu) | 3 ▾ |
| | ☑ | Assigned To | 4 ▾ |
| | ☑ | Status | 5 ▾ |
| | ☑ | Exposure | 6 ▾ |
| | ☑ | Category | 7 ▾ |
| | ☑ | Due Date | 8 ▾ |
| | ☑ | Reporting level | 9 ▾ |
| | ☑ | Contingency Plan | 10 ▾ |
| | ☑ | Description | 11 ▾ |
| | ☑ | Mitigation Plan | 12 ▾ |

3. Define a filter to display all the risks that have a due date of, for example, **[Today]-15** days and **[Today]+30** days:

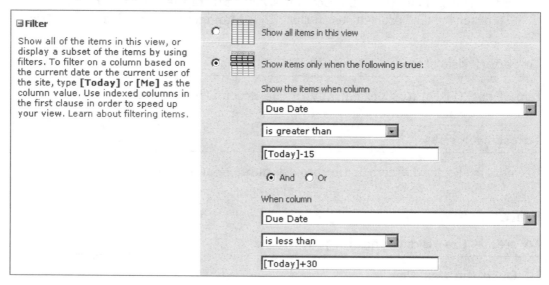

4. Group the risks by the **Assigned To** field or by the **Category** field.

## To add the risks monitoring view to the project home page:

1. On the project home page, from the **Site Actions** menu, select **Edit Page**:

2. On the page that opens, click **Add a Web Part**:

3. On the next page, check the **Risks** box and then click **Add**:

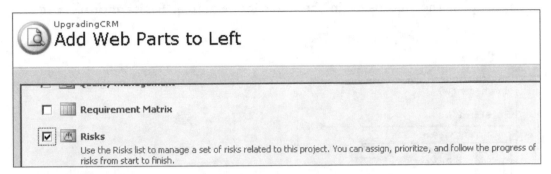

4. Drag the web part to its location on the page (for example, put it under the schedule web part).

5. From the **Edit** menu, select **Modify Shared Web Part**:

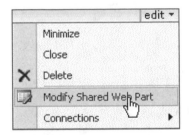

The following menu appears on the right-hand side of the page:

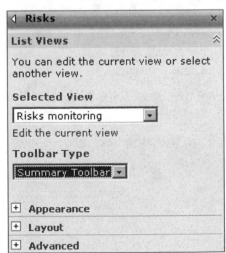

6. From the **Selected View** drop-down list, select the view that you want to appear on the web page (in the following example, **Risks monitoring**):

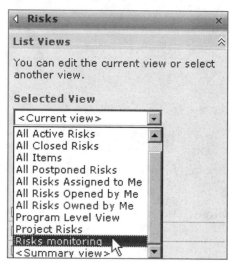

7. Click **OK**. The page is updated.

# Procurement: Contract Administration

The contract administration process ensures that a supplier delivers exactly what was asked for in the contract when it is due.

## Objectives

◆ To regularly check terms and conditions of the contract

◆ To ensure that changes made to the contract are dealt with using the change request procedure

◆ To verify that status reports are provided by the supplier

◆ To check planned vs. actual procedures

## Procedures

### To hold status meetings:

1. Receive status reports from each supplier and check the planned vs. actual and vs. contractual obligations of the deliverable due dates, costs, quality, and so on.

2. Save status reports in the reports folder of the procurement management document library:

3. Hold meetings with suppliers on a regular basis.

4. After each meeting with a supplier, make sure that all the decisions made in the meeting are documented in minutes of the meeting.

5. Save the minutes of meeting documents either in the procurement management document library or, if you have opened a workspace for these meetings, in the meeting workspace.

---

 In many cases, it is advisable to hold some of the meetings at the supplier's facilities, in order to check project progress in person instead of only by reviewing reports.

---

6. Manage action items resulting from the meetings.

### To check supplier quality:

1. Check quality of products received from each supplier.

2. If necessary, perform periodic vendor quality audits.

### To verify invoices:

1. Check all invoices received from suppliers on cost reimbursement contracts (cost plus, time and materials, and so on).

2. Monitor supplier resources and receive reports on resources.

3. If necessary, perform cost audits.

### To monitor contracts:

Monitor contract performance to check compliance with contract terms and conditions.

### To monitor change control:

Make sure that all changes are managed as defined by the change control process included in the contract.

## Prerequisites

There are no prerequisites for these procedures.

# Closing Process

## Overview

Some closing processes are performed at the end of one or more phases of a program/project. Others are performed only at the end of an entire program/project.

During the closing process, the deliverables of the program/project are verified to comply with the program/project requirements and scope. When all of the deliverables are accepted by the client, administrative closure is performed.

During project closure, the planned benefits of the program/project are delivered, program accomplishments are measured and reported on, and the handover of program activities to the customer is completed.

Key completion criteria are included in the program management plan developed during the planning phase.

The future ability of an organization to plan and implement projects depends on its ability to document programs/projects and use the document database to guide the planning and implementation of future programs/projects.

The procedures in this process are carried out:

◆ When a major phase is completed—verification of deliverables is carried out only at project termination

◆ When a project is completed

◆ When a project is terminated

Closure is managed and monitored using the closure checklist, to ensure that all activities required for closure are completed.

## Workflow

To provide a solution that meets the requirements that are defined for the closing process, the features/functions listed in Table 8.1 must be implemented.

### Table 8.1. Closing Feature/Function Processes

| Requirement | Solution Feature/ Function Guidelines | Relevant Procedure |
|---|---|---|
| **Integration Management** | | |
| Sponsor closure letter | Use Microsoft Word to write the document | "To issue the sponsor closure letter" |
| Create and manage the project closure checklist | Use the Windows Share-Point Services list to create the checklist | ◆ "To add items to the project closure checklist" <br> ◆ "To update the project closure checklist" |
| Hold the lessons learned meeting and save the results to the database | Use the Windows Share-Point Services document library to save the lessons learned documents | "To conduct lessons learned sessions" |
| Issue the end of program/project/phase report | Use Microsoft Word to create the report | "To create the end of program/project/phase report" |

## Table 8.1. Closing Feature/Function Processes (continued)

| Requirement | Solution Feature/ Function Guidelines | Relevant Procedure |
|---|---|---|
| **Scope Management** | | |
| Verify that all the deliverables have been delivered | Use the Windows SharePoint Services document library to save the formal documentation | ◆ "To ensure that all the deliverables have been delivered" <br> ◆ "To gain project acceptance" |
| Close the contract | Use Microsoft Word to document all relevant contract closures and use the Windows SharePoint Services document library to save the formal documentation | "To close the contract" |
| **Time Management** | | |
| Close the project plan | Use Project Professional to close tasks | "To terminate project activities" |
| **Cost Management** | | |
| Close all work packages and budget codes | Use Project Web Access to close the budget codes for reporting | "To close reporting codes" |
| **Human Resource Management** | | |
| Assign resources to other projects | | "To reassign team members" |
| **Communication Management** | | |
| Save all relevant information in the database for future use | Use the Windows SharePoint Services document library to save the data | "To save the project information to the database" |

**Table 8.1. Closing Feature/Function Processes (continued)**

| Requirement | Solution Feature/ Function Guidelines | Relevant Procedure |
|---|---|---|
| Close all open action items | Use the Windows Share-Point Services document library to close open action items or use the Windows SharePoint Services action items list to close open action items | "To close the action items log" |
| **Risk Management** | | |
| Close risks | Use the Windows Share-Point Services risks list to close risks | "To close the risk manage-ment activities" |
| **Procurement Management** | | |
| Close contracts with subcontractors | Use the Windows Share-Point Services document library to save all related documents | "To verify that all the deliverables have been received from sub-contractors" |

# Integration Management

## Objectives

◆ To verify that program/project/phase objectives have been met, including deliverables as appropriate

◆ To ensure that stakeholders are satisfied

◆ To communicate to stakeholders that the program/project/phase is complete

## Procedures

### To issue the sponsor closure letter:

The project sponsor carries out this activity.

1. Issue a closure letter to the client. The letter states that the program/project has been completed, deliverables have been delivered, and the final invoice has been issued.

2. Upload the letter to the project closure document library.

### To add items to the project closure checklist:

The organization may have a generic project closure checklist that was predefined for projects in the organization. You may want to add some specific items relevant to your program/project.

1. Open the **Project Web Access** home page.

2. Select the project workspace.

3. In the **Lists** section of the quick launch menu, click **Closure Checklist**:

4.  To add a new item to the checklist, from the **New** drop-down list, select **New Item**:

The following page will open:

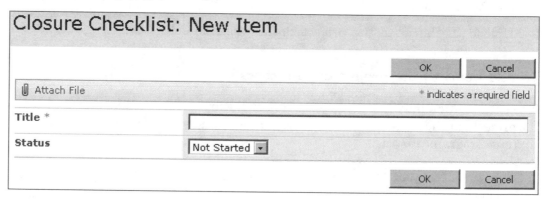

5.  Type the titles of the checklist items that you want to add.

6.  Repeat steps 4 and 5 until all required items have been added to the checklist.

### To update the project closure checklist:

As checklist items are acted upon, update their status in the checklist.

### To conduct lessons learned sessions:

1.  Gather information regarding time and schedule management, plans, actual data, etc.

2.  In a series of lessons learned sessions, analyze the information, and make a list of activities that went well and activities that did not go well.

3. The agenda and template for these sessions can be found in the project closure document library:

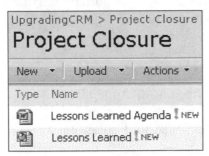

4. Conduct these meetings with the different forums (steering committee, team members, project managers) in order to gather more information and different point of views

5. Categorize the list of activities by project stage.

6. Where possible, determine:
   ◆ For things that went well, why these activities were successful.
   ◆ For things that did not go well, why these activities caused problems. Avoid blaming individuals; instead, concentrate on situations and events or triggers.

7. Document the lessons learned.

8. Save the document in the project closure document library.

## To create the end of program/project/phase report:

Create a report and archive the relevant materials. A template for such a report can be found in the project closure document library.

Examples of relevant materials include:

◆ Cost reports

◆ Status reports

◆ Risks

### Prerequisites

Prerequisites for the above procedures are creation of a document library and creation of a checklist for project/program/phase closure.

### To create the project closure document library:

Follow the procedure for creating a document library in Appendix A.3.

1. Upload the templates for lessons learned meetings, and create an agenda for lessons learned meetings.

2. Upload the agenda to the project closure document library.

3. Create a template for the presentation of the lessons learned.

4. Upload the template to the project closure document library.

5. Create a template for the end of phase/project/program report.

6. Upload the template to the project closure document library:

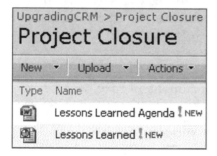

### To create the project closure checklist:

Create a closure checklist that includes the fields listed in Table 8.2. Follow the procedure for creating a new list in Appendix A.7.

**Table 8.2. Closure Checklist**

| Field Name | Description | Field Type |
|---|---|---|
| Title | Description of the item | Multiple-line text field |
| Status | Status of the item<br>Possible values:<br>◆ Not Started<br>◆ In Progress<br>◆ Completed<br>◆ N/A | Choice (value list) |

The following is a partial example of a checklist:

## Closure Checklist

| New ▾ | Actions ▾ | Settings ▾ | View: **All Items** ▾ |
|---|---|

| ◻ Title | Status |
|---|---|
| Close budget codes ! NEW | Not Started |
| Issue Project Sponsor closure document ! NEW | Not Started |
| Reassign the QA team to Project X ! NEW | Not Started |
| Write evaluation letters to the team members' functional managers ! NEW | Not Started |
| Write thank you letters to the team members ! NEW | Not Started |
| Archive documents ! NEW | Not Started |
| Did the customer approve all the deliverables? ! NEW | Not Started |
| Conduct lessons learned meeting ! NEW | Not Started |
| Issue lessons learned document ! NEW | Not Started |
| Check requirements matrix to see completion of activities ! NEW | Not Started |
| Check contract to see all items delivered ! NEW | Not Started |
| Receive final acceptance note from the customer ! NEW | Not Started |

## Scope Management: Deliverables Closure

### Objective

◆ To ensure that all the deliverables have been completed and delivered

### Procedures

#### To ensure that all the deliverables have been delivered:

1. Ensure that all the deliverables have been delivered to and approved by their intended recipients.

2. Ensure that all the deliverables have been stored and that versioning has been updated.

3. Ensure that the deliverables tracking log has been completed with the required information.

#### To gain project acceptance:

Ensure that the program/project manager, customer decision makers, and project sponsor acknowledge that all deliverables produced during project execution have been completed and delivered to the end user.

#### To close the contract:

Ensure that all open items in the contract are closed.

1. Verify that all deliverables are delivered.

2. Gain project acceptance.

3. Save the acceptance documents in the project closure document library.

### Prerequisites

There are no prerequisites for these procedures.

## Time Management

### Objective

◆ To ensure that the time and schedule management process is closed down and that the corresponding documents are archived

### Procedure

**To terminate project activities:**

Verify that all activities in the project plan have been completed.

### Prerequisites

There are no prerequisites for this procedure.

## Cost Management

In the cost closure process, the following must be completed:

◆ Pay the final invoices of the subcontractors

◆ Issue the final invoice to the customer

◆ Receive the final payment from the customer

◆ Close the budget reporting codes used in the project

◆ Dispose of the project assets

◆ Report final profit and loss

### Objective

◆ To close all of the financial activities of the project

## Procedure

### To close reporting codes:

When a reporting code has been closed, progress can no longer be reported against it, except for activities for which the reporting type is either "done" or "not done".

1. Open the **Project Web Access** home page.

2. Select the project workspace.

3. In the quick launch menu, click **Project Center**:

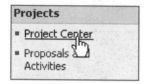

4. Select the project.

5. From the **Actions** drop-down list, select **Close Tasks to Updates**:

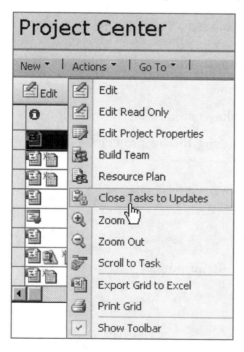

The **Close Tasks to Update** page opens:

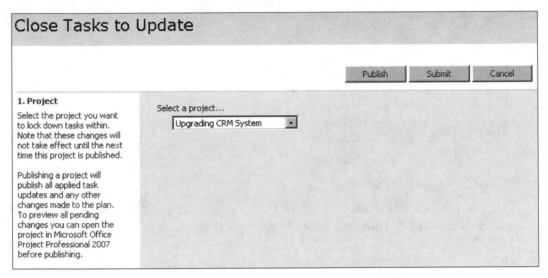

6. Select the project.

7. Select the tasks that you want to close for reporting:

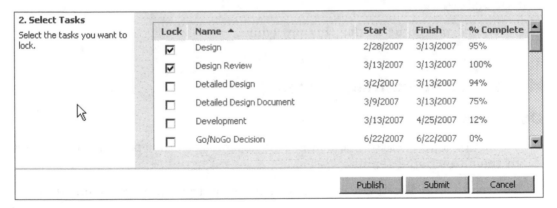

8. Click **Publish**.

9. Open the project for editing in Project Professional.

10. From the **File** menu, select **Publish...**:

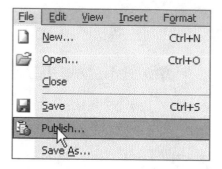

11. Close Project Professional.

12. In the project schedule in Project Professional, the  icon is displayed next to activities that are locked for reporting:

| | ⊟ Upgrading the CRM Software |
|---|---|
| 🗹 🗹 | Design Review |

## Prerequisites

There are no prerequisites for this procedure.

# Human Resource Management

## Objectives

◆ To ensure that the team members are reassigned to other projects or returned to their functional teams

◆ To ensure that the team members know what their next assignment is

## Procedure

### To reassign team members:

1. Make sure that all the team members are either reassigned to other projects or returned to their functional teams.

2. Evaluate the team members.

3. Write "thank-you" letters to the team members.

## Prerequisites

There are no prerequisites for this procedure.

# Communication Management

## Objective

◆ To save all the project information in the project workspace for future use and for knowledge management

## Procedure

### To save the project information to the database:

Check to see that all relevant project information, documentation, and presentations are stored in the project workspace. Documents and files that are not should be uploaded to the correct document libraries for future use.

## Prerequisites

There are no prerequisites for this procedure.

# Action Items

## Objective

◆ To ensure that the action items log is closed and archived

## Procedure

### To close the action items log:

1. Update the action items log to include:
   ◆ Descriptions of the activities carried out
   ◆ Deliverables provided
2. Close the items in the log.

## Prerequisites

There are no prerequisites for this procedure.

# Risk Management

## Objectives

◆ To ensure that all risks are closed and the risks tracking log is archived

◆ To ensure that at the end of each significant stage (such as development, system test, different phases of the project life cycle in a multiphase project), lessons learned from the risk management process are evaluated for implementation as quality improvement activities

## Procedure

### To close the risk management activities:

1. Update the risks log to include:
   ◆ Descriptions of the activities carried out
   ◆ Solutions provided
   ◆ Plans implemented

2. Close the items in the log.

## Prerequisites

There are no prerequisites for this procedure.

# Procurement Management

## Objective

◆ To close all contracts with subcontractors and complete all related financial activities

## Procedure

**To verify that all deliverables have been received from subcontractors:**

1. Review contracts and statements of work in the procurement management document library:

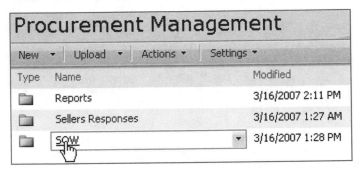

2. Perform an audit to ensure that all contracted deliverables have been delivered per the quality requirements specified.

3. Issue a letter to notify each subcontractor that all deliverables have been accepted.

4. Save the letters in the procurement management document library.

5. With the support of the purchasing and legal departments, pay all final invoices and close all contracts.

## Prerequisites

There are no prerequisites for this procedure.

# Converting Your Sample Site to Be the Default Project Workspace

The following procedure enables you to save your sample site as a site template that Project Server will use to create a new project workspace whenever a new project plan is published on that server.

You will need to use Microsoft Office SharePoint Designer 2007 in order to enable Project Server to use your sample site as a site template.

**To make your sample site the default project workspace:**

1. Log in to the machine where Windows SharePoint Server is installed.

2. Open the project workspace you used as your sample project site (for example, in this book "Upgrading the CRM System").

3.  Open the site in Microsoft SharePoint Designer by clicking the **Edit with Microsoft SharePoint Designer** icon located on the Internet browser toolbar.

4.  Click **Site > Site Settings...**:

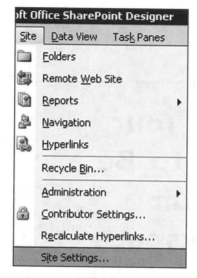

The **Site Settings** window opens.

5. Choose the **Parameters** tab in the **Site Settings** window:

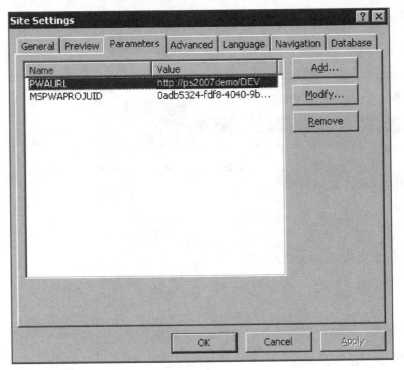

6. Choose the **PWAURL** entry and click **Modify**:

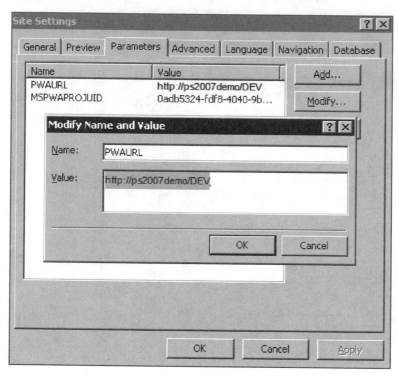

7. Clear the value in the **Value** field and click **OK**.

8. Choose the **MSPWAPROJUID** entry and click **Modify**:

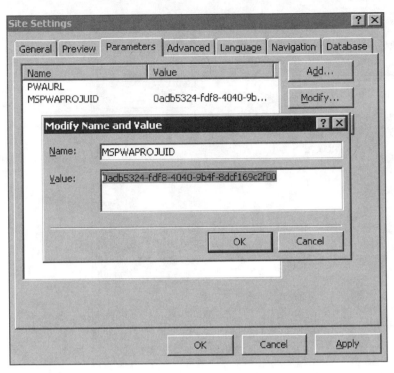

9. Clear the value in the **Value** field and click **OK**:

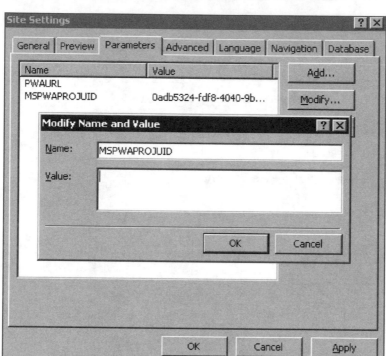

10. Click **OK** and then **File > Save** to save your changes.

11. Click **File > Close Site**.

12. Return to your project workspace and select **Site Actions > Site Settings**:

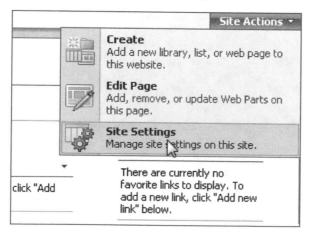

13. In the **Look and Feel** section, click **Save Site as Template**. The following screen will open:

| File Name | File name: |
|---|---|
| Enter the name for this template file. | PWS .stp |
| **Name and Description** | Template name: |
| The name and description of this template will be displayed on the Web site template picker page when users create new Web sites. | Org Project Workspace |
| | Template description: |
| **Include Content** | ☑ Include Content |
| Include content in your template if you want new Web sites created from this | |

14. Enter the **File name** of the template file.

15. Enter the name and description of the site, such as "<OrgName>Project Workspace". The name and description of this template will be displayed on the web site template picker page when users create new web sites.

16. Check the **Include Content** box. This will include the contents of all lists and document libraries in the web site.

17. On the **Operation Completed Successfully** page, click the **Go to the site template gallery** link. The site template gallery now lists your template:

Click the project workspace name and save the file to your local drive (for example, C:\PMO).

18. Select **Start > Run**, type "CMD", and click **OK**.

19. Use CD (change directory command in CMD) to navigate to the directory where the stsadm.exe file resides. In most cases, the directory is C:\Program Files\Common Files\Microsoft Shared\web server extensions\12\BIN:

Type "stsadm.exe -o addtemplate -filename <template filename> -title <template title>" (for example, "stsadm.exe -o addtemplate -filename c:\PMO\PWS.stp -title OrgProjectWorkspace"):

20. Upon successful completion of the operation, type "IISRESET" and press **Enter** on the keyboard to restart the IIS service.

21. Open Project Web Access and select **Server Settings** from the quick launch menu.

22. In the **Operational Policies** section, click **Project Workspace Provisioning Settings**.

23. From the **Default Project Workspace template** drop-down list, select the project workspace you have added:

24. Click **Save**.

## To verify that the sample site was successfully added to Project Server:

1. Create a new project plan.

2. Save the plan on the server.

3. Publish the plan.

4. Open Project Web Access.

5. Open the project workspace of the new plan you have published.

# 10

# Testing and Deploying the Enterprise Project Management Solution

## Testing the Solution with a Pilot Team/Project

In this stage, your solution is tested by a pilot team for a period of several months in order to prepare the solution for organization-wide deployment. Figure 10.1 illustrates the testing solution process.

So far, you have established the methodology and supporting tools. You have a system, and now you want to start deploying it. The first stage is to pilot the system.

The PMO is ready to test it "for real". The EPM implementation steering committee must verify that what you have defined is correct, and then you can move to the pilot phase.

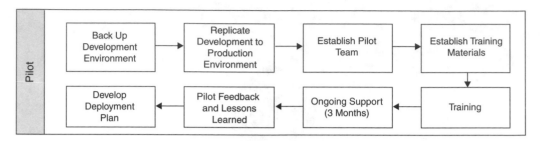

**Figure 10.1. Testing Solution Process**

## Back Up the Development Environment

Ask your IT department to back up the SQL databases of your development environment.

## Replicate the Development Environment to the Production Environment

Ask your IT department to restore the SQL databases of your development environment to the production environment.

## Establish the Pilot Team

The steering committee selects a project or projects for the pilot.

The pilot project should:

◆ Be typical for the organization; if there are several divisions with different types of typical projects, then there should be a pilot project for each division, to ensure that the solution fits most typical projects in the organization

◆ Be at the beginning of its life cycle—in the initiation phase

◆ Preferably be cross-functional

The pilot team includes project managers and the team members.

# Establish Training Materials

Prepare the training material for the following presentations and workshops:

- Presentation for the pilot project managers
- One- to two-day hands-on workshop
- Workshop for the pilot project team members
- Presentation for the pilot project steering committee and senior management

# Training

This section describes the process of implementing EPM in the pilot project.

## Presentation for the Pilot Project Managers

### *Purpose*

- To ensure the project managers' support for the pilot and EPM implementation
- To explain to the project managers what is expected of them in the course of the pilot project

### *Duration*

- Two to three hours

### *Syllabus*

- The rationale behind the tool, its advantages, and it possibilities

## One- to Two-Day Hands-on Workshop

### *Purpose*

- To explain the methodology and the EPM procedures
- To help the pilot project managers understand what is expected of them

### Duration

◆ One to two days

### Syllabus (Sample Topics)

◆ Brief description of the project management methodology used in the tool

◆ How to open a new project in the EPM system

◆ How to build resource teams from enterprise resources

◆ How to upload documents to the EPM system

◆ How to connect risks to the project schedule

◆ How to open a project from a template

◆ How to publish a project

◆ Other

## Workshop for the Pilot Project Team Members

### Purpose

◆ To ensure the team members' support for the pilot and EPM implementation

◆ To explain to the pilot team members what is expected of them in the course of the pilot project

### Duration

◆ Five hours

### Syllabus

◆ The rationale behind the tool, its advantages, and it possibilities

◆ Expectations from the team members

◆ Progress reports

◆ Risks

◆ Requests for new tasks

◆ Other

### Presentation for the Pilot Project Steering Committee and Senior Management

#### Purpose

◆ To ensure senior management support for the pilot and EPM implementation

◆ To describe the benefits of the system

#### Duration

◆ Two to three hours (can be one-on-one)

#### Syllabus

◆ The rationale behind the tool, its advantages, and it possibilities

◆ Viewing reports and making decisions based on those reports

## Ongoing Support (Three Months)

After the project managers and team members have completed the workshops, they create a project using the EPM system. They allocate resources, upload documents to the project home page, and use templates.

The PMO team provides support by helping with implementation of the system and collecting requests and critical issues (those that must be handled immediately). Requests that are not critical for the operation are collected and considered for implementation later on.

The pilot team holds status meetings and steering committee meetings in order to check whether the system is useful and supports their needs.

The pilot team works with the system for about three months, updating the status at least once a week. The system implementation team (PMO) provides support on a regular basis.

## Pilot Feedback and Lessons Learned

After the above period, the system implementation team collects all the requirements and comments raised during the pilot period. The team also sends a questionnaire to the pilot project managers, team members, and executives to verify their satisfaction with the system. This survey can be created on the pilot project home page.

Before the survey is distributed, there must be agreement on the passing grade in terms of whether the system provides a solution for the organization, to ensure buy-in and to continue with the implementation.

## Develop the Deployment Plan

A go/no-go decision is made regarding system implementation in the organization.

If the decision is to proceed, a deployment plan is developed that includes at least the following:

◆ Time frame—phases of deployment

◆ The projects to be implemented and at what phase

◆ The level of support to be given to the project teams

◆ Who will support which group of projects

◆ Training plan

◆ Version update points

## Deploying the Solution to Organization Units

After the pilot stage is over, the solution is fine-tuned based on the feedback received from the pilot team and is then deployed according to the deployment plan.

It is recommended that the system be deployed gradually. The deployment process is similar to the pilot process—presentations, training, workshops, and support from the PMO team—but with a larger number of projects. The projects to be deployed should be defined in the first stage.

A lessons learned session should be held after every project deployed. If there is a need for improvement and fine-tuning, this should be done before moving on to the next stage.

# Appendices

# Appendix A:
# Common Procedures

This appendix describes the graphical user interface (GUI) procedures used to:

1. Define enterprise custom fields
2. Create lookup tables for enterprise custom fields
3. Create a document library
4. Change document metadata
5. Change document library settings
6. Upload a document to a document library
7. Create a new list
8. Change a column name in a list
9. Add a choice column to a list
10. Add a yes/no (check box) column to a list
11. Add a text column
12. Add a multiple lines of text column
13. Add a lookup column
14. Add a number column
15. Add a currency column
16. Add a calculated column
17. Add a "person or group" column
18. Add a date column
19. Change the order of columns in a list
20. Modify an existing list

21. Create a list view
22. Modify an existing column
23. Create a folder in an existing document library

## 1. To define enterprise custom fields:

1. Navigate to Project Web Access (development environment).

2. In the left pane menu, select **Server Settings**:

3. On the **Server Settings** page, under the **Enterprise Data** column, select **Enterprise Custom Field Definition**:

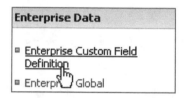

4. On the following page, under **Enterprise Custom Fields**, select **New Field:**

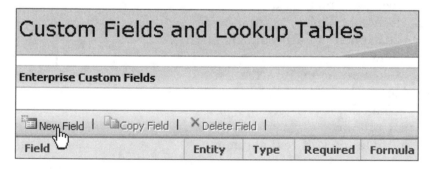

The **New Custom Field** page opens.

5.  Fill in the data for the new field:

| Name | |
| --- | --- |
| **Name**<br>Type a unique name for the custom field. | Name<br>`_Responsible Division` |
| **Entity and Type**<br>The entity and type for this custom field. | Entity<br>`Task`<br><br>Type<br>`Text` |
| **Custom Attributes**<br>Choose whether the field has a lookup table, a calculated formula, or neither. | ○ None<br>◉ Lookup Table `OBS`<br>☐ Use a value from the table as the default entry for the field<br>Default Value [        ] `...`<br>☐ Only allow codes with no subordinate values<br>☐ Allow multiple values to be selected from lookup table<br><br>○ Formula |
| **Calculation for Assignment Rows**<br>You can choose how this field gets rolled down to assignments. | ◉ None<br>○ Roll down, unless manually specified |
| **Values to Display**<br>Choose whether you want just the data or graphical indicators to be displayed. Graphical indicators are not displayed in all areas of Project Web Access. | ◉ Data<br>○ Graphical indicators |

In the example above, the **Name** of the field is "_Responsible Division". **Entity** is **Task**, and **Type** is **Text**. In the **Custom Attributes** field, **Lookup Table** "OBS" is entered.

---

 If you are choosing to use a lookup table, create that table **prior** to creating the custom field.

---

6. Fill in the information required.

7. Click **Save**.

## 2. To create lookup tables for enterprise custom fields:

1. Navigate to Project Web Access (development environment).

2. In the left pane menu, select **Server Settings**:

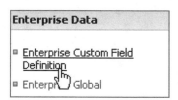

3. On the **Server Settings** page, under the **Enterprise Data** column, select **Enterprise Custom Field Definition**:

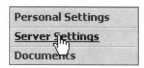

4. On the following page, under **Lookup Tables for Custom Fields**, select **New Lookup Table**:

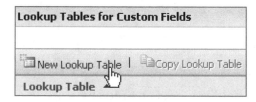

The **New Lookup Table** page opens:

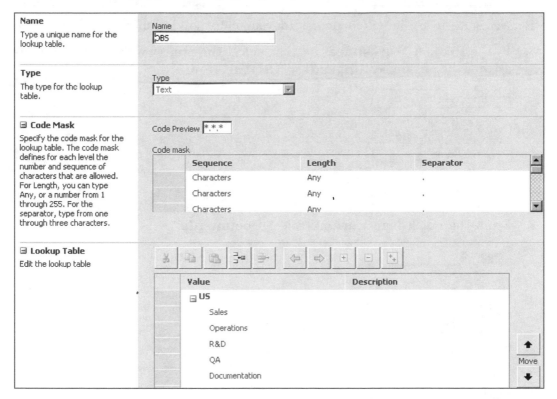

5.  Fill in the data. The example above shows the "OBS" lookup table.

6.  Fill in the values of the lookup table.

7.  Click **Save**.

### 3. To create a document library:

1. Navigate to Project Web Access (development environment).

2. In the **Project Workspaces** section, select the project workspace you have created (for example, **Upgrading CRM System**):

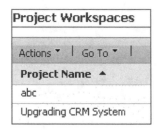

3. From the quick launch menu, select **Documents**:

4. Click **Create**:

5. In the **Libraries** section, select **Document Library**:

The **New** page opens:

```
Upgrading CRM System > Create > New
New
```

**Name and Description**

Type a new name as you want it to appear in headings and links throughout the site. Type descriptive text that will help site visitors use this document library.

Name:

```
Project Initiation
```

Description:

```
Includes the documentation
produced in the project initiation
phase
```

**Navigation**

Specify whether a link to this document library appears in the Quick Launch.

Display this document library on the Quick Launch?

⦿ Yes    ○ No

**Document Version History**

Specify whether a version is created each time you edit a file in this document library.   Learn about versions.

Create a version each time you edit a file in this document library?

○ Yes    ⦿ No

**Document Template**

Select a document template to determine the default for all new files created in this document library.

Document Template:

```
Microsoft Office Word 97-2003 document
```

[ Create ]   [ Cancel ]

6.  In the **Name** field, type the name of the document library (for example, "Project Initiation").

7.  In the **Description** field, type a description of the library.

8.  In the **Navigation** field, select the **Yes** option button (if you want the library to appear in the quick launch menu).

9. If you want to manage the document versions, select the **Yes** option button in the **Document Version History** field.

10. Click **Create**. The new document library is displayed in the **Documents** section:

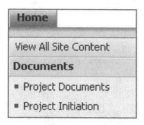

### 4. To change document metadata:

1. On the document library's home page, from the **Settings** menu, select **Document Library Settings**:

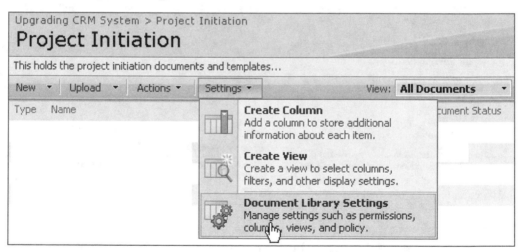

The **Customize <Document Library Name>** page opens.

2. In this section, you can choose to add columns, manage views, or customize columns to reflect the information that you want for your documentation:

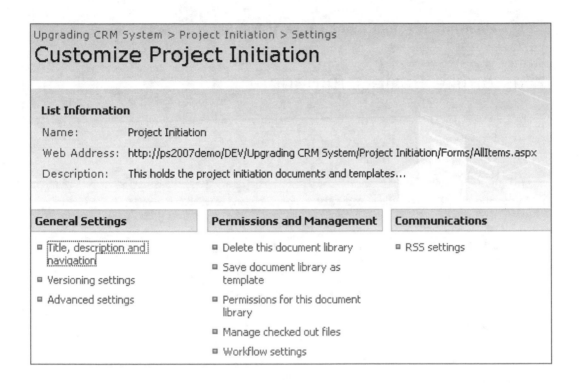

## 5. To change document library settings:

1. On the document library's home page, from the **Settings** menu, select **Document Library Settings**:

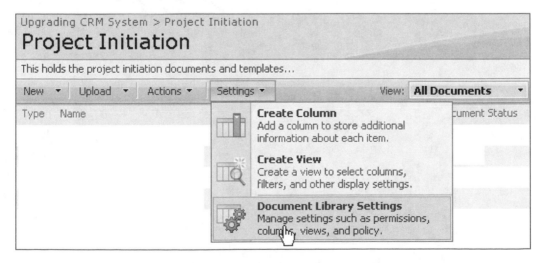

The **Customize <Document Library Name>** page opens:

Upgrading CRM System > Project Initiation > Settings

# Customize Project Initiation

### List Information

Name:            Project Initiation

Web Address:     http://ps2007demo/DEV/Upgrading CRM System/Project Initiation/Forms/AllItems.aspx

Description:     This holds the project initiation documents and templates...

| General Settings | Permissions and Management | Communications |
|---|---|---|
| ▫ Title, description and navigation | ▫ Delete this document library | ▫ RSS settings |
| ▫ Versioning settings | ▫ Save document library as template | |
| ▫ Advanced settings | ▫ Permissions for this document library | |
| | ▫ Manage checked out files | |
| | ▫ Workflow settings | |

## Columns

A column stores information about each document in the document library. The following columns are currently available in this document library:

| Column (click to edit) | Type | Required |
|---|---|---|
| Title | Single line of text | |
| Document Status | Choice | |
| Created By | Person or Group | |
| Modified By | Person or Group | |
| Checked Out To | Person or Group | |

- Create column
- Add from existing site columns
- Column ordering
- Indexed columns

## Views

A view of a document library allows you to see a particular selection of items or to see the items sorted in a particular order. Views currently configured for this document library:

| View (click to edit) | Default View |
|---|---|
| All Documents | ✔ |
| Explorer View | |
| By Status | |

- Create view

2. To add a column to the document library, click the **Create column** link:

**Columns**

A column stores information about each document in the document library. The following columns are currently available in this document library:

| Column (click to edit) | Type | Required |
|---|---|---|
| Title | Single line of text | |
| Document Status | Choice | |
| Created By | Person or Group | |
| Modified By | Person or Group | |
| Checked Out To | Person or Group | |

▫ Create column
▫ Add from existing site columns
▫ Column ordering
▫ Indexed columns

The **Create Column** page opens:

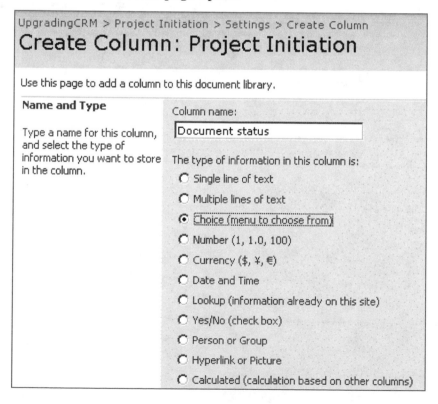

UpgradingCRM > Project Initiation > Settings > Create Column
# Create Column: Project Initiation

Use this page to add a column to this document library.

**Name and Type**

Type a name for this column, and select the type of information you want to store in the column.

Column name:

Document status

The type of information in this column is:

○ Single line of text
○ Multiple lines of text
◉ Choice (menu to choose from)
○ Number (1, 1.0, 100)
○ Currency ($, ¥, €)
○ Date and Time
○ Lookup (information already on this site)
○ Yes/No (check box)
○ Person or Group
○ Hyperlink or Picture
○ Calculated (calculation based on other columns)

3. In the **Column name** field, type a name for the new column.

4. Select the type of information to be stored in the column (text, choice, etc.). In the example above, **Choice (menu to choose from)** is selected.

5. In the **Additional Column Settings** section, in the **Description** field, type a brief description of the column:

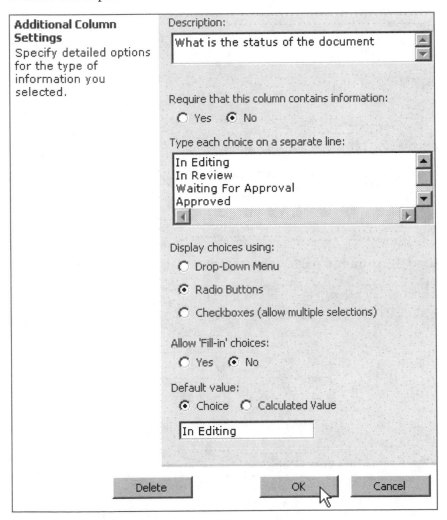

6. Define whether the column is mandatory (by selecting **Yes** under **Require that this column contains information**).

7. Add the choices.

8. Click **OK**.

### 6. To upload a document to a document library:

1. In the **Documents** section, click the **<Document Library Name>** link (for example, **Project Management Plan**):

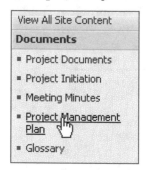

The **<Document Library Name>** page opens. Click **Upload**:

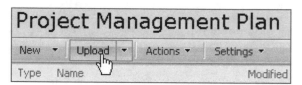

2. The **Upload Document** page opens. Click the **Browse...** button:

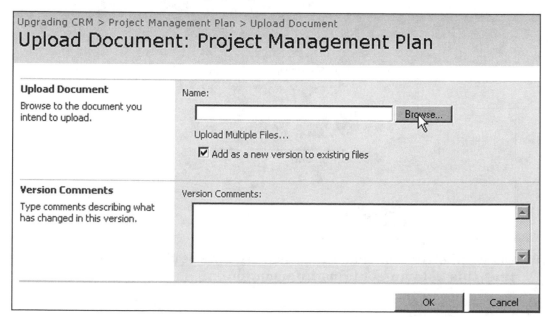

3. The **Choose file** dialog opens:

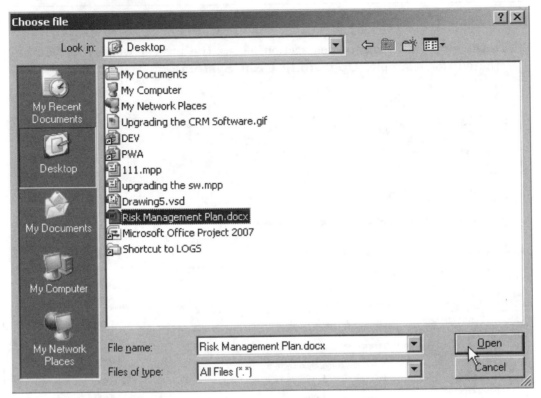

4. Select the file that you want to upload (for example, **Risk Management Plan.docx**) and click **Open**.

5. On the **Upload Document** page, click **OK**. The document is uploaded to the document library:

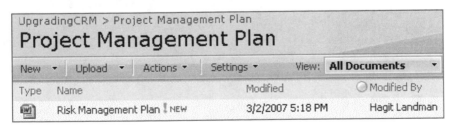

## 7. To create a new list:

1. Navigate to the Project Web Access development environment.

2. In the **Project Workspaces** section, select the project workspace you have created (for example, **Upgrading CRM System**):

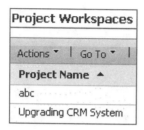

The selected project's workspace opens:

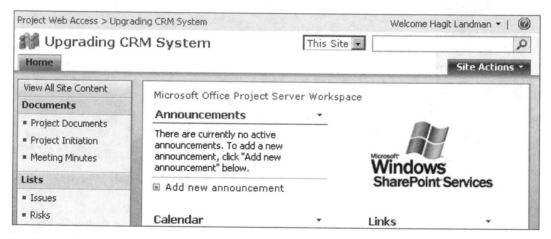

3. From the quick launch menu, select **Lists**:

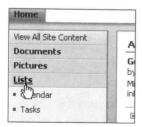

The **All Site Content** page opens.

4. Click **Create**:

5. Click **Custom List**:

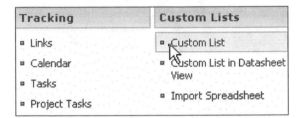

The **New** page opens:

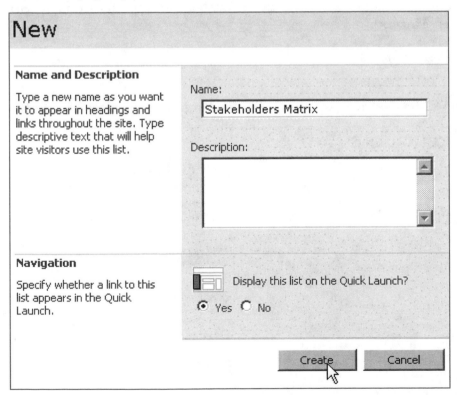

6. In the **Name** field, type a name for the list (for example, "Stakeholders Matrix").

7. In the **Description** field, type a description of the list.

8. If you want the list to appear in the quick launch menu, select the **Yes** option button in the **Navigation** section.

9. Click **Create**. The **<List Name>** page opens:

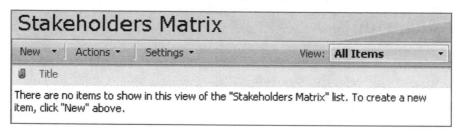

### 8. To change a column name in a list:

1. On the project home page, click the **<List Name>** link (for example, **Stakeholders Matrix**):

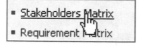

2. On the **<List Name>** page, from the **Settings** menu, select **List Settings**:

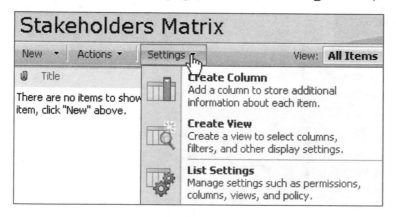

3. In the **Columns** section, click the **Title** link:

4. In the **Column name** field, type over the current column name with the new name (for example, type "Stakeholder Name" to replace "Title").

5. Click **OK**.

## 9. To add a choice column to a list:

1. On the project home page, from the quick launch menu, select the list you want to add a choice column to (for example, **Stakeholders Matrix**).

2. On the **<List Name>** page, from the **Settings** menu, select **List Settings**:

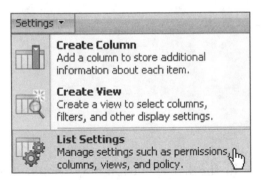

3. In the **Columns** section, click the **Create column** link:

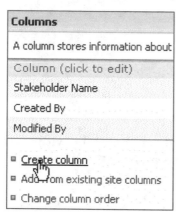

The **Additional Column Settings** page opens.

4. In the **Column name** field, type a name for the new column (for example, "Stakeholder Type").

5. Select the **Choice (menu to choose from)** option button:

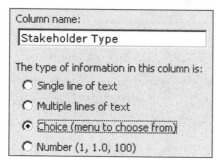

6. Enter the values you want to appear in the list (for example, "Vendor/Supplier", "Team Leader", etc.):

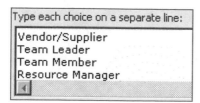

7. Click **OK**.

## 10. To add a yes/no (check box) column to a list:

1. On the project home page, from the quick launch menu, select the list you want to add a choice column to (for example, **Stakeholders Matrix**).

2. On the **<List Name>** page, from the **Settings** menu, select **Create Column**:

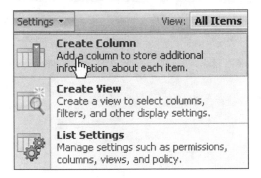

   The **Create Column** page opens.

3. In the **Column name** field, type a name for the column (for example, "Belong to Organization?").

4. Select the **Yes/No (check box)** option button:

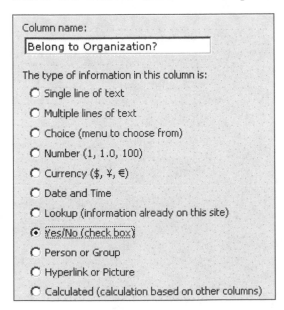

5. Click **OK**.

## 11. To add a text column:

1. On the project home page, from the quick launch menu, select the list you want to add a choice column to (for example, **Stakeholders Matrix**).

2. On the **<List Name>** page, from the **Settings** menu, select **Create Column**:

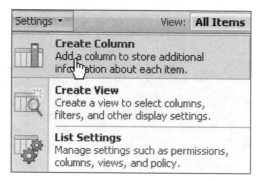

   The **Create Column** page opens.

3. In the **Column name** field, type a name for the column (for example, "If No, Company Name").

4. Select the **Single line of text** option button:

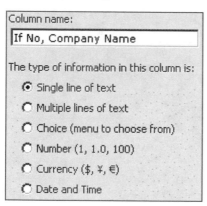

5. In the **Default value** section, select the **Text** or **Calculated Value** option button:

**Additional Column Settings**
Specify detailed options for the type of information you selected.

Description:

Require that this column contains information:
○ Yes  ● No

Maximum number of characters:
255

Default value:
● Text  ○ Calculated Value

[ Delete ]   [ OK ]   [ Cancel ]

6. Click **OK**.

## 12. To add a multiple lines of text column:

1. Use the procedure in Appendix A.11 to add a text column.

2. In the **Column name** field, type a name for the column (for example, "Title and Role in Organization").

3. Select the **Multiple lines of text** option button:

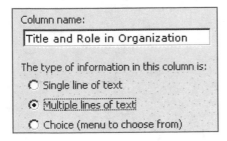

Column name:
Title and Role in Organization

The type of information in this column is:
○ Single line of text
● Multiple lines of text
○ Choice (menu to choose from)

## 13. To add a lookup column:

1. On the project home page, from the quick launch menu, select the list you want to add a choice column to (for example, **Stakeholders Matrix**).

2. On the **<List Name>** page, from the **Settings** menu, select **Create Column**:

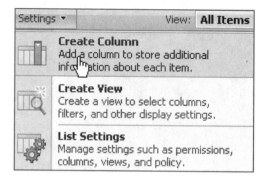

The **Create Column** page opens.

3. In the **Column name** field, type a name for the column (for example, "Relevant Stakeholder").

4. Select the **Lookup (information already on this site)** option button:

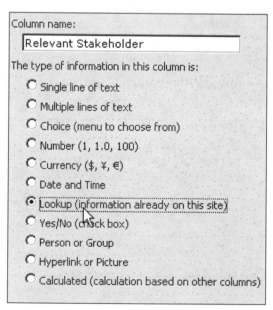

5. From the **Get information from** drop-down list, select **Stakeholders Matrix**:

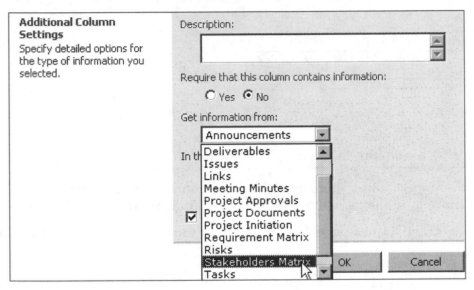

6. From the **In this column** drop-down list, select **Stakeholder Name (linked to item)**:

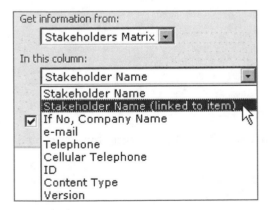

This enables you to choose a field from the list selected. In the example above, it enables you to choose a stakeholder name from the stakeholders matrix list. It is recommended that you choose **(linked to item)**, so that when you click on the stakeholder name, the relevant "stakeholder matrix" information which is linked to this stakeholder will be displayed.

7. To allow multiple values for the column, check the **Allow multiple values** box:

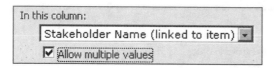

8. Click **OK**.

## 14. To add a number column:

1. On the project home page, from the quick launch menu, select the list you want to add a choice column to (for example, **Stakeholders Matrix**).

2. On the **<List Name>** page, from the **Settings** menu, select **Create Column**:

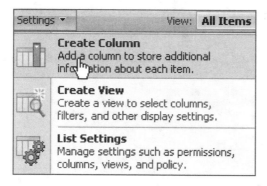

The **Create Column** page opens.

3. In the **Column name** field, type a name for the column (for example, "In-house Work Effort Estimate").

4. Select the **Number** option button:

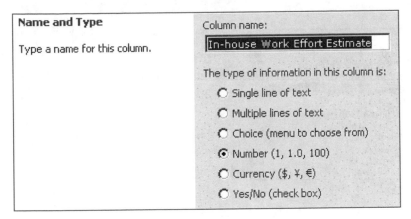

5. Click **OK**.

## 15. To add a currency column:

1. Use steps 1 and 2 of the procedure in Appendix A.14 to add a number column.

2. In the **Column name** field, type the name of the column (for example, "Average In House MP Cost per Hour").

3. Select the **Currency** option button:

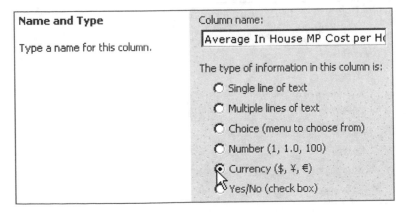

4. From the **Currency format** drop-down list, select the required format:

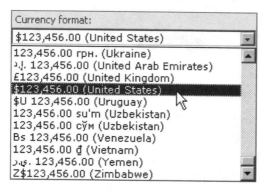

5. Click **OK**.

---

### 16. To add a calculated column:

---

1. Use steps 1 and 2 of the procedure in Appendix A.14 to add a number column.

2. In the **Column name** field, type the name of the column (for example, "Total In-house MP Costs").

3. Select the **Calculated** option button:

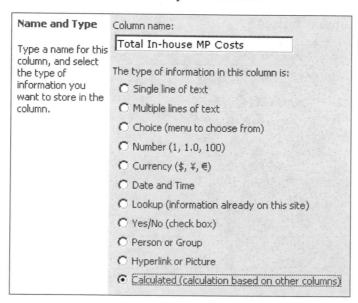

4. Select the columns you want to use in the calculation formula and click **Add to formula**:

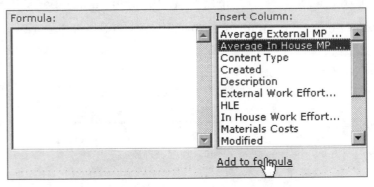

5. Build the formula and click **Add to formula**:

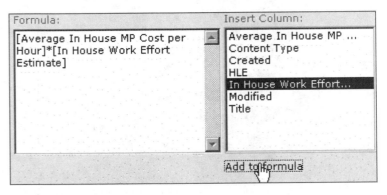

6. Select the data type you want the formula to return (for example, select the **Currency** option button):

> The data type returned from this formula is:
> ○ Single line of text
> ○ Number (1, 1.0, 100)
> ⊙ Currency ($, ¥, €)
> ○ Date and Time
> ○ Yes/No

7. Click **OK**.

## 17. To add a "person or group" column:

1. Use steps 1 and 2 of the procedure in Appendix A.14 to add a number column.

2. In the **Column name** field, type a name for the column (for example, "Approver Name").

3. Select the **Person or Group** option button:

| Name and Type | Column name: |
|---|---|
| Type a name for this column, and select the type of information you want to store in the column. | Approver Name |
| | The type of information in this column is: |
| | ○ Single line of text |
| | ○ Multiple lines of text |
| | ○ Choice (menu to choose from) |
| | ○ Number (1, 1.0, 100) |
| | ○ Currency ($, ¥, €) |
| | ○ Date and Time |
| | ○ Lookup (information already on this site) |
| | ○ Yes/No (check box) |
| | ⦿ Person or Group |
| | ○ Hyperlink or Picture |
| | ○ Calculated (calculation based on other columns) |

4. Select the list of names you want to choose from and the type of personal data you want to be displayed:

5. Click **OK**.

## 18. To add a date column:

1. Use steps 1 and 2 of the procedure in Appendix A.14 to add a number column.

2. In the **Column name** field, type a name for the column (for example, "Approval Date").

3. Select the **Date and Time** option button:

| Name and Type | Column name: |
|---|---|
| Type a name for this column, and select the type of information you want to store in the column. | Approval Date |
| | The type of information in this column is: |
| | ○ Single line of text |
| | ○ Multiple lines of text |
| | ○ Choice (menu to choose from) |
| | ○ Number (1, 1.0, 100) |
| | ○ Currency ($, ¥, €) |
| | ◉ Date and Time |
| | ○ Lookup (information already on this site) |
| | ○ Yes/No (check box) |
| | ○ Person or Group |
| | ○ Hyperlink or Picture |
| | ○ Calculated (calculation based on other columns) |

4. Select the **Date and Time Format** and the **Default value** (usually **Today's Date**):

5. Click **OK**.

### 19. To change the order of columns in a list:

1. On the project home page, from the quick launch menu, select the list for which you want to change the column order (for example, **Stakeholders Matrix**).

2. On the **<List Name>** page, from the **Settings** menu, select **List Settings**:

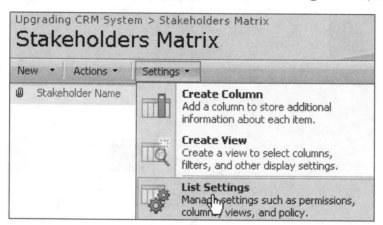

3. On the page that opens, click the **Column ordering** link:

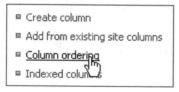

The **Change Field Order** page opens:

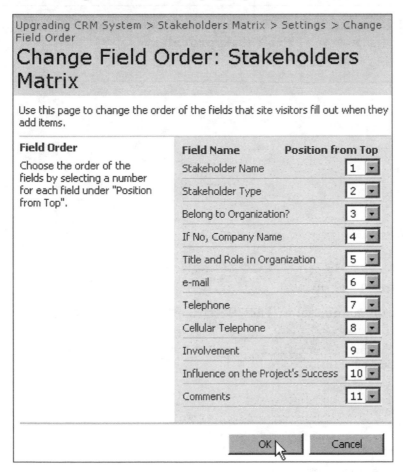

4. Use the **Position from Top** drop-down lists to define the order of the columns in the list.

5. Click **OK**.

## 20. To modify an existing list:

1. On the project home page, from the quick launch menu, select the list you want to modify (for example, **Project Approvals**):

The **<List Name>** page opens.

2. From the **Settings** menu, select **List Settings**:

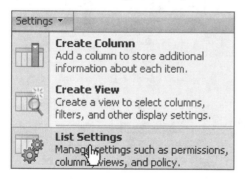

The **Customize <List Name>** page opens:

Upgrading CRM System > Project Approvals > Settings

# Customize Project Approvals

## List Information

Name:  Project Approvals

Web Address:  http://ps2007demo/DEV/Upgrading CRM System/Lists/Project Approvals/AllItems.aspx

Description:

| General Settings | Permissions and Management | Communications |
|---|---|---|
| ▫ Title, description and navigation | ▫ Delete this list | ▫ RSS settings |
| ▫ Versioning settings | ▫ Save list as template | |
| ▫ Advanced settings | ▫ Permissions for this list | |
| | ▫ Workflow settings | |

## Columns

A column stores information about each item in the list. The following columns are currently available in this list:

| Column (click to edit) | Type | Required |
|---|---|---|
| Title | Single line of text | ✔ |
| Name of Approver | Single line of text | |
| Approved? | Yes/No | |
| Approval Date | Date and Time | |
| Comments | Multiple lines of text | |
| Created By | Person or Group | |
| Modified By | Person or Group | |

▫ Create column

▫ Add from existing site columns

▫ Column ordering

▫ Indexed columns

## Views

A view of a list allows you to see a particular selection of items or to see the items sorted in a particular order. Views currently configured for this list:

| View (click to edit) | Default View |
|---|---|
| All Items | ✔ |

▫ Create view

3. Select the modification you want to make.

4. Follow the wizard prompts.

5. Click **OK**.

## 21. To create a list view:

1. On the project home page, from the quick launch menu, select the list for which you want to create a view (for example, **Requirement Matrix**):

The **<List Name>** page opens.

2. From the **Settings** menu, select **Create View**:

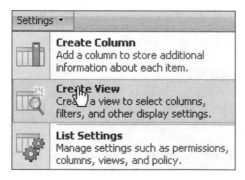

The **Create View** page opens:

Upgrading CRM System > Requirement Matrix > Settings > View Type

# Create View: Requirement Matrix

Use this page to select the type of view you want to create for your data.

### Choose a view format

 Standard View
View data on a Web page. You can choose from a list of display styles.

 Datasheet View
View data in an editable spreadsheet format that is convenient for bulk editing and quick customization.

 Calendar View
View data as a daily, weekly, or monthly calendar.

 Gantt View
View list items in a Gantt chart to see a graphical representation of how a team's tasks relate over time.

 Access View
Start Microsoft Office Access to create forms and reports that are based on this list.

### Start from an existing view

▪ All Items

3. Under **Choose a view format**, select the view format (for example, **Standard View**). The following page opens:

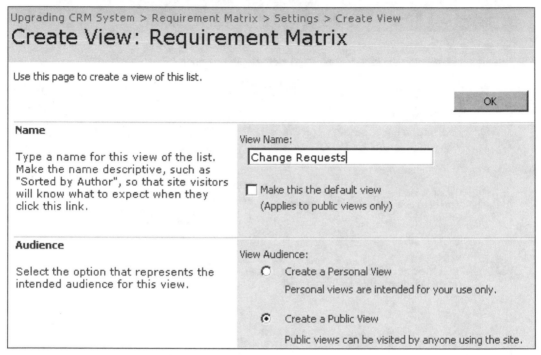

4. In the **View Name** field, type a name for the view (in the example above, "Change Requests").

5. Under **Display**, select the columns you want to appear in the view, and define the sort order under **Position from Left**:

| | Display | Column Name | Position from Left |
|---|---|---|---|
| **Columns** | | | |
| Select or clear the check box next to each column you want to show or hide in this view. To specify the order of the columns, select a number in the **Position from left** box. | ✓ | Attachments | 1 |
| | ✓ | Title (linked to item with edit menu) | 2 |
| | ✓ | Description | 3 |
| | ✓ | Requirements Type | 4 |
| | ✓ | Relevant Stakeholder | 5 |
| | ✓ | Requirement's Origin | 6 |
| | ✓ | Requirement's Reference | 7 |
| | ✓ | Responsible Department | 8 |

6. Define whether you want to use a filter in the view. In the example below, all rows where the value of the **Requirement's Origin** field is "Change Request" are included:

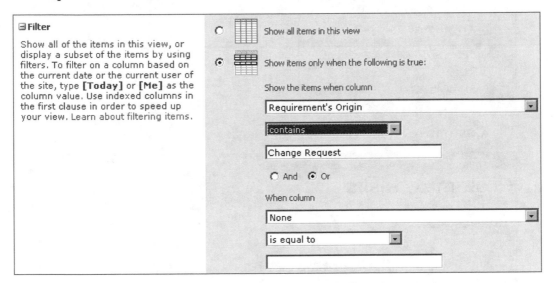

7. Define rules to apply to the list, such as **Group By**, **Totals**, and so on:

8. Click **OK**.

## 22. To modify an existing column:

1. On the project home page, from the quick launch menu, select the list in which you want to modify a column (for example, **Risks**).

2. From the **Settings** menu, select **List Settings**:

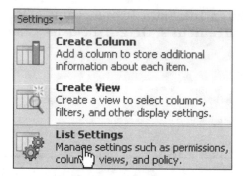

The **Customize &lt;List Name&gt;** page opens:

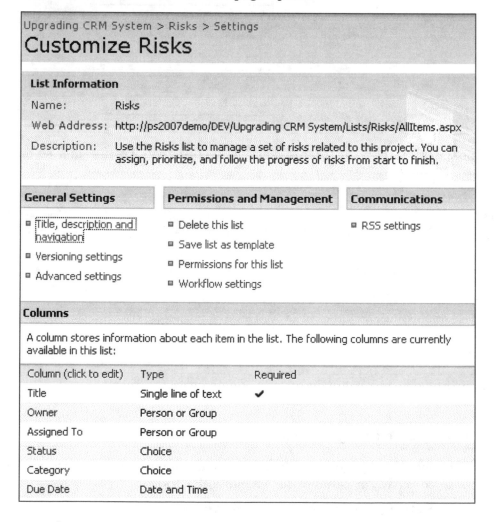

3. In the **Columns** section on that page, click on the column you want to modify (for example, **Category**):

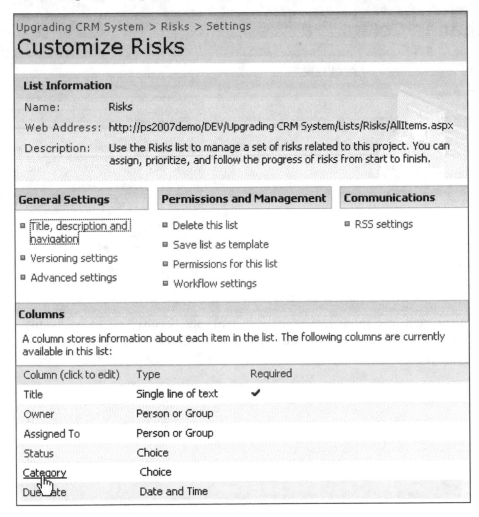

The **Change Column** page opens:

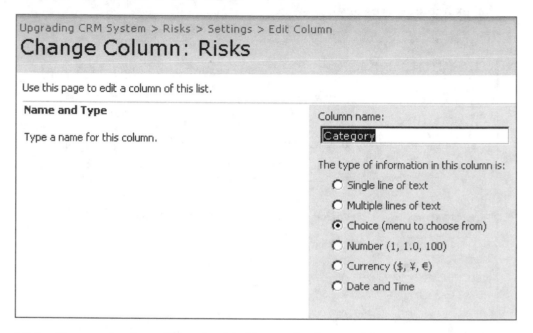

4. Make the required modification(s). For example, a column can be modified by changing the value list by adding a value or deleting a value.

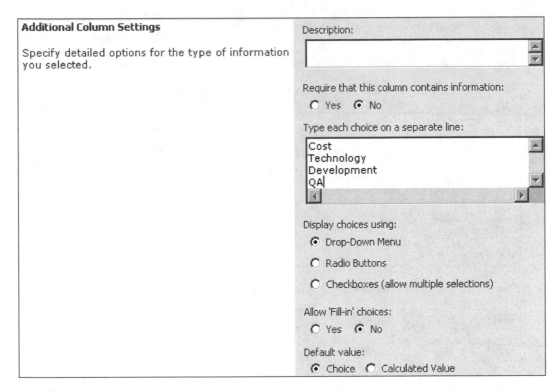

5.  Click **OK**.

## 23. To create a folder in an existing document library:

1.  On the project home page, from the **Documents** section, select the document library where you want to create a folder (for example, **Project Management Plan**):

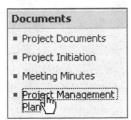

The **<Document Library Name>** page opens:

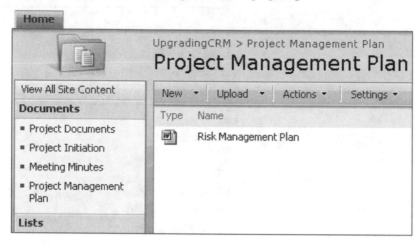

2. From the **New** menu, select **New Folder**:

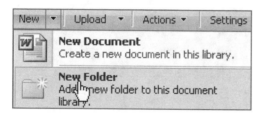

The **New Folder** page opens:

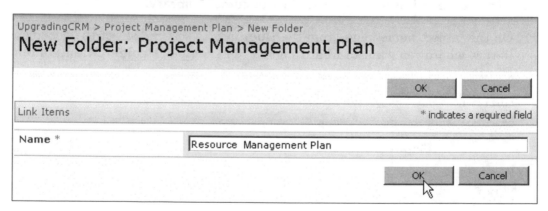

3. In the **Name** field, type a name for the new folder (for example, "Resource Management Plan").

4. Click **OK**.

# Appendix B: Troubleshooting

## Project Open Read-Write in Another Session— Projects Force Check-in

Sometimes, if you do not check-in your project plan or close Project Professional correctly (without saving the plan and checking the project in or discarding the changes), Project Server leaves the plan checked out. The next time you open the plan, you will get the following message:

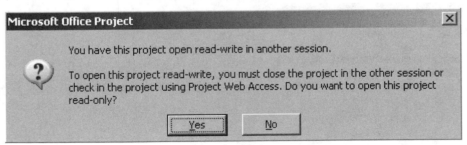

## To force check-in:

1. Navigate to the **Project Web Access** home page.

2. Select **Server Settings**:

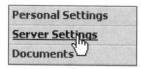

3. On the **Server Settings** page, under **Database Administration**, click on the **Force Check-in Enterprise Objects** option:

4. Select the object you want to force check-in (for example, **Enterprise Projects**):

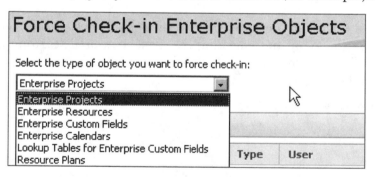

5.  Check the box to the left of the project you want to force check-in and click on **Check In**:

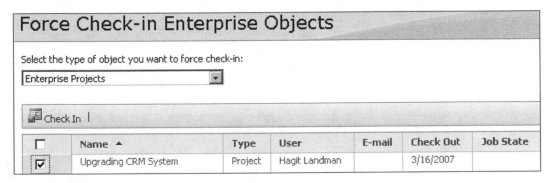

The system will ask you whether you are sure you want to check-in these items:

6.  Click **OK**. The system processes the request. You can see the **Job State**:

| | Name ▲ | Type | User | E-mail | Check Out | Job State |
|---|---|---|---|---|---|---|
| ☐ | Upgrading CRM System | Project | Hagit Landman | | 3/16/2007 | Processing |

As soon as the process is completed, the name of the object no longer appears in that list.

# Index